Babylon, NY 11702

4/3/2012

MW00465513

The Gondola
Philadelphia
& the Battle
of Lake Champlain

NUMBER SIX
Studies in Nautical Archaeology

Cheryl Ward, General Editor

Series Editorial Board:
Kevin J. Crisman
Donny L. Hamilton
Frederick M. Hocker
J. Richard Steffy
Frederick H. van Doornick, Jr.
Shelley Wachsmann

*A complete listing of books in print
in this series appears on the last page.*

The Gondola
PHILADELPHIA
& the
Battle of
Lake Champlain

JOHN R. BRATTEN

TEXAS A&M UNIVERSITY PRESS • *College Station*

Copyright © 2002
by John R. Bratten
Manufactured in the
United States of America
All rights reserved
first edition

The paper used in this book meets the minimum requirements
of the American National Standard for Permanence
of Paper for Printed Library Materials, z39.48-1984.
Binding materials have been chosen for durability.

Library of Congress Cataloging-in-Publication Data

Bratten, John R.
     The gondola Philadelphia and the Battle of Lake Champlain / John R.
Bratten.—1st ed.
          p. cm. — (Studies in nautical archaeology ; no. 6)
     Includes bibliographical references and index.
     ISBN 1-58544-147-3 (cloth : alk. paper)
          1. Philadelphia (Gunboat)   2. Valcour Island, Battle of, 1776.
3. United States—History—Revolution, 1775–1783—Naval operations.
4. Underwater archaeology—Champlain, Lake.   5. Excavations
(Archaeology)—Champlain, Lake.   I. Title.   II. Series.
VA65.P48B73   2002
359.8'32'0973—dc21   2001005630

TO WILLIAM LLOYD BRATTEN, SR.

CONTENTS

ILLUSTRATIONS

TABLES

ACKNOWLEDGMENTS

Many people have helped during this study. I am extremely grateful to Kevin J. Crisman for his invaluable suggestions and unfailing encouragement throughout the course of this project, in addition to my graduate studies at Texas A&M University. I am also indebted to the other members of my dissertation committee: Donny L. Hamilton, David Carlson, and James C. Bradford. Financial assistance was provided by a grant from the Institute of Nautical Archaeology, Texas A&M University, and administered by the Nautical Archaeology Program. My thanks to Cheryl Ward who was serving as series editor for her assistance in the publication process.

Staff members of the Lake Champlain Maritime Museum were essential to the completion of this research. Art Cohn, director of the museum, was helpful in all aspects of primary data collection. I am also obliged to Grace Barberis, Don DeWees, Laurie Eddy, Dale Henry, Erick Tichonuk, and Gwen Tichonuk. Their assistance during the course of this project is graciously acknowledged.

Research at the Smithsonian Institution was completed with the help of Paul Johnston, Harold Langley, and Phillip Lundeberg. Beth Richwine and Nan Card provided access to the *Philadelphia*'s conservation and accession records. Don Wickman of Rutland, Vermont, shared archival information related to the history of the *Philadelphia* and her crew. Roger Taylor, captain of the *Philadelphia II*, provided information relevant to the replica's handling abilities.

Additional thanks go to my colleagues in Florida, Judith Bense and Roger C. Smith, who provided me with some time and space to finish this project. Jay Clune reviewed each chapter and offered a number of helpful suggestions. Special thanks also to James W. Hunter III, Bonnie Martin, and Lee McKenzie of the University of West Florida Archaeology Institute who provided assistance with graphics and photocopying.

Many others deserve my thanks for assistance with this manuscript. I particularly recognize: Dennis Bratten, Tim Chapman, Bob Corbett, J. Coz Cozzi, Harv Dickey, Debra Jo Hailey, Tommy Hailey, Bailey Harris, Mark Hartmann, Richard Everett, Marianne Franklin, David Grant, Dora Johnson, Hera Konstantinou, Scott McLaughlin, Tom Muir, Gigi Naggatz, David and Hailey Robinson, Della Scott-Ireton, C. Wayne Smith, Richard Wills, and Kieran Wilmes.

I also express a general thanks to many others who helped in various ways to make this edition possible. My deepest thanks is reserved for Norma J. Harris, for encouragement and understanding.

The Gondola
Philadelphia
& the Battle
of Lake Champlain

INTRODUCTION

The Continental gondola *Philadelphia* is the oldest intact warship on display in North America. This small craft, only 54 feet in length, was part of the flotilla that frustrated Britain's first major effort to divide and subdue her rebellious American subjects by cutting off New England from the middle and southern colonies. The Americans launched the *Philadelphia* from the American shipyard at Skenesborough (now Whitehall), New York, into the waters of Lake Champlain on July 30, 1776. The Continental Congress had ordered the construction of the *Philadelphia* and her sister ships on June 17, 1776, when it instructed General Philip Schuyler, commander of the American forces in New York, "to build, with all expedition, as many gallies and armed vessels as . . . shall be sufficient to make us indisputably masters of the lakes Champlain and George."[1] Congress's order came with the realization that the American attempt to take Quebec and neutralize British Canada in the first year of the Revolutionary War had failed. Schuyler, anticipating the possible need for vessels to aid in the retreat of the army, had begun preparations in late May for the construction of gondolas by sending carpenters from Fort George, New York, to Skenesborough.[2]

Fearing an imminent British invasion through the Lake Champlain corridor, the Marine Committee of Congress ordered additional shipwrights to Skenesborough in mid-June. At that time, Schuyler optimistically predicted that once more carpenters arrived it would be possible to build five gondolas a week.[3] However, only two gondolas had been sent to Fort Ticonderoga by July 15. This fact prompted General Horatio Gates, field commander of the Northern Army, to complain that the sixty carpenters at work at Skenesborough "must be very ill-attended to, or very ignorant of their business, not to do more work."[4] Gates had already written to Brigadier General Benedict Arnold expressing his wish that Arnold take charge of the building program at Skenesborough.[5]

In late July both the shipbuilding program and command of the fleet fell to Arnold. He instructed the nearly two hundred ship and house carpenters at Skenesborough to turn their attention to the construction of larger galleys. Meanwhile, Arnold's British counterpart, Sir Guy Carleton, governor general of Canada and commander of the British forces, was assembling vessels at St. Jean on the Richelieu River in preparation for a thrust southward, down Lake Champlain, to cut off New England from the southern colonies.

When the British invasion of Lake Champlain began, Arnold anchored his fleet at Valcour Island near the New York shore. On October 11, 1776, the battle commenced. The Americans fought skillfully and determinedly, but the superior firepower of the British squadron proved decisive. One hour after the battle ended, the badly damaged *Philadelphia* sank.[6] Arnold and most of his men escaped in a daring nighttime retreat by rowing their ships between the British fleet and the New York shore. By the end of the three-day engagement only four of the original seventeen ships that formed the American fleet returned to the shelter of Fort Ticonderoga.

The British victory, however, was incomplete. Realizing it was too late in the season to lay siege to Fort Ticonderoga, Carleton returned to Canada. A second invasion in 1777 swept quickly through the Champlain Valley, but the campaign of British commander John Burgoyne ended in disaster at Saratoga, where Burgoyne surrendered his entire army to Horatio Gates on October 17, 1777.

Many historians point to the naval contest for Lake Champlain in 1776 as the foundation for Burgoyne's defeat the following year. Had Arnold not forced the British to enter into a lengthy shipbuilding race, thus sacrificing a campaign season, the Americans would not have had time to build their army to the strength necessary for victory at Saratoga. The sacrifice of the *Philadelphia* and other vessels in Arnold's fleet served its purpose.

The gunboat *Philadelphia* remained at the bottom of Lake Champlain until 1935, when Colonel Lorenzo Hagglund raised her, placed the hull on a barge, and created a floating exhibit that toured the Hudson River and Lake Champlain for many years.[7] In 1961 the Smithsonian Institution acquired the *Philadelphia* and made her a central exhibit at the National Museum of History and Technology (later the National Museum of American History).[8]

Many of the ships of Arnold's fleet have been located, and many salvaged, but only the *Philadelphia* is intact and on public display. This vessel is an exceptional resource for students of the Revolutionary War and eighteenth-century maritime studies, well deserving of complete documentation, analysis, and reconstruction. For the first time the many separate elements of the *Philadelphia*'s story have been combined into one study.

Chapter 1

HISTORY OF THE MILITARY AND NAVAL EVENTS LEADING TO THE AMERICAN DEFENSE OF LAKE CHAMPLAIN IN 1776

During the first two centuries of European colonization of North America, Lake Champlain was the key to transportation across the wilderness area between Canada and the continent's eastern seaboard. The valley between the Adirondacks and the Green Mountains was a waterway between the colonies of Britain and France. Connected to the St. Lawrence via the Richelieu River, Lake Champlain provided an easily navigable route to New England and New York via the Hudson River (fig. 1.1).

Long before European explorers came, the Iroquois inhabited the Hudson Valley, and the Algonquins inhabited the St. Lawrence River Valley. From north and south, the two tribes traveled along the lake in search of furs or food, with the Iroquois claiming the western shore and the Algonquins the eastern shore.[1]

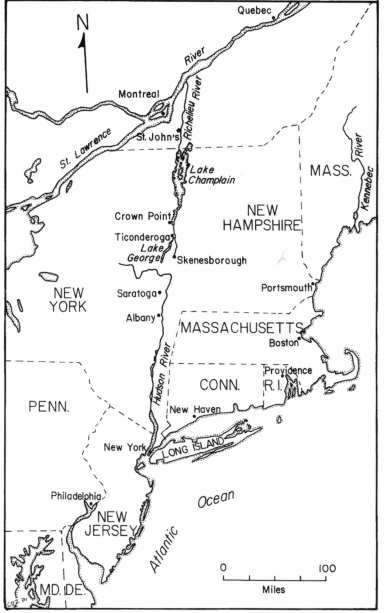

In September, 1609, Henry Hudson, an English explorer in the employ of the Dutch, sailed to the uppermost limit of navigation on the river that now bears his name. Hudson may have been aware of the lakes that lay but a few miles to the north of where he ended his exploration. As a result of this expedition, the Dutch concluded a treaty with the Iroquois and established a trading post, called Fort Nassau, on Castle Island in the Hudson River, south of present-day Albany, New York. In 1624 several Walloon families settled at the Dutch post of Fort Orange (later, Albany).

Just a few months before Hudson made his historic voyage into the interior with the ship *Half Moon*, a French explorer entered the Champlain Valley from the north. Samuel de Champlain, with two French companions and some sixty Algonquins, had paddled south from Quebec, the first permanent colony in New France, to raid the Iroquois. Near the southern end of the lake named after the explorer, the party met a large force of Iroquois. Loading his arquebus with four balls, Champlain, at the head of the Algonquins, marched to within thirty paces of the defenders. With a single shot he killed two of the opposing chiefs and wounded a third.[2] Amazed at the power of these astonishing French weapons, the Iroquois fled. According to most historians, this encounter would set the stage for the later alliance of the Iroquois with the British against the French. One historian writes, "It was inevitable, however, that the French should ally themselves with the people among whom they had to live, and, in the end, defend them against the raids of their enemy."[3]

For the next one hundred years, the French settled the St. Lawrence Valley and engaged in the fur trade with the Native Americans. Eventually, their trading interests led them farther south into the Champlain Valley. To protect their new markets, the French began construction of a stockade in 1730 that, with later additions, became Fort St. Frédéric.[4] In 1755 the French began construction of a second fort, Carillon, at the southern end of Lake Champlain. As the French pushed south, the British pressed north, making the Champlain Valley a contested region.

In 1758 Fort Carillon became the center of French resistance against a mixed force of nearly 15,000 British and provincial troops invading from the Hudson Valley in 900 bateaux and 100 whale boats. In early July the British army lost 2,000 men, including George Viscount Howe, their most gallant general. To further strengthen their hold on the lake, the French built a small naval squadron consisting of 4 65-ton sloops (the *Musquelongy, Esturgeon, Brochette,* and *Waggon*) and a 70-ton schooner (the *Vigilante*).[5]

In July, 1759, General Jeffrey Amherst finally took Fort Carillon. The British immediately occupied the fort and renamed it Fort Ticonderoga. Similarly, they captured Fort St. Frédéric and renamed it Crown Point.[6] Before the British could continue their advance north into Canada, however, it was necessary to take control of Lake Champlain. Amherst therefore "ordered the construction of a 155-ton brig, the *Duke of Cumberland,* and a 115-ton sloop, the *Boscawen,* at the King's Shipyard at Ticonderoga."[7] Once the two vessels were launched, the British sailed in search of the French fleet. In what has been called a "questionable maneuver," the French intentionally scuttled three of their sloops without a fight when they spotted the British vessels.[8] The British immediately raised the sloops and pressed them into service. The capture of the greater portion of the French fleet signaled the end of the French occupation of the Champlain Valley. In 1760 three British armies, one of them Colonel William Haviland's from Ticonderoga, moved against Montreal.[9] The 1763 Treaty of Paris, which ended the Seven Years' War, made all of Canada British. For a short time peace returned to the Champlain Valley.

The use of Lake Champlain as an invasion route was not soon forgotten. In 1767 Guy Carleton, governor general of Canada, wrote to General Thomas Gage, commander in chief of the British forces in America, recommending that he "strengthen the vital posts at Crown Point, Ticonderoga and Fort George, as well as the terminal citadels at Quebec and New York City, [and that] . . . old forts must be repaired and new ones constructed at the terminal points in order to secure communications with Great Britain."[10]

As tensions began to mount between the colonists and Great Britain during the spring of 1774, General Frederick Haldimand (acting commander in chief during Thomas Gage's absence) suggested that two regiments be ordered from Quebec to Crown Point with the idea of rebuilding that fort.[11] Like Carleton, Haldimand realized that a British garrison on Lake Champlain would ensure an open line of communications with Canada and provide access to the more remote settlements of the northern colonies should they decide to stage any violence against the British from these outposts.[12] Shortly afterward, Lord Dartmouth, secretary of state for the colonies, advised Gage that proposals for the repair of both Crown Point and Ticonderoga would be considered.[13]

By the fall of 1774 increasing unrest among the colonists prompted Dartmouth to order Gage to restore both Ticonderoga and Crown Point to their original state of military readiness.[14] Gage did not receive these orders until winter had moved into the valley, restricting troop movements thereafter. Gage took a rather leisurely approach to the reconstruction, perhaps because of the general inactivity of the winter season. His only orders to Captain William Delaplace at Ticonderoga were to be alert in the event of trouble.[15]

The British decided by mid-April, 1775, to occupy any forts and defensive locations that might benefit the rebels.[16] Four regiments of foot soldiers that were intended to reinforce Gage's troops in Boston were instead directed to New York to take control of the Lake Champlain–Hudson River corridor and to prevent any military movement to New England from the middle colonies.[17] On April 19 Gage ordered Carleton to send the Tenth Regiment to Ticonderoga or Crown Point as soon as possible.[18] Gage was confident that his troops would be able to hold the Champlain Valley or at the least "make a diversion on the frontiers as the service shall require."[19] Carleton received these orders a month later, only to discover on the next day that they were no longer appropriate since Benedict Arnold and his men were already camped along the lakeshore.[20] The colonial leaders had also seen the importance of the Lake Champlain installations and had taken the first action.

In 1775 the garrison at Fort Ticonderoga had fewer than fifty British troops under an elderly officer, Captain William Delaplace. On May 10, scarcely three weeks since the outbreak of fighting at Lexington and Concord, the captain and his men earned their place in history by being the first British troops to surrender to the American rebels. Ethan Allen, a land speculator from Vermont and leader of the famed Green Mountain Boys, formed a joint, if strained, leadership with Arnold, who was commissioned by the Massachusetts Committee of Safety. The two men led an American force of eighty-three men across the lake by night. At three o'clock in the morning the Americans dashed into the sleeping fortress. Legend holds that in response to the baffled Captain Delaplace's demand of "In whose name do you come?" Allen answered, "In the name of

the Great Jehovah and the Continental Congress."[21] The War of
Independence had begun on Lake Champlain.

With the capture of Ticonderoga, American insurgents had seized
the gateway to British Canada for their embryo republic. At the
same time they had gained a valuable store of military supplies.
The guns of Ticonderoga, rusty from disuse but still serviceable,
formed the main artillery strength of General Washington's army
outside Boston.[22]

Captain Samuel Herrick with a force of thirty men captured the
village of Skenesborough without any exchange of gunfire.[23] A more
valuable prize collected by Herrick was a small schooner belonging
to the town's founder, Philip Skene.[24] Captain Herrick and his men
took the schooner, renamed the *Liberty*, to Ticonderoga.

The *Liberty* arrived at Ticonderoga on May 13, 1775. She provided Arnold with a haven from which to command without the
interference of Allen. The relationship between Arnold and Allen
was tense. Arnold not only felt that he had been cheated out of
command but also disapproved of the drunken behavior of Allen's
Green Mountain Boys. Arnold's experience at sea allowed him to
claim the vessel and use it to expand the reach of the Americans
onto other parts of the lake, especially down the Richelieu to the
northern terminus of navigation at St. Jean. With the fall of the
undermanned garrison at Crown Point on May 12, St. Jean was
the only significant post on the lake still under British control.[25]

On the morning of May 18, Arnold surprised the British at St.
Jean. In an official report to Gage, Guy Carleton told his superior
that "one Dominick Arnold, said to be a Native of Connecticut,
and Known Horse Jockey, who has been several times in this Prov-
ince, and is well acquainted with every Avenue to it landed at St.
Johns, captured one sergeant and ten men, plus the sloop."[26] The
sloop to which Carleton referred was about 70 tons and mounted
two 6-pounders. The Americans renamed it the *Enterprise*.[27] In
addition, Arnold and his thirty-five-man force captured two brass
fieldpieces and nine small boats, five of which they burned.

The British quickly regrouped, and within a few days four hundred regulars moved up the Richelieu and secured St. Jean.[28] Ru-
mors of a British counterattack from Canada prompted the Continental Congress to order the evacuation of the Champlain forts
and the withdrawal of American forces to an east-west line at the

southern end of Lake George. In Congress's haste to make a decision, its members examined only the most recent evidence and did not carefully devise their strategy.[29] The legislatures of New York and the New England states, along with Arnold and Allen, loudly protested the withdrawal, believing it would leave the northern states vulnerable to British invasion.[30] Congress heard the voices of the states and officers and on June 27 ordered that St. Jean be retaken, as well as Montreal and any other strategic positions that would help to secure the colonies.[31] Colonel Benjamin Hinman arrived at Ticonderoga in late May with one thousand Connecticut troops and asked Arnold to turn over command of American forces on the lake. Arnold refused to relinquish command and was immediately dismissed, after which he left the lake and returned to his Connecticut home.

On June 17, 1775, shortly after the Battle of Bunker Hill (which was actually fought on nearby Breed's Hill, Charlestown, Massachusetts), the Second Continental Congress named George Washington commander in chief of the American forces. He assumed command in July and succeeded in capturing Boston from the British in March, 1776. With the congressional organization of the American army, Philip Schuyler found himself a major general and commander of the American forces in New York, responsible for leading an invasion into Canada.[32]

By July 17 Schuyler had visited Fort George, New York, and left instructions for its further preparedness. After a similar inspection of the garrisons on Lake Champlain, Schuyler requested that additional supplies and equipment be sent north to prepare for the Canadian expedition. In anticipation of transporting troops down Lake Champlain and into Canada, Schuyler ordered the construction of bateaux at Lake George. By mid-August the American naval force on the lake consisted of enough bateaux to carry thirteen hundred troops, the schooner *Liberty*, sloop *Enterprise*, two newly constructed flat-bottomed gunboats (the gondolas *Hancock* and *Schuyler*), and an assortment of smaller vessels, including two armed bateaux.[33]

Schuyler's second in command, Brigadier General Richard Montgomery, arrived in August. By this time, the British were making their own efforts toward a lake invasion by beginning the construction of two lake vessels at St. Jean. On August 28, Montgomery left

Ticonderoga with twelve hundred men to attack St. Jean. The task would be far more difficult now that the British had reinforced the garrison with cannons and troops. After spending seven weeks in an unsuccessful attempt to capture the outpost, Montgomery finally managed to cut the fort off from its Chambly and Montreal supply lines, forcing the St. Jean commanders to capitulate on November 2. It was the greatest American victory yet in the Revolution. Included among the captured military and naval equipment was the recently finished schooner *Royal Savage* (which the Americans had sunk with a 13-inch mortar on October 14) and a row galley still on the stocks but ready for launching. The Americans raised the schooner and renamed it the *Yankee*, but the designation quickly returned to its original British sobriquet, the *Royal Savage*.[34] They designated the row galley the *Douglas* in honor of Major William Douglas, the "commodore" of the small American fleet. Later at Ticonderoga it would be rigged as a schooner and renamed the *Revenge*.[35]

A second plan to push north and attack Canada came out of a meeting between Colonel Arnold and George Washington at the latter's Cambridge, Massachusetts, headquarters in early September. At his own request, Arnold was given his first independent command and placed in charge of a plan to attack Quebec. In mid-September Arnold led eleven hundred men through the wilderness of Maine. After an arduous trip Arnold arrived at Quebec on November 9 with slightly more than six hundred effective troops. General Richard Montgomery's troops were pushing toward Quebec after taking the undefended city of Montreal on November 13. Together the combined forces of Arnold and Montgomery attacked Carleton's stronghold in the heavily fortified city of Quebec on New Year's Eve in a blinding snowstorm. The attack was a disaster. Montgomery and several of his officers died in battle; Arnold suffered a serious leg wound; and British governor Guy Carleton captured more than four hundred American soldiers. The American army pulled back and retired three miles up the river to establish a land blockade of Quebec. With Quebec cut off from the sea by ice, the Continental troops camped near the Plains of Abraham and continued to surround the city until May, 1776.

On May 6, 1776, the British reinforcement fleet arrived at Quebec after carefully negotiating its way through the late spring ice of the St. Lawrence River. The transport ships landed eighteen hundred fresh troops, forcing the sick, starving, unclothed, and suffering Americans who had passed the winter in the field to retreat to Sorel, about a hundred miles southwest of Quebec on the St. Lawrence River. By June 17 the remains of the American army had retreated to St. Jean, burning the fort and barracks before moving on to Isle aux Noix and finally retreating up the lake to Crown Point.

The invasion cost the Americans five thousand men from the original force of thirteen thousand, some to British guns, some to disease, and still others to British capture.[36] At least three thousand of the retreating soldiers suffered from wounds and sickness, and the remaining five thousand from exhaustion and demoralization. In the words of the noted naval historian Alfred Thayer Mahan, the Royal Navy's relief of Quebec had "decided the fate of Canada."[37] For the time being, however, the Americans held Lake Champlain. All that stood between the British army and the rebelling northern colonies were four small vessels, the *Liberty, Enterprise, Royal Savage,* and *Revenge.* These vessels held control on the lake. But the British would soon begin to regroup, and the American response would determine how long the schooners would maintain their supremacy.

Chapter 2

BUILDING THE
AMERICAN FLEET

On June 17, 1776, General Philip Schuyler began formally carrying out the order of the Continental Congress to build a fleet of vessels for Lake Champlain.[1] He had already ordered preparations, as early as May of that year, by sending thirty carpenters from Fort George, New York, to Skenesborough.[2] He wrote General George Washington, commander in chief of the American forces, that "altho' Nothing is prepared for building them—I hope nevertheless to finish one in a short Time."[3] Schuyler admitted, however, that he knew next to nothing about constructing vessels and requested that an experienced shipwright be sent to oversee the construction.

As far as resources were concerned, Schuyler's choice of Skenesborough for the site of the American shipyard was excellent. Located at the head of Lake Champlain where Wood Creek empties into South Bay, the area abounded in large tracts of timber (fig. 2.1). The small community had been established in 1765 through a British land warrant rewarding Major Philip Skene for his field service in the French wars.[4] The initial tract grew to twenty-five thousand acres, and as a result of Skene's mercantile ambitions, became the largest pre-Revolutionary lake settlement.[5] The grounds housed Skene's mansion house, barns for storing crops and housing cattle and horses, and cleared meadows. But of greater significance for the construction of naval vessels was the presence of two sawmills and an iron forge. In Skene's own words, the furnace and bloomery were capable "of turning out the best iron bar in the colonies."[6] Iron ore for the forge came from a nearby six-hundred-acre section of land that Skene had purchased close to modern-day Port Henry, New York.

To augment the construction force at Skenesborough, Schuyler wrote to Colonel Cornelius D. Wynkoop (then commander at Fort Ticonderoga) for additional carpenters, a blacksmith, and tools.[7] Unable to oversee construction of the gondolas himself, Schuyler ordered Hermanus Schuyler (apparently no relation), the assistant deputy commissary general of the Northern Department, to Skenesborough on June 7.[8] Hermanus Schuyler's orders were explicit:

> [T]ake Charge of the Carpenters, Ax-men, Teamsters & Blacksmiths at that place and do every Thing in your power to forward the Building of the Gundaloes and to procure plank and whatever may be necessary—the Saw Mill must be immediately repaired—a Mr Granger who resides in that Neighbourhood understands the work well; him you must procure and add as many of the other Carpenters now there, as can work at it, that it may be finished the soonest possible.
>
> You will employ the Oxen in drawing the Timber necessary to construct the Vessel with and try to procure as many Oak Logs before the Mill is finished as you possibly can; the larger and longer they are the better.
>
> Take a List of all the people employed under your Direction, distinguishing the Carpenters from the Ax-men, and those from the Teamsters, and discharge such as may be unfit for Service either by Disease Drunkenness or Laziness, and keep an exact Checque Book, and call over the Names of every person at Sunrise before they go to Work.
>
> You must provide a Master Sawyer for the Mill & the sawing must go on by Night as well as by Day and that the Sawyers may not play Tricks count the Logs on the Log-Way at Sunset, and again at Sunrise in the Morning and then you will be able to know if the Sawyers have done their Duty.
>
> You should now and then visit them in the Night. Let the greatest Care be taken to guard against accidents by Fire, and

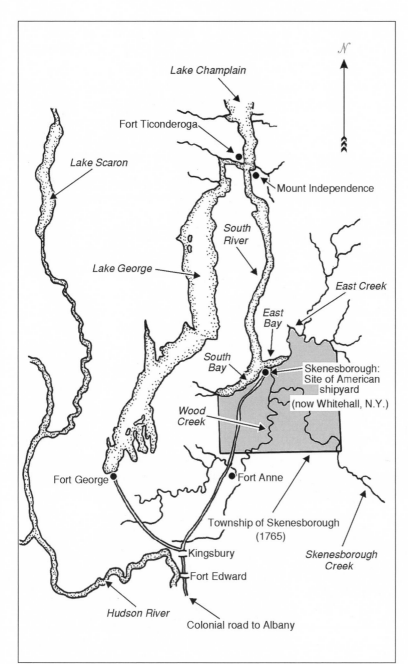

Fig. 2.1.
Skenesborough
and its environs,
circa 1776. After
Howard P.
Hoffman, A
Graphic
Presentation of
the Continental
Gondola
Philadelphia:
American
Gunboat of 1776
(Washington,
D.C.:
Smithsonian
Institution, 1982),
sheet 1.

charge the Sawyers that if any Thing gives Way in the Night not to go to Bed or lay down to sleep, as many Mills have been burnt for Want of this precaution—Keep always two Barrels full of Water in the Mill with a Bucket in each.

Frequently examine the Stores, and see what you are likely to want and write for it in Time. I expect to be frequently informed how the Work goes on: how many Logs you have their Dimensions and when you expect the Mill will begin to saw.

You can write either by the Way of Ticonderoga or Wood Creek, as you will have frequent oppertunities both ways.[9]

On June 12 General Schuyler wrote Washington to express his fears of the imminent evacuation of Canada by the American troops following their unsuccessful attempt to establish a land blockade outside the city of Quebec.[10] The major general also reemphasized the necessity of the work at Skenesborough by stating, "I am however humbly of Opinion That we still ought to Build the Gundaloes, and Make every preparation to prevent the Enemys Crossing the Lake and penetrating into the Colonies Which I think will Certainly be our own Fault if they do."[11] He also informed Washington that Brigadier General Benedict Arnold had written from Canada with the news that the British were already preparing to assemble gunboats for a lake invasion.[12] The British task would be made much easier since the vessels were to be constructed from prefabricated parts that had already been shipped from England.

The "Gundaloes" to which Schuyler referred were gunboats and, more often than not, called gondolas. These vessels were easily, quickly, and cheaply built, for they had flat bottoms, nearly flat sides, and were double ended. They were powered by long oars, known as sweeps, but could sail when the wind was fair. Historical sources reveal that there were many colloquial spellings of the word *gondola*. These include: "gundalow," "gun'low," "gondela," "gundalow," "gundaloa," "'gundeloe," and "gunlo."[13] The most common spelling in New England was gundalow, commonly pronounced in two syllables—"gun'low." It is readily apparent that the word "gondola" came from the Mediterranean where it described the long, narrow, flat-bottomed boat with a high prow and stern used on the Venetian canals for passenger traffic and general yachting. The only similarities between the American gondola and its

Mediterranean counterpart, however, were that both were of shallow draft and often propelled by rowing or poling.

As evidenced in early New England accounts, newspapers, and town histories, colonial settlers quickly adopted the name to describe the various flat-bottomed lighters that were used to transport passengers and their goods over rivers and arms of the sea. Howard Chapelle believes that the configuration of the Skenesborough gondolas was modeled on the contemporary English pram or American bateau.[14] In their larger form as a gondola, these flat-bottomed boats provided large capacity for limited draft and possessed the ability to ground without damage, making them desirable for the shallow and sheltered waters in Lake Champlain. They could not only carry a large number of troops but also support several large cannons.

By June 13 the first American gondola (later to be called the *New Haven*) had its flat bottom finished. The stem and sternpost had been set in place and the knees were ready to install the following day.[15] Construction of the second gondola (the *Providence*) was proceeding at the same time. Although the woodcutters had cut and dragged enough timber for both of them, Hermanus Schuyler wrote that without "a Dozen of Whip Saws & Files sent up with all possible Dispatch" the sawmills would be unable to keep up with the carpenters' demands.[16]

General Schuyler's foresight, and the subsequent letters of Generals Benedict Arnold and John Sullivan to George Washington, prompted Congress's Marine Committee to order additional shipwrights and a master carpenter to Skenesborough in mid-June.[17] Congress further specified that the master carpenter should be acquainted with the construction of the eleven "galleys" that had been built in 1775 by John Wharton, Emanuel Eyre, and other Philadelphia shipbuilders for the defense of the Delaware River.[18]

In spite of General Schuyler's concern about the situation along the lake, he remained at Fort George directing the work at Skenesborough by dispatch. Hermanus Schuyler, however, was never fully informed as to how many vessels would be needed and appeared fearful that he might waste time by cutting too much wood. Schuyler instructed the former quartermaster to continue cutting oak logs until enough had been stockpiled to complete five more gondolas.[19] As before, his letter to Hermanus Schuyler emphasized the importance of the work. He ordered that "the Mill must Constantly be kept going & If You have not strength to Team enough, Employ more,— Remember that Altho Every thing is to be done with the Greatest Oeconomy.—*Yet the Work must be done.*"[20]

As soon as Hermanus Schuyler finished the first gondola, he was to send it to Fort Ticonderoga for masting and rigging. A contemporary map suggests that this was accomplished across from Fort Ticonderoga on the Vermont side of the lake at the area later to be fortified and called Mount Independence. Philip Schuyler indicated that the gondolas must be "fixed to receive the Guns in the Manner those of last Year were."[21] Apparently he was referring to the *Schuyler* and *Hancock*, which had been built in 1775 at Lake George just before the Canadian invasion. The two gondolas were approximately 60 feet long and of a size Schuyler considered to be capable of supporting five 12-pounders each.[22] Due to a shortage of cannons the Americans outfitted the two vessels with only one 12-pounder in the bow and twelve swivels on the sides.[23] Ultimately, the Skenesborough gondolas were armed with three cannons: a 12-pounder in the bow and two 9-pounders on the midship deck. This arrangement of three heavy guns per gondola was identical to Arnold's plan for the gondolas whose construction he supervised at Chambly in May.[24]

While the work continued at Skenesborough seven days a week, in accordance with Schuyler's orders, the American retreat from Canada was well under way. Arnold fled Montreal on June 15 with three hundred men. By June 24 Brigadier General John Sullivan's troops had fallen back to Isle aux Noix. He wrote Washington:

> I think it would be by far, the Best to remove to Crown Point, Fortify that, Build Row-gallies to Command the Lakes. . . . I know of no better Method than to Secure the Important posts of Ticondaroga & Crown point, & by building a Number of Arm'd Vessels, Command the Lakes, Otherwise the forces now in Canada, Will be brought down upon us, As quick as Possible, having nothing now to Oppose them in that Colony—They have a Number of Batteaus fram'd Which they brought from three Rivers, They will Doubtless Construct Some Arm'd Vessels, & then Endeavour to penetrate the Country Toward New York, This I am persuaded They will Attempt, But am Sure they can

never Effect, Unless we Neglect to Secure the important posts now in our power.[25]

Sullivan's advice did not go unheeded. But he would soon be dismayed to learn that he had been replaced by Major General Horatio Gates as the commander of the American army in the field following his retreat.[26]

On June 26 the first gondola was launched at Skenesborough. The second was being planked, and enough logs had been to cut to see to the start of several others. It had taken a little more than three weeks to begin the necessary processes of harvesting, cutting, and shaping the green wood into two of the simply designed gondolas. Philip Schuyler was optimistic enough to write Washington that he would "build one every six Days."[27] Schuyler's confidence was due to his having written to Connecticut governor Jonathan Trumbull for fifty more ship carpenters and a similar number from Massachusetts Bay.[28] The new carpenters were to be organized into gangs of twenty-five each and paid at the rate of those already engaged in the service, one-third of a dollar per day, commencing from the time the companies left home, allowing the rate of one day for twenty miles.[29]

The proffered salary was not high enough, however. To entice the shipwrights away from their lucrative (and potentially healthier) positions in the privateer trade, the Marine Committee of Congress offered thirty-four and two-thirds dollars per month.[30] The wage was incredibly high. According to William Fowler, the shipwrights working at Lake Champlain were the most highly paid in America. In fact, aside from Commodore Esek Hopkins, they would earn "more than any enlisted man or officer in the entire Continental navy" and five times that of the common Massachusetts soldier stationed at Ticonderoga.[31] Beyond the high salary, the carpenters negotiated to receive one month's pay in advance and one and a half rations per day. Before the carpenters even began their march to Skenesborough, formal contracts had to be signed. The shipwrights agreed to "begin work at sunrise and to continue until sunset, with the exception of an hour break for breakfast and an hour and a half break for dinner. Rations were to include a pound and a quarter of beef or pork, a pound and a half of flour, and a half pint of rum. In addition, four pints of peas and a pint of molasses were to be distributed to each carpenter on a weekly basis."[32]

Beyond the rushed work of building the gondolas, the Americans faced the task of finding the equipment needed to rig and arm the small fleet of larger vessels that were already in their possession. To this difficult task, Philip Schuyler assigned his personal aide, Captain Richard Varick. Varick began the process in early May by writing to John McKesson, secretary to the New York Provincial Congress for "a suit of sails, of certain dimensions, for a pettiauger, and as much rope as will rig two Albany sloops, (cables, shrouds and hawsers excepted) and also enough for two large pettiaugers; blocks for all."[33]

The requisition was probably for additional rigging needed for the *Royal Savage;* the row galley captured at St. Jean, later to be called the *Revenge;* and the two gondolas Arnold was building at Chambly. General Sullivan burned the latter two vessels just before he retreated to St. Jean.[34] When this rigging arrived, it was probably used for the first two gondolas built at Skenesborough.

Hermanus Schuyler sent the second gondola to Ticonderoga on June 30 and launched the third that same day. He reported dimensions for the first two gondolas as 50 feet long, 15 feet in beam, and 4½ feet deep, essentially equal to those for the *Philadelphia.*[35] Based on the supply of wood already cut, Captain Henry Bradt (head carpenter at Skenesborough) predicted that a gondola could be launched every week, weather permitting.[36]

On the day the Americans declared their independence from Great Britain, Philip Schuyler was writing the orders for the new carpenters coming from Massachusetts and Connecticut. Each company of twenty-five men was to put itself under the command of Hermanus Schuyler and take charge of constructing a gondola.[37]

At the end of June the American army completed its retreat from Canada. Over a period of several days, bateaux ferried seven to eight thousand men from Isle aux Noix to Crown Point. On July 7 Major General Philip Schuyler, Major General Horatio Gates, Brigadier General Benedict Arnold, Brigadier General John Sullivan, and Baron Frederick Wilhelm de Woedtke met at Crown Point in a council of war to discuss the state of affairs on the lake. They deemed that Crown Point was not tenable and determined that it could not be made so that summer.[38] They further determined that colonial troops should be moved to Ticonderoga and the "Strong Ground" (Mount Independence) on the east side of the lake.[39] To ensure that the Americans could retain control of the lake and, by that, prevent the British from penetrating into the New England colonies, the colonial officers decided that the construction of more formidable row galleys to augment the smaller gondolas should begin immediately.

By June 9 Arnold was working closely with Gates to improve the efficiency of the American shipbuilding effort. Arnold detailed oar makers to the woods near Crown Point to find suitable material for making the oars and sweeps that would be needed for the gondolas.[40] He ordered that Captain Edward Williams and his gang of blacksmiths be sent from Crown Point to Skenesborough.[41] The armorers, under the charge of Lieutenant Solomon Bowman, were to remain at Fort Ticonderoga where the new vessels were being fitted with cannons. Arnold also ordered that Lieutenant Benjamin Beal's thirty-four house carpenters and Mr. Noah Nichols's eight wheelwrights remain under the orders of Colonel Jeduthan Baldwin, chief engineer at Ticonderoga, to see to the production of gun carriages for the fleet. He sent thirty-four other house carpenters under the supervision of Thayer (probably Captain Simeon Thayer from Providence, Rhode Island) to Skenesborough, along with Richard Fittock's gang of thirteen ship carpenters. Lieutenant Curtis and thirteen additional ship carpenters were to remain at Ticonderoga under the direction of Captain Jacobus Wynkoop.[42]

To determine the state of readiness of the British forces, General Sullivan sent Colonel Thomas Hartley from Crown Point to scout out the northern end of the lake. At Cumberland Head, Hartley's party destroyed a small quantity of ship timber to keep it from falling into the hands of the British. At William Hay's clearing, opposite Valcour Island, his troops seized a quantity of "good Plank and crooked Timber" and carried it to Crown Point in bateaux.[43] An additional one thousand board feet of timber was left in the swamps to be retrieved over the next winter. Hartley reported to Arnold that General Guy Carleton and Brigadier General Simon Fraser were repairing the works at St. Jean, and a number of Hanoverian and British regulars were employed in cutting wood between St. Jean and Isle aux Noix for the British shipbuilding effort.

Just after the council of war, the Americans began to construct an enormous earthwork on the east side of the lake across from Fort Ticonderoga. From there, Colonel John Trumbull expressed his concerns about the American shipbuilding effort to his father Jonathan Trumbull, governor of Connecticut:

> How we shall maintain our Naval superiority I must confess myself much at a Loss.—Tis true we build a thing *calld* a Gondola, perhaps as much as one in a Week—but where is our Rigging for them, where our Guns, we have to be sure, a great Train of Artillery, but they are very few of them mounted on Carriages, & our Materials & Conveniences for making them are very slender. We have Carpenters, shipbuilders, & Blacksmiths in plenty, but neither places for them to work in nor Materials in that plenty we ought to have. . . .
>
> To oppose the Enemy on the Lake,—we have a schooner of twelve Carriage Guns—a sloop of Eight; two small Schooners to Carry four or six each & three Gondolas—The large Schooner will be in good sailing order in two or three Days—the sloop is a most unmanageable thing,—tis not possible to beat up against a head wind, in her—the two small schooners are Arm'd, Gondolas are Arm'd,—& even the Carri[ages] of their Guns are yet to be made—
>
> The Enemy we find are at St. Johns repairing the works at the place, & building three schooners & two sloops, they have, no doubt every thing ready to their hands, the Rigging made, the Guns mounted, & only the wooden work to perform,—in which I fear they will have the advantage of us.[44]

Notwithstanding the lack of equipment and rigging, Schuyler predicted in mid-June that once the additional carpenters arrived it would be possible to build five gondolas a week.[45] Even though three gondolas had been completed, only two arrived at Fort Ticonderoga by July 15. This prompted General Horatio Gates, commander of the Northern Army, to complain that the sixty carpenters at work at Skenesborough "must be very ill-attended to, or very ignorant of their business, not to do more work."[46] Gates wrote to Arnold from Ticonderoga to express his anxiety for the latter's early return from Crown Point because he felt that "maintaining our naval Superiority is of the last Importance."[47] By this, Gates meant that the gondolas were of the utmost importance and desired Arnold to personally oversee their construction.

By July 16 Governor Nicholas Cooke of Rhode Island had responded to Congress's request for carpenters. Captain Barnard Eddy enlisted twenty men at a rate of pay equal to that which the Marine Committee had given to the Philadelphia shipwrights.[48] By the time Eddy's men began their march to Skenesborough, the number of Rhode Island carpenters had grown to fifty, all supplied with tools and arms.

At the end of June the *Royal Savage, Enterprise, Revenge*, and *Liberty* aided in the evacuation of the troops from Canada. Gates wrote that what had "hitherto been solely employ'd as Floating Waggons" must be brought from Crown Point and armed. New carriages for the cannons were made at Ticonderoga "out of Wood taken from the Swamp."[49] The *Royal Savage*, armed with four 6-pounders and eight 4-pounders, was ready to sail by July 15 (fig. 2.2). The smaller *Revenge* had four 4-pounders and four 2-pounders. Although it would later be designated as the hospital sloop, the *Enterprise* had twelve 4-pounders. The *Liberty* had the smallest broadside weight of all: two 4-pounders and six 2-pounders.

Horatio Gates was singularly unimpressed with the two gondolas that Schuyler had sent forward to Ticonderoga. He wrote Hancock: "The Gondolas General Schuyler has Order'd to be built, as he had no Model to direct him, are in nothing but in name like those at Philadelphia, the Rigging and Artillery are all to be Fix'd here, and when done, they seem to be Vessels very unweildly to move, & very indifferent for the purpose intended. Two are Finished, & Two more will be Finish'd this Week; if the Enemy gives us time to do all this, it will be well, if not, This wretched Army will probably be yet more unfortunate."[50]

The responsibility for seeing that the American fleet was properly rigged and armed fell to Colonel Jeduthan Baldwin, chief engineer at Ticonderoga. His journal entry for July 28 states: "I have my hands & mind constantly employed night & Day except when I am a Sleep & then sometimes I dream."[51] Baldwin may also have been responsible for overseeing the assembly and rigging of the cutter *Lee* at Ticonderoga (fig. 2.3). The frames for the vessel came from another craft the Americans had been building at St. Jean. During the American retreat, Arnold had wisely numbered the frames and carried them back to the south.

Fig. 2.2. The schooner Royal Savage. Illustration by James W. Hunter III after an original drawing included in the Schuyler Papers, New York Public Library.

Per Horatio Gates's request, Benedict Arnold arrived at Skenesborough on July 23 to oversee and evaluate the fleet construction progress. By this date, four gondolas had been launched. Two others, including the *Philadelphia*, were nearly finished. Thirty fresh carpenters had just arrived from Connecticut. Arnold ordered their leader, Captain Winslow, to begin the construction of the first "Spanish Galley."[52] According to Hermanus Schuyler, the galley was "to be 63 feet long 18 feet beam holl [sic] 74 inch waist."[53] To honor the Connecticut shipwrights' governor it would later be named *Trumbull*. On the night of July 24, fifty-two additional carpenters arrived from Philadelphia. Their captain was Thomas Casdrop (or Casdorp) of Casdrop and Fullerton, the company that had built the *Chatham* and *Effingham* (variously called row galleys, armed boats, or gondolas) for the Pennsylvania state navy.[54] Casdrop's crew started work the next morning on the second galley (the *Congress*). At the same time, a Captain Titcomb brought another fifty carpenters from Massachusetts Bay to construct the third galley (the *Washington;* fig. 2.4). To satisfy their most immediate needs, Hermanus Schuyler wrote to General Schuyler for iron, steel, and "about a tun of Rum."[55]

Benedict Arnold also sent General Schuyler a list of the articles that would be needed to complete the vessels. Relying on his former business connections, Arnold suggested that sailcloth could be obtained from Thomas Mumford of New London, Connecticut, and cordage from Mr. Mortimer of Middletown, Connecticut. Arnold emphasized to Schuyler that while many of the articles on his list might seem like "triffles," they were absolutely necessary and could not be procured near the lake.[56]

To obtain desperately needed rigging for the vessels, Schuyler ordered Richard Varick to attempt to procure it from the owners of the sloops at Albany, New York. Schuyler reasoned that since their

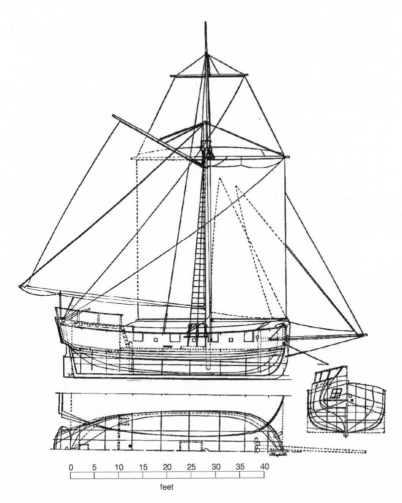

*Fig. 2.3. The
cutter* Lee. *After
a reconstruction
by Howard I.
Chapelle based on
an admiralty
drawing made
after her capture.
Courtesy of the
Smithsonian
Institution,
NMAH/AFH.*

0   5   10   15   20   25   30   35   40

feet

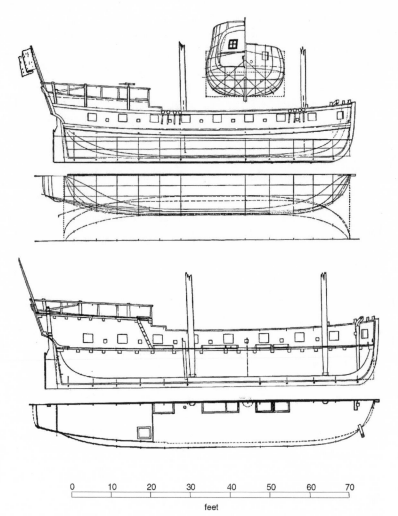

Fig. 2.4. The galley Washington. After a reconstruction by Howard I. Chapelle. Courtesy of the Smithsonian Institution, NMAH/AFH.

navigation had been stopped following the British occupation of New York City every sloop owner would aid the effort. If it proved impossible to purchase used blocks, Varick was to have block makers at Albany fabricate new blocks. In the event that the cordage and sailcloth could not be obtained in Albany, Varick was to approach the ship carpenters at Poughkeepsie, New York.

It was a difficult shopping list to fill. Besides the sailcloth and the cordage, Varick was also searching all of New York state and Connecticut for the wide variety of other materials needed to supply Arnold's fleet, the troops at Ticonderoga, Mount Independence, and the small garrison that remained at Crown Point. Eventually gunpowder and buckshot came from Albany and junk (pieces of old cable or cordage used to make gaskets, swabs, and oakum), oakum, pitch, iron, and steel from Fort George. The yard at Poughkeepsie furnished six coils of slow match; six dozen large sails, bolt rope, and marline needles; a hundredweight (112 pounds) of twine; some blocks; and a quantity of oakum and other articles.[57] A portion of the many anchors and cables needed came from Captain Peter Post of Esopus, New York, a small community about sixty miles south of Albany on the Hudson River.[58]

Jacobus Van Zandt, manager of the Poughkeepsie yard, regretfully informed Varick that he would be able unable to supply the pistols, cutlasses, sheet lead, quick match, portfires, cod lines, sheet copper, and swivel guns Varick had requested since "the Fire Craft & other Vessels we have been fixing here has Consumed largely of our Stores."[59] Van Zandt suggested that General Schuyler write to Judge Porter, manager of the Salisbury ironworks for the swivels since he had been assured that a large number of them had been cast for government use. Varick noted to George Washington that he immediately sent an express message to both the Salisbury ironworks and the "Forges & Furnaces at Livingstons Manor" for swivel guns, grapeshot, bar shot, and chain shot.[60] Varick also obtained anchors, cables, and cordage from the sloop owners and merchants at Albany and Schenectady.[61] Bateaux carried all these items, including a set of bellows, blacksmith tools, grindstones, spades, and axes, on the Hudson River; wagons carried them overland on the last leg to Skenesborough.[62]

The *Philadelphia* was the fifth of eight gunboats under Arnold's command. Like the others before it, the *Philadelphia* was constructed by Schuyler's carpenters in approximately three weeks, a remarkable feat considering the host of problems they faced. The *Philadelphia*'s builders complained of the necessity of having to stand in line each morning waiting to sharpen their axes on the few grindstones available to them. Woodcutters protested that the soldiers who "went into the woods to help them . . . would sit down by the trees instead of working."[63] By the time of the *Philadelphia*'s construction, ax-men ventured up to twelve miles to secure the oak crooks needed for the seventy-eight knees of each gunboat.[64] Although Benedict Arnold is usually given the credit for overseeing the construction of the *Philadelphia*, his first contact with the vessel came only three days short of its planned launching. After inspecting Schuyler's latest gondola, he delayed its launch and ordered a gun platform installed in the stern for the installation of a mortar to complement the three cannons that would be added at Ticonderoga.[65]

After the extra work on the mortar platform was completed, the *Philadelphia* was launched on July 30. Captain Cornelius Wynkoop wrote to Gates: "I have sent you one gondola more down, which the carpenters have named after me."[66] Obviously, the name did not stick, for on the first list of vessels built on Lake Champlain in 1776, all the gondolas but one have the names of cities or states (table 2.1). The *Spitfire* was the lone exception. The names may have been chosen to honor the colonial troops who were serving from those places or, more likely, the homes of the carpenters who had built them. At least one other vessel had its name changed. The list compiled on August 7 designates a galley *Schuyler*. This is the only reference to a galley of that name; all future lists designate the galleys as the *Trumbull, Congress, Washington*, and *Gates*. Perhaps General Schuyler suggested the name change himself since one of the gondolas built at Lake George in 1775 had been named *Schuyler*.

The *Philadelphia* was likely the gondola that military engineer Jeduthan Baldwin described on August 1: "at Sunset one howet [howitzer] was fired on board a large Gundalow by way of experiment, the Shell brok in the air, one 13 inch Bomb was also thrown from the same Gundelow on bord of which were about 20 men, when the Bomb went of[f] the Morter Split & the upper part went above 20 feet high in the Air over the mens heads into the water & hurt no man. the piece that blowd of[f] weighd near a ton, I was nigh & saw the men fall when the morter burst, & it was a great wonder no man was kild."[67]

The *Philadelphia* has several square openings cut into its inner planking in the aft end of the vessel, suggesting that Arnold's mortar platform was removed following the mishap. To trim the vessel, a number of stones were then placed under the quarterdeck to counteract the weight of the 12-pounder bow gun. The idea of arming the gondolas with mortars was given up when the only other large mortar available to the Americans also blew apart during a test firing on Mount Independence the morning of August 2.[68]

TABLE 2.1

*List of the Navy of the United States of America on Lake Cham[p]lain
Aug. 7th 1776*

	C. Guns	Swivels	and Men
1. Row Gally. *Congress*	6.	16	80
2. do *Washington*	6.	16	80
3. do *Schuyler*	6.	16	80
4. do *Lee*	6.	10	65
Schooner *Royal Savage*	12.	10	60
	G. Guns	Swivels	and Men
Sloop *Enterprize*	10	10	60
Schooner *Revenge*	8	10	40
Schr *Liberty*	8	8	35
Gondola *Newhaven*	3	8	45
do *Providence*	3	8	45
do *Boston*	3	8	45
do *Spitfire*	3	8	45
do *Philada*	3	8	45
do *Connecticut*	3	8	45
do *New Jersey*	3	8	45
do *New York*	3	8	45

NB. each Gally Mounts 2. 24 pounders, 2. 12 pounders & 2 — 6 pounders,
each Gondola 1. 12 & 2. 9 pounders
The Sloop & Schooner carry 3 — 4 & 6 pounders
6 Gondola's end compleat—one Gally Launched
The Sloop & Schooners compleated—the whole will be ready compleated
in the course of this month & four other Gally's will be compleated by the
middle of September.

Source: Clark, Morgan, and Crawford, *Naval Documents,* 6:96–98.

Arnold wrote to Schuyler at the end of July with the news that
there were now two hundred carpenters working at Skenesborough.
Construction of the four galleys was well under way. Arnold described them as similar to those built in Philadelphia and hoped to
arm each with two 24-pounders, two 18-pounders, and two other
lighter cannons.[69] In addition, he planned to build four more galleys that would require a similar complement of cannons. In regard
to the ordnance supply, Arnold wrote: "We have only Eleven pieces
& 10 twelve Pounders, which May Answer tho Not so well as heavier

Guns—If they are substituted, Eleven Pieces will still be wanting with shot &ca—which I wish May be sent up if they Can possibly be procured."[70]

Evidently, Philip Schuyler and Richard Varick failed to obtain the heavy cannons that Arnold desired. By the time the galleys were armed, not a single 24-pounder was included in Arnold's fleet. The armament needs for the galley *Gates* alone indicate the vast expense and effort that was required to build the defensive force the Americans hoped would be enough to stop the British invasion through the Champlain Valley (table 2.2).

With the steady increase of American vessels on the lake, there was optimism about the Americans remaining "masters of the lakes." Colonel Anthony Wayne wrote Benjamin Franklin from Ticonderoga: "We are indefatigable in preparing to meet the Enemy by Water—the Superiority in a Naval force on this Lake is an object of the first moment—it has been hitherto shamefully neglected, but now in a fair way of becoming formidable as we have at present three Schooners & one Sloop well appointed & mann'd with people drafted from the several Regiments; they carry from 8 to 16 Guns, each which together with four Gondolas already built will be no contemptible fleet in the Sea."[71]

Benedict Arnold wrote to Horatio Gates on August 7 that he was very pleased with the progress made toward completing the galleys. The *Trumbull* had already been launched, and he expected to launch three more in two weeks or less.[72] He predicted that a shortage of iron and planking would be the only thing that would retard the work.[73] In actuality, the procurement of enough rigging materials would be the most difficult part and would not be completely accomplished until October 11.[74] At the time of the *Philadelphia*'s construction, Arnold was still optimistic about the gondolas. He planned to build a total of ten, each to be armed with three or four heavy cannons and fourteen swivels.[75] Once the carpenters began working on the galleys, however, he changed his mind and ordered that no more gondolas should be put on the stocks, since "they take a large quantity of Plank, & retard the Building of the Gallies, which are of more Consequence."[76] Gondola construction ended with a total of eight vessels. Arnold was still planning, however, to build a total of eight galleys. He

TABLE 2.2
Supplies for the Galley Washington

2 18 pound Iron Cannon
2 12 ditto   do   do
2 9 ditto   do   do
4 4 ditto   do   do
20 round Shott for 18 pounder
20 ditto   do   for 12 ditto
20 ditto   do   for 9 ditto
20 ditto   do   for 4 do
10 Doublehead Shott for 18
10   Ditto ditto for 12
1–2 pound cannon
8 swivels
40 Swivels Shott Round
10 2 pound do do
10 Cannister Shott for 18
10 ditto do for 12
20 ditto do for 9
40 ditto do for 4
40 Paper cartridges fill'd for . . . 18 lb.
40 ditto do do for 12
50 ditto do do for 9
60 ditto do do for 4
80 ditto do do for 2
300 ditto do do for swivels
Rammers & Spunges
       2 for 18 pounders
       2 for 12 pounders
       2 for 9 pounders
       4 for 4 pounders
       1 for 2 pounders
       8 for Swivels
8 Lead Aprons for Cannons
2 Priming Wires & Brushes
20 Unfilled Flannel Cartridges for 12 poundr.
10 Doubleheaded Shott for 9 pdr omitted
1 Cartridge to Each Cannon Fill'd with Damaged powder
1 Barrel Contg 1 hundred Wt. 4 Quire Cannon powder

1 Ladle for 18 pounder
1 do for 12 do
1 do for 9 do
2 do for 4 do
1 do for 2 do
2 do for swivels
1 Worm for 18 pounders
1 do for 12 do
2 do for 9 do
4 do for 4....do
2 do for 2. . .do
2 do for Swivels
24 Handspikes
8 powder Horns
8 Linstocks
10 Priming Wires
3 Coils Slow Match
6 Portfires
12 Tubes
3200 Musquet Cartridges
200 Flints
Cartridge paper
1 Musquet & Bayonet
1 Rifle Gun

                    John Thacher Capt.

Source: "Supplies for the Galley *Washington,*" *Bulletin of the Fort Ticonderoga Museum* 4 (1936):21–22.

wrote to Schuyler to praise Captain Varick's efforts to supply the shipwrights and blacksmiths to that date, but in his estimate another 12 to 15 tons of iron would still be needed to see the galleys through to completion. He suggested to Schuyler that time could be saved if about 6 to 8 tons of the iron could be sent up in ready-made spikes from 5 to 7 inches long, mainly 6 inches.[77]

In total, 159 carpenters arrived from Philadelphia and Connecticut. Out of the 50 that traveled from Providence, Rhode Island, with Captain Barnard Eddy, only 11 were fit enough to work. The other 39 were at Williamstown, Massachusetts, suffering from smallpox. Hermanus Schuyler requested that Philip Schuyler prevent their coming to Skenesborough as he feared they would infect the other workers.[78] When Gates learned of this news from General David Waterbury, he responded at once by asking Governor Trumbull to write to Governor Cooke to dismiss them immediately.[79] "Pay," he said, "they do not deserve a penny, [and] should on no Account be permitted to come to Skenesborough, I am confidently assured we can do without them."[80] At this period there was much self-inoculation by soldiers, which consisted of infecting one's self with matter from a mild case of smallpox. The infected then usually underwent a mild attack of the disease and secured future immunity. Despite stringent orders against the practice, it could not be stopped.[81]

In the latter part of August the shipbuilding effort at Skenesborough began to slow down. Hermanus Schuyler wrote on August 25 that 55 of the blacksmiths had taken sick and were unable to make the ironwork as fast as the carpenters required it.[82] He also admitted that Captain Titcomb's crew was down from 50 to 20 able men. Both Winslow's and Casdrop's crews were also suffering a great deal from the "ague" (probably malaria). Upon being informed of the illness, General Schuyler ordered a physician to Skenesborough to examine the sick carpenters and discharge those who were "not likely to be of future Service—the Expense being very high."[83]

Later in the month one of Captain Casdrop's ensigns was involved in an unspecified dispute with a colonel from the regular troops. Evidently, the disagreement was serious; the ensign was placed under guard and taken to Ticonderoga to be tried. Prior to this incident, the highly paid carpenters apparently felt that they were not subject to regular military discipline. As a result of the affair and the continuing sickness, the carpenters became very uneasy and anxious to go home.[84] Despite the problems, Casdrop's crew launched the *Congress* on the first of September.[85]

The launch of a third galley occurred just before the end of the month. In order to see the fourth galley completed more quickly, Horatio Gates ordered the entire carpenter force to finish the vessel.[86] Essentially, all the shipbuilding activities at Skenesborough ended on October 2 when the *Gates* departed for Ticonderoga to be rigged and armed. As Horatio Gates expressed it, the Americans had done all they could that season to meet the British invasion by water. There was discussion, however, of continuing the shipbuilding effort over the winter.[87] Benedict Arnold wrote to Gates from Valcour Island on October 10:

> I am extremely glad you have represented to Congress and General Schuyler the absolute necessity of augmenting our navy on the Lake. It appears to me to be an object of the utmost importance. I hope measures will be immediately taken for that purpose. There is water between Crown Point and Point-aux-Fer for vessels of the largest size. I am of the opinion that row galleys are of the best construction and cheapest for this Lake. Perhaps it may be well to have one frigate of thirty-six guns; she may carry eighteen pounders on the lake, and will be superior to any vessel that can be built at and floated from St. John's. Carpenters ought to be immediately employed to cut timber and plank, and three hundred set at work at Skeensborough, the 1st of Feb. Of these matters I hope we shall have time to confer hereafter.[88]

The Battle of Valcour Island, however, changed the American defensive strategy (see chap. 5). After October 13 the Americans would concentrate all their attention on increasing the defensive strength of Fort Ticonderoga and Mount Independence.

The shipbuilding effort had taken almost exactly four months. In that short time, the Americans had managed to build eight gondolas, four galleys, and finish the construction of the cutter *Lee*. Although Benedict Arnold would still be requesting additional supplies and ordnance as late as October 10, the entire American fleet of seventeen vessels had for the most part been rigged and armed. That this was possible was due mainly to the efforts of Captain Richard Varick, but General Schuyler had certainly aided the work, especially through his close contact with Governor Jonathan Trumbull.

The Gondola
Philadelphia

Chapter 3

BUILDING THE
BRITISH FLEET

The British shipbuilding effort began at almost the same time the Americans started building gondolas at Skenesborough, New York. In fact, the British should have been ahead of the Americans, because British governor Guy Carleton had written to Vice Admiral Samuel Graves in Boston as early as July, 1775, asking for two "Sloops of War, and an additional number of Shipwrights and Seamen, in order to build Vessels and regain the Navigation of the Lakes and drive out the Rebels."[1] Graves was unable to fill Carleton's request and it was apparently forwarded to the British Admiralty Office.[2] Besides the sloops, Carleton's requisition specified that enough materials should be sent to Quebec to build, "at least four hundred Batteaux from 36 to 40 feet in length, and 6 or 7 feet in Breadth on the Beam."[3] It was not necessary to send planking and timber for the vessels because the admiralty knew that such materials could be easily obtained in Canada. Carleton received at least some building materials in early May, 1776, when Charles Douglas's transport fleet arrived to relieve the then-besieged city of Quebec. Additional materials arrived in late May and early June.

Following the American retreat from Canada, the British army quickly made camp on the banks of the Richelieu River at Isle aux Noix, Chambly, and St. Jean.[4] No time was wasted in repairing the facilities. The British assigned two hundred men to reconstruct the two old redoubts and ship stages at St. Jean because the Americans had destroyed the docks, yards, and boats before abandoning the post.[5]

The biggest obstacle facing the British in their preparations to place a fleet on Lake Champlain was the fact that their existing fleet could only sail up the Richelieu River as far as Chambly. Beyond that point, a twelve-mile stretch of rapids and shallow water on the river prevented any further progress to St. Jean and Lake Champlain by water. The British were faced with two choices: they could start from scratch and build a new fleet of ships at St. Jean, much as the Americans were doing at Skenesborough, or they could attempt to carry part of their existing force either through or around the St. Thérèse rapids between Chambly and St. Jean. Captain Charles Douglas, commander of the St. Lawrence fleet, believed the first choice would be a mistake.[6] With the short time available to the British that summer, the best they could hope to build at St. Jean would be several small vessels. What Douglas believed the British really needed were a few large vessels, ones powerful enough to confront and overwhelm the weaker fleet the Americans were putting together.

In the end the British decided to do both. New vessels would be built at the St. Jean shipyard, but Douglas was determined to transport warships around the portage. After a quick survey of the Richelieu River, it was deemed necessary to build a road so the vessels could be carried overland. "By all these means," wrote Douglas, the British would acquire "an absolute dominion over Lake Champlain."[7]

The first vessel to be carried across the portage was the 14-gun schooner *Lady Maria*. Named for General Guy Carleton's wife, the schooner had been captured by the Americans in November, 1775, on the St. Lawrence and retaken by the British following the American retreat. The *Maria* had a length on deck of 66 feet; a 52-foot-2¼-inch length of keel; a beam of 21 feet, 6 inches; and a depth of hold of 8 to 8½ feet.[8] When originally built, the vessel was fitted out with eight gunports on a side, five sweep ports, a cutwater, and a figurehead. Charles Douglas ordered the *Maria*'s captain, Lieutenant John Starke, to bring the vessel to St. Jean.[9] If necessary, Starke, working under the direction of Captain Thomas Pringle, was to take down the schooner to nearly the waterline to ensure that it would be light enough to be rolled along the portage on logs. When the road proved too soft to support even that weight, Starke stripped down the partially dismantled vessel to its floor heads.[10]

In a similar manner the schooner *Carleton* and gondola *Loyal Convert* (fig. 3.1) were transported to St. Jean and reassembled. The *Carleton* was a topsail schooner, 59 feet, 2 inches on deck; 46 feet, 10 inches on the keel; 20 feet in breadth; and 6 to 6½ feet deep in the hold.[11] The vessel had seven gunports on a side and was eventually armed with twelve 6-pounders.[12] The British plan of the vessel suggests that it was very similar to the *Maria* but lacked the sweep ports, cutwater, and figurehead of the former. Both vessels had a short quarterdeck. Like the *Maria*, the *Carleton* had been captured by the Americans in November, 1775, and retaken by the British in June, 1776.[13] The *Loyal Convert* (or *Royal Convert*), a captured American gondola,[14] may have been either the *Hancock* or the *Schuyler*, the two armed gondolas Philip Schuyler had built at Lake George in 1775.[15] According to Howard Chapelle, the *Loyal Convert* measured 62 feet, 10 inches on the deck; 50 feet, 8 inches on the keel; 20 feet, 3 inches in beam; and had a depth of hold of 3 feet, 7½ inches.[16] This overall length matches very closely with the corresponding dimensions Schuyler reported for the *Hancock* and the *Schuyler*.[17] The gondola was armed at St. Jean with six broadside 9-pounders and one 24-pounder bow gun taken from the army.[18]

In a remarkable feat of engineering, the 180-ton *Inflexible* was also carried up to the lake. After receiving intelligence reports of the progress the Americans were making toward their own fleet, Governor Guy Carleton insisted on the *Inflexible*'s transport to St. Jean.[19] The vessel had already been under construction at Quebec "where her floors were all laid, and some of her timbers put in."[20] Lieutenant John Schank, captain of the armed ship *Canceaux*, ordered his carpenters to dismantle the partially built *Inflexible* so the ship's timbers could be shipped to St. Jean in thirty longboats.[21] According to Lieutenant James Hadden, *Inflexible*'s "keel was laid the second time on the morning of Sept. 2d, 1776, and by sunset on that day, not only was she as far advanced in her new location as she had been at Quebec, but a considerable quantity of fresh timber was also got out and formed into futtocks, top timbers, beams, planks, &c,; as it was no uncommon thing for trees, growing at

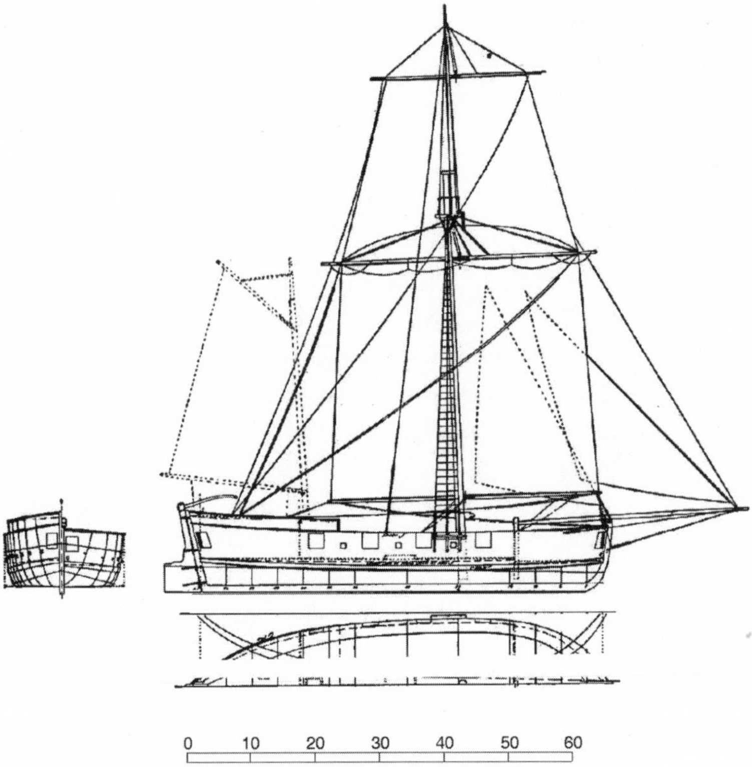

Fig. 3.1. The gondola Loyal Convert. *After a reconstruction by Howard I. Chapell. Courtesy of the Smithsonian Institution, NMAH/AFH.*

dawn of day, to form parts of the ship before night."[22]

Captain Charles Douglas ordered Schank to take the *Canceaux* to Chambly, where all her stores, sails, anchors, and crew were transferred to St. Jean for duty with the *Inflexible*.[23] Until the *Inflexible* was ready to sail, Schank served as the superintendent of the shipyard.[24] Schank's workforce was drawn from the St. Lawrence River fleet. Hundreds of carpenters, riggers, sail makers, and caulkers arrived to assemble the vessels. More than six hundred experienced sailors waited to man them.

Lieutenant William Twiss of the Engineers Corps was also ordered to the St. Jean's shipyard. Upon his arrival he was given directions for building the army's transport boats: "a common flat bottom called a King's Boat or Royal Boat, calculated to carry from thirty to forty men with stores and provisions, with this only difference, that the Bow of each Boat is to be made square resembling an English Punt, for the conveniency of disembarking the Troops, by the means of a kind of broad gang board, with Loopholes made in it for Musquetry, and which may serve as a Mantelet when advancing towards an Enemy, and must be made strong accordingly."[25] It is unknown how many flat-bottomed boats were built to these specifications at St. Jean. A British document entitled "Force on the Lake [Champlain] Tolerably Exact, on Septr 18th. 1776" specifies that "450 Batoes" were to be used for the "conveyance of the Troops."[26]

By the middle of August the *Maria* had been reassembled and launched onto Lake Champlain. Two weeks later, the *Carleton*, the *Loyal Convert*, and most of the gunboats followed. According to one researcher the *Inflexible* took longer. After the keel had been relaid at St. Jean, Schank ordered it extended eight or nine feet so the vessel would draw less water than had been originally planned.[27]

German company surgeon J. F. Wasmus, who watched the launching of the *Inflexible* on September 29, wrote: "At 10 o'clock this morning, the frigate Inflexible was launched. It was beautiful to see how she had been set on a sled-like machine, which had been rendered slippery with tallow and soap. With much effort, the ship got into motion but went into the water with great speed and cast anchor in the Riviére Richelieu. And now there sounded a cry of hurrah, done 3 times by the sailors and workmen."[28]

Captain Charles Douglas was extremely impressed with both Schank and the *Inflexible*. He wrote to Philemon Pownoll, captain of the frigate *Blonde* (anchored in the St. Lawrence River), about the imminent departure of the British fleet: "As the Inflexible is of the party, I am not uneasy about the event. . . . All the Carpenters work bestow'd upon her; until launching; did not exceed 12 men's labor for 16 days—By Lieutenant Schank's contrivance and close unremitting diligence."[29]

One large vessel was built entirely at St. Jean. The radeau *Thunderer* was a large, scow-like vessel designed to carry the heaviest armament of the fleet: six 24-pounders, six 12-pounders, and two howitzers (fig. 3.2).[30] The *Thunderer* had an overall length on deck of 91 feet, 9 inches; 72 feet on the keel; 33 feet, 4 inches in breadth; and 6 feet, 8 inches deep in the hold.[31] The nearly flat-bottomed vessel (Howard Chapelle calculated approximately 6 inches deadrise) had raking ends comparable to more modern scows.[32]

To round out the fleet, the British assembled at St. Jean twenty to twenty-eight gunboats, each armed with a brass fieldpiece (24- to 9-pounders), some with howitzers (fig. 3.3).[33] Ten of these gunboats (complete, but disassembled) had arrived from England on the frigate *Tartar* on July 7.[34] The British took four longboats from the transport fleet on the St. Lawrence River and fitted them with carriage guns to serve as armed tenders. Another twenty-four unarmed longboats to carry provisions for the fleet rounded out the flotilla.

It was a remarkable feat of engineering. In less than ninety days, the British had built and armed an invasion fleet. Lieutenant Thomas Pringle, formerly captain of the armed ship the *Lord Howe*, commanded the new fleet. Seasoned sailors manned the large British vessels, but soldiers manned the bateaux and gunboats. Guy Carleton's troops, the Hesse-Hanau artillerymen in particular, practiced their rowing skills on the St. Lawrence so they could propel themselves up Lake Champlain.[35]

Governor Carleton continued to receive updates on the position of the American fleet. The first British vessels sailed for Isle

Fig. 3.2. The radeau Thunderer. *After a reconstruction by Howard I. Chapelle based on an admiralty drawing. Courtesy of the Smithsonian Institution, NMAH/AFH.*

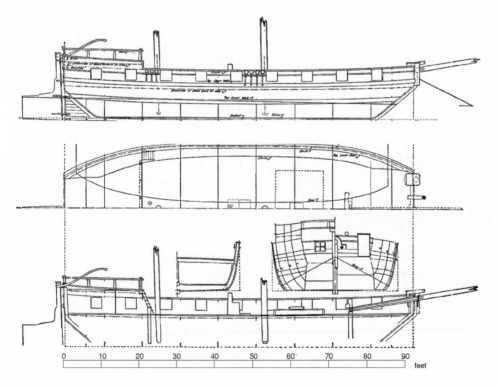

0 10 20 30 40 50 60· 70 80 90
feet

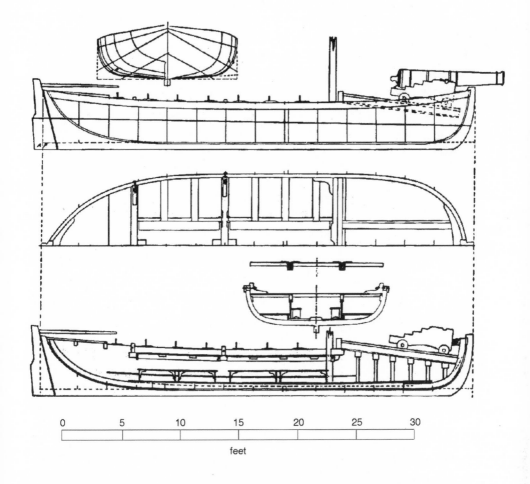

aux Noix on October 4. The smaller gondolas and gunboats soon followed, but the Germans had some difficulties in loading their bateaux and had to be transferred to the *Thunderer*.[36] After leaving the Richelieu River, the British fleet sailed cautiously onto Lake Champlain. By October 9 they anchored together at Isle La Motte; on the tenth Carleton moved his fleet to a point near Grand Island. That night he received word that one of the American ships had been spotted near Valcour Island. The two newly constructed British and American fleets would meet in battle the following day.

Fig. 3.3. Admiralty drawing of a boat to carry one carriage gun forward. Courtesy of the Smithsonian Institution, NMAH/AFH.

Chapter 4

THE AMERICAN FLEET
PREPARES FOR
CONFRONTATION

On August 7, 1776, shortly after the Americans declared their independence from Great Britain, Major General Horatio Gates wrote Benedict Arnold's sailing orders: "Upon your Arrival at Crown-Point you will proceed with the Fleet [of] the United States under your Command, down Lake Champlain." Gates made emphatically clear to Arnold that "It is a defensive War we are carrying on; therefore, no wanton risque, or unnecessary Display of the Power of the Fleet, is at any Time, to influence your Conduct." The fleet was not to be stationed any farther north than Isle aux Têtes and was to be kept far enough from shore so it could not be damaged from land-based artillery. Arnold's ultimate goal was to prevent the enemy's invasion, and if attacked by the British he was to "act with such cool determined Valour, as will give them Reason to repent their Temerity."[1]

Acting on Gates's orders, Arnold arrived at Crown Point on August 16 to take command of the fleet, unaware that General Philip Schuyler had already assigned the responsibility to Jacobus Wynkoop, captain of the *Royal Savage*.[2] The next afternoon, Arnold received a message from Lieutenant Colonel Thomas Hartley indicating that the British were approaching. A group of Hartley's men acting as a covering guard for a gang of oar makers had spotted a British scouting party seven miles farther down the lake and had lit a signal fire to alert Crown Point to the possibility of an invasion.[3] Arnold immediately ordered Hartley to take one hundred men and secure the retreat of the oar makers. He instructed Captains Seamon (also spelled Seaman) and Premier to take the *Revenge* and the *Liberty* down the lake for seven or eight miles to search for the enemy. After seeing the two schooners weigh anchor, Wynkoop immediately fired a shot from the *Royal Savage*, bringing the vessels to. Upon questioning the two captains, Wynkoop sent a hastily written note to Arnold exclaiming that he was the only person who had the authority to issue a sailing order. Arnold immediately responded to Wynkoop with a note of his own in which he remarked: "you surely must be out of your senses to say no Orders shal be obey'd but yours, do you Imagine that Congress have given you a Superiour Command over the Commander in chief."[4]

Arnold's note, in which he also threatened to arrest Wynkoop, brought no immediate reaction from the captain, either in reply or in orders to the two schooners. Arnold therefore boarded the *Royal Savage* to confront Wynkoop in person. After reading Gates's instructions to Arnold, Wynkoop finally relented and ordered the two schooners under way.[5]

However, Wynkoop, still believing he was in the right, appealed to Gates that night for redress. Arnold did the same. After reading both officers' accounts of the incident, Gates became furious and ordered Arnold to arrest Wynkoop and send him to Ticonderoga.[6] Wynkoop's reputation as a commander was already tarnished. Earlier that month while scanning the lake with his telescope he had spotted what he thought were the sails of the approaching British fleet. With the use of a speaking trumpet he shouted out an alarm to all the vessels at Crown Point. However, when Captain Isaac Seamon climbed to the top mast of the *Revenge* with a telescope he determined that what Wynkoop had taken to be sails was only a large flock of white seagulls.[7]

Arnold dutifully sent Wynkoop to Ticonderoga but admitted to Gates that the captain was really of the opinion that neither he nor Gates had the authority to command him. Gates wrote to Philip Schuyler indicating that he was going to send Wynkoop to Albany, where "I dare say you will without Scruple, forthwith dismiss him [from] the Service—He ought, upon no account, to be employed again." Gates added that many officers at Ticonderoga considered Wynkoop totally unfit to command a single vessel.[8] It was Arnold's wish, however, that Wynkoop return home without being cashiered. Wynkoop eventually arrived at Albany with an appeal to submit to Congress. The Marine Committee of the Continental Congress, however, appears to have ignored his "memorial." Wynkoop left the lake service, but not with the embarrassment of being cashiered as Gates had suggested.

In response to Wynkoop's ordeal, Philip Schuyler wrote: "Altho' I believed Wynkoop to be brave and industrious and equal to the Command of what Vessels we had when I recommended him, yet I was so far from being sufficiently acquainted whether he was equal to the Command of such a Number of Vessels as we have now there, that I learnt [of] General Arnold's Appointment with great Satisfaction and very much approved of it."[9]

On August 18 Gates assigned Brigadier General David Waterbury, Jr., as second in command of the fleet. Gates had confidence that there would be no dispute between the two because Arnold and Waterbury were upon the best terms.[10] As a replacement for Wynkoop on the *Royal Savage*, Gates recommended Colonel Edward Wigglesworth and also that he be third officer in overall command. Wigglesworth was known to be a good seaman and, according to Gates, "much of a Gentleman [of] unimpeached good Character."[11] However, Arnold had already taken the *Royal Savage* as his flagship and appointed David Hawley as captain.[12] Hawley had brought along the majority of his crew with him from Connecticut. Wigglesworth arrived later and took command of the *Trumbull*.

Arnold's first task as fleet commander was to find a pilot and a surgeon. He wrote to Dr. Thomas Potts at Fort George for a surgeon and one "Robert Aitkinson," a patient at the hospital, who was known to be an exceedingly good pilot.[13] Dr. Stephen McCrea became first surgeon to the fleet, with Mr. Francis Hagen acting as assistant.[14] McCrea brought his own medical instruments and medicines, but Arnold was forced to rent instruments for the assistant.

The *Washington* had just been finished at Skenesborough, and its builder, Captain Titcomb, asked to captain the galley.[15] Arnold denied the request because he thought it best that Titcomb remain with his gang to finish the fourth galley. Instead, Captain John

Thatcher of Colonel Heman Swift's Connecticut regiment became the commander of the *Washington*.[16] Because of delays in rigging the galley, Thatcher and Waterbury did not join Arnold with the *Washington* until October 6.

Before the gondolas were sent to Crown Point, at least one of the green crews had an opportunity for training. On the morning of August 5, while off the east redoubt of Mount Independence, Captain Simonds ordered his crew to fire the cannons onboard the gondola *Providence*. The crew fired the bow and port gun without mishap, but when it came time to reload, gunner's mate Solomon Dyer, who was serving the sponge for the 12-pounder bow gun, suffered a deadly accident. While Dyer was ramming a new gunpowder cartridge down the barrel, the improperly cleaned gun fired prematurely. According to the gondola's ensign, Dyer was standing in front of the gun when it went off, blowing "Boath his hands & one nee almost of[f]."[17] A search failed to find the gunner's body, and it was two days before Dyer's remains floated up and he could be given a proper burial.[18]

A Connecticut officer recorded additional activities of the American fleet from the time of their outfitting until the Battle of Valcour Island. The journal of Ensign Bayze Wells of the gondola *Providence* provides a daily record of the fleet's preparation and movement down the lake. Wells notes that early on the morning of August 24, with most of the fleet at Crown Point, Arnold ordered every vessel to prepare to sail.[19] The gondola *Philadelphia* under the command of Captain Benjamin Rue had joined the fleet four days earlier. The *Connecticut*, the sixth gondola built at Skenesborough, had just arrived under the command of Captain Joshua Grant, making a total of ten vessels ready for service.[20]

Arnold was still short of his desired complement of seamen and marines. To make up the deficiency he temporarily drafted a detachment of troops from Colonel Thomas Hartley's force at Crown Point. Preparations for sailing took almost the entire day, so not until sunset of the twenty-fourth did the fleet finally get under way. Arnold led the way in the *Royal Savage*, followed by the *Enterprise* and the gondolas *New Haven, Boston, Providence, Spitfire, Philadelphia,* and *Connecticut*. The schooners *Revenge* and *Liberty* brought up the rear. The fleet sailed down the lake for four miles and anchored for the night in four fathoms of water.[21]

By the night of August 25, Arnold's fleet arrived at Willsborough (now Willsboro), New York.[22] That same night a violent storm came out of the northeast. By 2:00 P.M. the next day, the fleet was forced to weigh anchor and return to Buttonmould Bay (now Button Bay), Vermont, for a safer anchorage. The storm proved to be a real test for the smaller gondolas. The *Connecticut* lost its mast and had to be taken in tow by the *Revenge*.[23] Unable to clear the shore, the *Spitfire* rode out the storm alone. Arnold was amazed to see the *Spitfire* the next day when Captain Ulmer brought the vessel in shorn of its trailing bateau.[24]

The storm continued unabated over the next two days, keeping the fleet wind bound. On the afternoon of August 29, Arnold invited all the captains and lieutenants to dine with him on shore. According to Wells, it was a "most Genteel feast" of roast pig, wine, punch, and cider.[25] After drinking to the health of Congress and Benedict Arnold, the officers named the small point of land and bay to their south after Arnold.

By August 31 the wind switched directions, enabling the fleet to resume its northerly course. Arnold hoisted a white pendant on the *Royal Savage*, ordering all captains to come aboard. Apparently, during the wind delay some troops went ashore and raided the area residents of household furniture and garden produce.[26] Arnold ordered Captains Seamon and Sumner ashore to ascertain the damage, so the locals could be reimbursed. Forthwith, no boats were allowed to the shore unless accompanied by an officer.

Arnold reported to Gates on September 2: "I hope soon to have it in my power to send you a very full Account of the Strength of the *Enemy* by Sea & land[.] I hope no time will be lost in forwarding, the three Gallies, when they have Joined us, I am very Confident, the Enemy will not Dare attempt Crossing the Lake . . . when the Enemy drive us back, to Tyonderoga, I have some thoughts of going to Congress, & beging leave to resign,—do you think they will make me a Major General—(Entre Nous)."[27]

At the time, Arnold had only scant intelligence of the British naval strength. It was the general opinion of most Americans that they were far ahead of the British in the shipbuilding race. That fact, coupled with the oncoming winter, led everyone to believe the British would not mount an attack that year but would instead strengthen their positions to the north and force the Americans to winter at Ticonderoga.

Gates sent further instructions to Arnold, ordering him to position his fleet in three divisions: Arnold in the center, Waterbury on the right, and Wigglesworth on the left. From this disposition, Gates believed the captains of the vessels would get "to know their Commanding Officers, and prevent any Confusion or dispute, about Command, in Case of an unlucky Shot, or other Accident should take care of the General."[28] The choice of the fleet's final defensive position was left entirely to Arnold.

On Monday, September 2, the American fleet sailed north, acting on a false alarm that the British were just four miles farther down the lake. Unmolested, the Americans continued to the lower end of Schuyler Island.[29] Acting cautiously, Arnold continued to send scout boats ahead of the fleet each day to determine if the British were in the area. By September 3 the fleet had made its way to Cumberland Head. During that day the scout boats encountered a party of twenty British soldiers and fired on them with three swivel guns.[30] Several riflemen from the fleet landed and searched the New York shore but apparently met with no resistance. By four o'clock, the fleet was anchored off Isle la Motte.

The next day, six American scout boats discovered that the British were placing cannons on an island to the north.[31] Arnold ordered the *Liberty* and the *Revenge* to determine the British strength. The two vessels soon returned with the news that several hundred British troops were on Isle aux Têtes about four miles to the north. When Arnold brought his vessels up in a line of battle, the enemy made a hasty retreat.[32]

Arnold continued to post scout boats at his front. The British were also sending out boats but with a "View of decoying" the American guard boats.[33] Presumably, the British were hoping to make an easy capture and gather intelligence about Arnold's real strength. Relying on his own intelligence sources, Arnold resisted pursuing the British vessels. Instead he sent Lieutenant Benjamin Whitcomb and three others to spy on St. Jean. While Whitcomb traveled by water on the western side of Isle la Motte, Ensign Thomas McCoy and his party of three scouted out the eastern approach to St. Jean.

On September 5 and 6 the crews of the gondolas went ashore to gather fascines (bundles of saplings) that Ensign Bayze Wells stated were to be placed "Round the fore Castle."[34] Arnold elaborated further on their use: they were to be fixed on the "Bows and Sides of the Gondolas to prevent the Enemies boarding and to keep off small shot."[35] The British had used the same tactic during the French and Indian War on Lake Champlain.[36]

Contrary to orders, Captain Sumner of the gondola *Boston* went ashore with eighteen men to gather fascines but neglected to wait until the other boats were ready. When Sumner's men landed, they were attacked by a "Party of Savages."[37] The British officer in charge offered quarter, but the Americans refused and were subsequently fired upon in their boat. Two Americans were killed and five more wounded, one of whom died soon after he was placed on the hospital sloop.[38] The rest of the fleet immediately fired into the woods where the British had lain in wait.[39] Afterward, Arnold sent a party ashore but found only a laced beaver hat and a button of the British Forty-Seventh Regiment. Later that afternoon the cutter *Lee* and the gondola *New Jersey* joined the fleet.

Now that Arnold had had an opportunity to observe the abilities of his men and fleet, he advised Gates of his present concerns and strategy and asked "will it not be prudent to send up one thousand or fifteen hundred Men, who might encamp on the Isle aux Mott, and be ready at all times to assist us if attacked?"[40] Oddly, Gates never responded to Arnold's suggestion of placing troops on Isle la Motte. Instead he cautioned Arnold to continue watching his flanks and to provide for the protection of resupply vessels.[41] Along with the promise that the galleys would soon be manned and dispatched north, Gates sent Arnold a copy of the Declaration of Independence. The document was to be given to the British if Arnold received an "*Order* to send a Flag to the Enemy; or have an Opportunity by the return of one of theirs."[42]

On September 8 the American fleet was stationed at Isle la Motte. Wigglesworth arrived by bateau the next day to begin his duties as third officer to the fleet. Two days later, the eighth and last gondola joined the fleet. Curiously, Ensign Wells referred to the *New York* as the *Sucsess [sic]*, which suggests that several vessels may have had their names changed after completion.[43]

By now the British had a very good idea of the number of American vessels and their general whereabouts. The Americans also knew the British were making further preparations to the north because on September 12 they heard reports of about sixty cannons from the vicinity of St. Jean or Isle aux Noix.[44] Five days later, Arnold received his first real intelligence of the British strength by water, "about Seven Sail allmost Compleat and A Large number of Large Battoes."[45] More specifically, "a Ship on the Stocks at St. John's, designed to mount Twenty Guns, Nine, and Twelve Pounders, several Schooners, and small Craft."[46] Arnold's informants were ignorant of the sizes of the vessels and the number of guns and crew, however. In an attempt to gather further information Arnold befriended someone he referred to as a "Frenchman," whom he had found in Mississquoi Bay, and sent him to St. Jean for information. Until Arnold received new intelligence, he planned to go to Valcour Island and wait for the three new galleys. Arnold had already scouted out the position and knew that it would leave him the option of a retreat if necessary. Gates approved openly of Arnold's plan but had earlier warned him: "The Enemy are Subtile, and quick at Expedients; they may endeavour to Impose False Friends upon you; your watch word, should never be given until Sun Sett, and all boats, at Day light, kept at a proper Distance, until their Crews are examined."[47]

Bateaux occasionally arrived from Crown Point with fresh provisions, but Arnold's men were running short of food. At one point, he wrote Gates that the only fresh provisions they had received lately were four "Beeves."[48] The crews still foraged ashore if given the chance. At an abandoned "french mans" farm, crewmen from five bateaux found some potatoes and corn.[49] Beyond the lack of provisions and tobacco, many of the crewmen were becoming ill due to their exposure on the open lake. Arnold was forced to send twenty-three of the more serious cases back to Ticonderoga.[50]

On September 19, while the American fleet lay off Bay St. Armand (north of Cumberland Head), Arnold ordered the schooner *Liberty* to patrol off Isle la Motte and join up with the fleet later that day. On its return, the vessel was hailed by a "man in french Dress"on the New York shoreline, opposite the southern end of Isle la Motte.[51] The unknown individual indicated that he was a British deserter and wished to board the vessel. Suspicious of a trap, Captain Premier ordered his boat to approach stern first, with "Swivels pointed & match lited."[52] Premier directed the stranger to swim out, but the man waded out only to his chest and indicated that he did not know how to swim. Unable to lure the boat in, he waded back to shore, gave "three Cahoops," to bring forth three to four hundred of the enemy dressed mostly as Native Americans.[53] Their surprise fire on the boat and schooner wounded five of the Americans. In retaliation, Premier fired upon the shore with grapeshot for nearly an hour.

A little later and a little farther down the lake, the *Liberty* came across two or three hundred Native Americans equipped with many birch bark canoes. Arnold feared the canoes because they could easily slip past him in the night and hide along the shore in the daytime. Following these last encounters with the British, Arnold told Gates: "I must renew my request For more Seamen & Gunners. . . . this emergency will Justify the measure."[54] Of the men already under his command, Arnold wrote: "We have but very indifferent Men, in general, [the] great part of those who shipped for Seamen know very little of the Matter."[55] His opinion did not improve until after the Battle of Valcour Island. It certainly did not change on September 20, when the nervous lieutenant of the *New York* mistakenly fired a swivel gun into the gondola *Providence.*[56] Fortunately, neither vessel suffered any damage nor were any crew members injured. On the same day, seaman Ansel Fox was "Cabbd twelve Strokes on his Naked Buttucks" for sleeping on watch.[57] Later, when a battle seemed imminent, four seamen announced that they would refuse to fight the British.[58] Arnold handed out punishment comparable to the strict and harsh treatment the British navy inflicted upon their sailors: the four mutinous seamen were whipped from vessel to vessel, receiving in total seventy-eight lashes.

On September 24, with the wind from the northwest, the fleet sailed for Valcour Island where it made a good anchorage in six fathoms of water. The next day, Arnold, secure in his new position, invited all the officers to dine with him on the island. While enjoying "a most agreable Entertainment," the Americans listened to sounds of British cannon fire to the north.[59]

Chapter 5

THE BATTLE OF
VALCOUR ISLAND

enedict Arnold brought his small fleet of galleys and gondolas to anchor in the half-milewide channel between
Valcour Island and the New York shoreline (fig. 5.1). The
geography of the position reflected Arnold's strategy for meeting
the British ships. Valcour Island is approximately two miles long
and one mile wide. The steep sides of the rocky island rise to nearly
180 feet above Lake Champlain's surface.[1] The island, then heavily
wooded, provided an excellent screen from a southbound fleet in
the main channel. A small promontory on the northwest side of the
island aided in the fleet's concealment from the north. Arnold
justified the defensive position to Major General Horatio Gates by
emphasizing "that few vessels can attack us at the same time, and
those will be exposed to the fire of the whole fleet."[2]

The galley *Trumbull* joined the fleet on September 30. After sailing down from Fort Ticonderoga, Captain Seth Warner informed
Arnold that he was not carrying the expected reinforcement of one
hundred additional sailors. An exasperated Arnold wrote to Gates:
"I hope to be excused (after the requisitions so often made) if with
five hundred men, half naked, I should not be able to beat the enemy with seven thousand men, well clothed, and a naval force, by
the best accounts, near equal to ours."[3]

After inspecting the new galley, Arnold wrote that although
"the *Trumbull* is a considerable addition to our fleet," it is "not

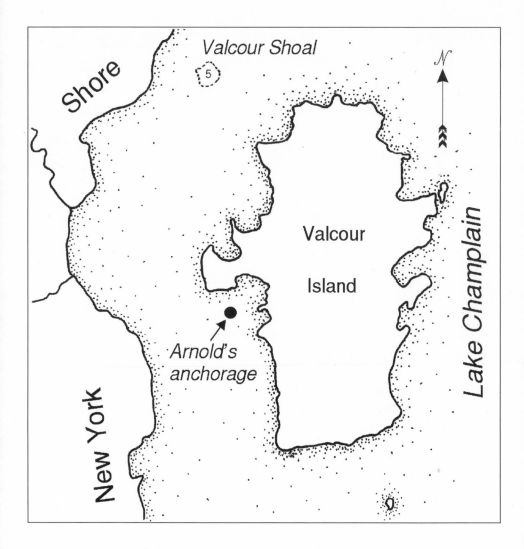

Fig. 5.1. Valcour Island. After Philip K. Lundeberg, The Gunboat Philadelphia and the Defense of Lake Champlain in 1776 (Basin Harbor, Vt.: Lake Champlain Maritime Museum, 1995), 22.

half finished or rigged; her cannon are much too small."[4] He reminded Gates that in July the original building plan called for eight galleys and that cordage had been requisitioned for all eight. Because only four galleys were constructed, Arnold stated: "I am surprised at their strange economy or infatuation below. Saving and negligence, I am afraid, will ruin us at last." The weather had turned windy and cold. Snow had already fallen on the fleet in late September.[5] Without an immediate resupply of adequate clothing and provisions Arnold felt that his "half naked" seamen and marines could not remain on station for more than two weeks. He therefore requested that Gates send the supplies down with the *Liberty*, a badly leaking schooner that had been captured more than a year before and had already been sent to Ticonderoga for recaulking.[6]

Brigadier General David Waterbury, Jr., joined the fleet on October 6, with the galleys *Washington* and *Congress*, captained by John Thatcher and James Arnold, respectively.[7] Waterbury, an experienced mariner from Stamford, Connecticut, had assumed his role as the fleet's overall second in command now that his duties at the Skenesborough shipyard had ended. Waterbury brought a letter from Gates responding to Arnold's complaints of a shortage of sailors, rigging, and provisions. In this letter, Gates admitted to Arnold that although two hundred seamen were promised from New York, none had been sent to Ticonderoga or were expected to arrive. Gates also explained that only half the requested cordage had been obtained. Consequently, the fourth and final galley, the *Gates*, was still incomplete. It was expected, however, that the final rigging could be completed at Fort Ticonderoga and the galley sent ahead in a week. As to the supplies and clothing, Gates wrote, "every article that you demanded in your last letter [is] on board the Liberty schooner except what is not [to] be had here; where it is not to be had, you and the princes of the earth must go unfinished."[8]

It was Gates's opinion that the British were not going to make an attack that season. He based this observation on the latest intelligence report received from Canada. In late September a Sergeant Stiles was sent north to spy upon the British encampments. Stiles had just returned from Isle aux Noix where, on September 30, he observed "upwards of Two Thousand Men on the Island."[9] He also reported a number of men erecting a battery of heavy cannons on River LaCole. Gates took the erection of the battery as a sign that the British were taking a defensive position.[10] Arnold agreed and indicated that the probability of a British attack that year would be dictated by the quickly approaching winter. He wrote Gates: "If the enemy do not make their appearance by the middle of this month [October], I have thought of returning to Button-Mould Bay, as I think they will not pretend to cross the Lake after that time." Arnold ended the letter, however, by adding: "We are prepared for them at all times, and if they attempt crossing the Lake, I make no doubt of giving a good account of them."[11]

Up to this point, the American estimates of the British naval and land forces had not been very reliable. The observations of Sergeant

Stiles generated an updated "Intelligence Report on the British Forces in Canada and on Lake Champlain" written at Valcour Island on approximately October 1.[12] The report correctly noted that ten thousand men had arrived in Canada from Europe. Of these, eight thousand were to join up with loyal Canadians for the invasion of the lakes. The detailed report also listed an accurate tally of the British naval force in Canada but did not include the newly built radeau *Thunderer.* It seems likely, however, that Arnold knew of the existence of the large raftlike vessel, as early as September 21, when rumor of its construction had reached Fort Ticonderoga.[13] All the other large vessels in the British fleet were listed, as were the smaller gunboats.

The inclement weather persisted, but Arnold's mood and outlook improved with the arrival of General David Waterbury and the two new galleys. Especially welcome to the fleet were fourteen barrels of rum and what Gates reputed to be the finest beef the region had to offer.[14]

Despite the lateness of the season and the erection of a defensive battery, the British force sailed from Canada on October 4. The British were fully aware that the American fleet was on the lake. Lieutenant William Digby's journal entry for October 6 notes that the Americans "were cruising off Cumberland Bay, about 20 miles above ours." Cumberland Bay was, in reality, approximately ten miles north of Arnold's true position at Valcour Island. Three days later, Digby indicated that "About 12 o'clock we heard the enemy very distinctly scaleing the guns on board their fleet, and soon hoped to make [them] exercise them in a different manner."[15] The reported position was again incorrect, placing the American fleet nearer to Grand Isle than Valcour Island.

With the arrival of the galleys, Arnold's fleet consisted of fifteen vessels: two schooners, three galleys, a sloop, a cutter, and eight gondolas (table 5.1). The *Enterprise* was designated as the fleet's hospital ship, with Dr. Stephen McCrea serving as fleet surgeon. The *Gates* was still at Fort Ticonderoga, as yet unfinished and unavailable. The *Liberty* had not yet sailed from Ticonderoga with the additional supplies of clothing and equipment.

Arnold reported to Gates on October 10 that he had not heard any recent intelligence of the British actions because the two canoes available to the fleet for small scouting parties had been lost.[16]

TABLE 5.1

The American Fleet at Valcour Island

Name	Type	Commander	Armament
Royal Savage	schooner	David Hawley	4 6-pounders; 8 4-pounders
Revenge	schooner	Isaac Seaman	4 4-pounders; 4 2-pounders
Enterprise	sloop	Thomas Dickenson	12 4-pounders
Lee	cutter	Robert Davis	1 12-pounder; 1 9-pounder 4 4-pounders
Trumbull	galley	Seth Warner	1 18-pounder; 1 12-pounder 2 9-pounders; 4 6-pounders
Congress	galley	James Arnold	2 18-pounders; 2 12-pounders 4 6-pounders
Washington	galley	John Thatcher	1 18-pounder; 1 12-pounders 2 9-pounders; 6 6-pounders
New Haven	gondola	Samuel Mansfield	1 12-pounder; 2 9-pounders
Providence	gondola	Isaiah Simonds	1 12-pounder; 2 9-pounders
Boston	gondola	Sumner	1 12-pounder; 2 9-pounders
Spitfire	gondola	Philip Ulmer	1 12-pounder; 2 9-pounders
Philadelphia	gondola	Benjamin Rue	1 12-pounder; 2 9-pounders
Connecticut	gondola	Joshua Grant	1 12-pounder; 2 9-pounders
New Jersey	gondola	Moses Grimes	1 12-pounder; 2 9-pounders
New York	gondola	John Reed	1 12-pounder; 2 9-pounders

Note: Arnold's desired complement of crewmen for the 15 vessels included 80 for each galley, 65 for the *Lee*, 50 for the *Royal Savage* and *Enterprise*, 45 for each gondola, and 35 for the *Revenge*. It is doubtful, however, that Arnold's total force of seamen and marines was anywhere near the 800 required. Although the *Philadelphia* was supposed to muster a total crew of 45, its final payroll indicates that only 44 men actually served.

Sources: Clark, Morgan, and Crawford, *Naval Documents*, 6:96–98; Lundeberg, *The Gunboat* Philadelphia *and the Defense of Lake Champlain*, 30.

Even though Arnold was unaware that the British had in fact sailed, he wisely sent the schooner *Revenge* down the lake to act as scout vessel. On Friday morning, October 11, Arnold transferred his flag from the *Royal Savage* to the newly built *Congress*. Sometime between seven and eight o'clock in the morning, the *Revenge* returned from her scouting mission, signaling the approach of the British fleet.[17] After receiving the report, David Waterbury immediately rowed over to the *Congress* and urged Arnold "to come to sail and fight them on a retreat in [the] main lake." Waterbury believed the superior numbers and strength of the British fleet would prove overwhelming because the Americans lay in such a disadvantageous position. "The enemy would be able to surround them on every side since they lay between the island and the New York shore," he reasoned.[18] Arnold was determined to fight the British from his preselected position even though the scouting report indicated that his forces were greatly outnumbered.

At 9:30 A.M. Arnold ordered Colonel Edward Wigglesworth, third in overall command, into the "yawl to go to windward and observe their motions."[19] When Wigglesworth returned at ten o'clock with the news that the British had rounded the island, Arnold ordered the *Royal Savage* and the three galleys under way. He planned to send the larger vessels to windward to draw the attention of the British and, if possible, gain a raking position on the enemy fleet. The eight gondolas, the *Lee*, and the *Enterprise* remained at anchor in a tight defensive arc in the middle of the channel. Aided by a strong northerly wind, the British ships were already in midchannel, two miles beyond the southern end of Valcour Island, before the crews detected the concealed American fleet.

Captain Thomas Pringle commanded the British naval force (table 5.2), and Governor General Guy Carleton, in overall charge of the invasion, rode in company on Pringle's flagship, the *Maria*, named in honor of Carleton's wife. In addition, the vanguard of the British invasion force consisted of four other large vessels: the schooner *Carleton;* the *Inflexible*, a three-masted, ship-rigged man-of-war; the radeau *Thunderer;* and the *Loyal Convert*, the aptly named gondola captured from the Americans the year before. The British also possessed a second gondola, noted in both Arnold's and Arthur St. Clair's reports; it was also counted among the British vessels first reported to the crew of the *Trumbull*.[20] Following closely behind the larger vessels were 20 to 24 gunboats, 4 longboats, and several smaller supply vessels. Nearly 1,000 British soldiers came after the main group in 40 or more bateaux to act as boarding parties should the need arise.[21] In addition, some 650 Native Americans, led by British officers, followed in a contingent of canoes. The British main army—7,000 men preparing some 300 to 400 bateaux—remained behind at Point au Fer.[22]

TABLE 5.2

The British Fleet at Valcour Island

Name	Type	Commander	Armament
Inflexible	ship	John Schank	18 12-pounders
Maria	schooner	John Starke	14 6-pounders
Carleton	schooner	James Dacres	12 6-pounders
Thunderer	radeau	Scott	6 24-pounders
			6 12-pounders
			2 howitzers
Loyal Convert	gondola	Edward Longcroft	7 9-pounders
unnamed	gondola	unknown	unknown
20–24 unnamed	gunboats	various	20–24 various, from 24-pounders to 9-pounders
4 unnamed	longboats	various	4 various

Note: The flotilla of 30 to 34 vessels was manned by a contingent of seamen from the British ships and transports at Quebec. Their numbers amounted to 8 officers, 19 petty officers, and 670 picked seamen, making in all 697 men from the regular navy. One hundred of these men were taken from the *Isis;* 70, from the *Blood;* 60, from the *Triton;* 30, from the *Garland;* 40, from the *Canceaux;* 18, from the *Magdalen, Brunswick,* and *Gaspee;* 90, from the *Treasury* and several armed brigs; 30, from the *Fell;* 9, from the *Charlotte;* 214, from transports; while 9 were volunteers.

Sources: Douglas to Stephens, October 21, 1776, in Clark, Morgan, and Crawford, *Naval Documents,* 6:1344–45; Chapelle, *History of the American Sailing Navy,* 53–54n; Lundeberg, *The Gunboat* Philadelphia *and the Defense of Lake Champlain,* 30.

Lieutenant Digby stated Thomas Pringle's order for proceeding up the lake as follows: "Three small boats in front of all as a party of observation, our schooners and armed vessel in line of battle following: Gun boats . . . The battallion of Grenadiers in flat bottomed boats, and in their rear, the remainder of the army in battows. One gun fired from a gun boat, was a signal to form 8 boats a breast; and two guns, a signal to form a line of boats." Frequent practice had made the otherwise land-based soldiers expert rowers, capable of performing the formations with good effect. The plan, however, was later "found not to answer so well," once the true position of the American fleet became known.[23]

Dr. Robert Knox, physician to the British fleet, claimed to be the first to sight the American fleet. In a letter written a few days after the battle, Knox recounted that "about ten o clock, as I was walking the Quarter deck with the Genl, I descried a vessel close in shore, which suddenly disappeared, and almost made me think I was deceived, but my glasses being good, I persisted in it, and induced the Commodore [Pringle] to send a Tender down, with orders, to fire a gun and heist a signal if he saw any ships; he no sooner arrived at ye mouth of ye river Valcour, than he fired."[24]

Pringle signaled the fleet to execute a turn to windward, then being north-northwest, in an attempt to weather the point of Valcour Island and engage the American ships.[25] The *Maria*, although described as "the best sailer" in the fleet, was among the least successful in performing this maneuver.[26] Thomas Pringle brought her to anchor at a prudent distance from the action; the ship's captain, Lieutenant John Starke, had refused to do so as he thought it an "act truly unbecoming on such an occasion."[27]

The British error in not sending out scout boats became readily apparent. As Arnold had predicted, Pringle had to sail his vessels into the wind to make an attack, a difficult maneuver if it was to be conducted with any sort of coordination between the vessels in the confined channel.

According to Pascal De Angelis, a thirteen-year-old Connecticut seaman serving on the *Trumbull*, Arnold gave the order for all the ships, which had been "standing off and on . . . to come to anchor in a line of battle."[28] Shortly after, the *Royal Savage*, due to the crew's mishandling, missed stays several times and did not get up into the line. Seizing the advantage, several of the British commanders immediately attacked the lone schooner. After the *Inflexible* "fired several broadsides with much effect," severing *Royal Savage*'s foremast and most of its rigging, Captain David Hawley was forced to run her aground on the southern end of Valcour Island.[29] Under the direct fire of the *Inflexible* and several British gunboats, the crew attempted to abandon the *Royal Savage* and seek out protective cover on the island. Simultaneously, Lieutenant Edward Longcroft, commander of the *Loyal Convert*, led a boarding party onto the stranded vessel and captured about twenty Americans who had not yet escaped. Longcroft then turned the *Royal Savage*'s guns upon the American fleet. When the British gunboats began firing on the escaping crew, four of the American vessels moved up in an attempt to protect the grounded schooner. As British lieutenant James Hadden described it, the British gunboats were at that point "in a cluster" within reach of the guns of the larger American vessels.[30] Pringle immediately signaled an order for the gunboats to drop back and form across the bay. Longcroft, however, continued to fight the captured schooner "till half of the men who boarded with him were kill'd."[31] Once the *Loyal Convert* fell to leeward, Pringle was forced to abandon the schooner. According to a later report by the British ship captains, the *Royal Savage* "was most shamefully lost" because Pringle did not send the assistance Edward Longcroft needed to get her offshore.[32]

The crews of the gunboats executed Thomas Pringle's order under heavy American fire from all vessels, galleys and gondolas alike. Captain George Pausch of the Hesse-Hanau artillery wrote that "several armed gondolas, which, one after another, emerged from a small bay of the island firing rapidly and effectively. Every once in a while they would vanish in order to get breath, and again suddenly reappear."[33] Although successful, the withdrawal of the gunboats was completely unsupported as all the other British vessels had "dropped too far to Leeward."[34]

Sometime between twelve and one o'clock, the *Carleton* came up into the anchorage by catching a chance wind veering off Valcour Island. The schooner, well in front of the gunboats, immediately opened fire with her modest battery of twelve 6-pounders.[35] The captain, Lieutenant James Dacres, anchored the *Carleton* broadside to the American defensive crescent with a spring on its cable.[36] Seventeen of the British gunboats followed the schooner up. Accounts from both sides indicate that it was at this point that the real battle began. Jahiel Stewart, viewing the battle from the deck of the American hospital sloop, wrote that when "one of the Regular Skooners Came up . . . the battel was verryey hot [and] the Cannon balls & grape Shot flew verrey thick."[37] With one large target at very close range, the Americans were able to concentrate their fire. According to Hadden, the *Carleton* received "the Enemies whole fire which continued without intermission for about an hour."[38] Very early in the action, Robert Brown, the *Carleton*'s second in command, lost an arm; soon after, Lieutenant Dacres fell, severely wounded and unconscious. Just as Dacres was about to be thrown overboard for dead, a nineteen-year-old midshipman named Edward Pellew intervened and saved his captain's life. Following Dacres's and Brown's injuries, Pellew succeeded to command.[39]

According to a biographer, Pellew, later the Admiral Viscount Exmouth,

> maintained the unequal contest until Captain Pringle, baffled in all his efforts to bring up the squadron, made the signal of recall. The *Carleton*, with two feet of water in its hold, and half the crew killed or wounded, was not in a condition to obey, being at the time near the shore, which was covered with enemy's marksmen, she hung in stays, and Mr. Pellew, not regarding the danger of making himself so conspicuous; sprang out on the bowsprit to push the jib over. The artillery-boats now took her in tow, while the enemy maintained a very heavy fire, being enabled to bear their guns upon her with more effect, as she increased her distance. A shot cut the tow-rope, and Mr. Pellew ordered some one to go and secure it; but seeing all hesitate, for indeed it appeared a death-service, he ran forward and did it himself.[40]

Eventually, the badly damaged *Carleton* was towed out of range by two of the *Inflexible*'s boats.

According to Dr. Robert Knox, about one o'clock in the afternoon, General Carleton became displeased with the *Maria*'s distance from the action.[41] This was the moment as well, according to Knox, in which both he and Carleton suffered a close call from an enemy shot. Knox was leaning on a boom alongside Carleton at the moment an 18-pound shot from the *Congress* passed perilously close. The shot slammed into the quarterdeck of the *Maria*, seriously wounding Thomas Carleton, the general's younger brother. Knox recorded the general's nonchalant reaction: "well Doctor, says he, how do you like a sea fight."[42] Following the incident, Pringle kept the *Maria* to her anchorage. As Starke and the other dissident captains later charged, she "lay too with the top sails, and [Pringle] was the only person in the fleet who showed no inclination to fight."[43]

It was assumed that the heavy armament of the radeau *Thunderer* would command respect from the Americans, but such was not the case. Lieutenant John Enys noted that the *Thunderer* was "totally useless she being flat bottomed and consequently could not work to Windward. We fired some few Shot at the time we first Saw their fleet but believe it might have been just well lett alone."[44]

Similarly, the *Inflexible* and the *Maria* also fired a number of shot during the battle but with little effect because both were too far off to hit any American targets. The real work of the battle had fallen to the British gunboats once the *Carleton* was towed out of the action. According to Hadden, "It was found that the Boat's advantage was not to come nearer than about 700 yards, as whenever they approached nearer, they were greatly annoyed by Grape Shot, tho' their Case could do little mischief."[45] Captain George Pausch of the Hesse-Hanau artillery was in charge of one British gunboat. He provides a vivid account of the gunboat action:

Our attack with about 27 batteaux armed with 24, 12 and 6 pound cannon and a few howitzers became very fierce; and, after getting to close quarters, very animated. . . . Close to one o'clock in the afternoon, this naval battle began to get very serious. Lieut Dufais came very near perishing with all his men; for a cannon ball from the enemy's guns going through his powder magazine, it blew up. He kept at a long distance to the right. The sergeant, who served the cannon, on my batteau, was the first one who saw the explosion, and called my attention to it as I was taking aim with my cannon. At first, I could not tell what men were on board; but directly, a chest went up into the air, and after the smoke had cleared away, I recognized the men by the cords around their hats. Dufais's batteau came back burning; and I hurried toward it to save, if possible, the Lieutenant and his men, for as additional misfortune, the batteau was full of water. All who could, jumped on board my batteau, which was being thus overloaded, came near sinking. At this moment, a Lieutenant of artillery by the name of Smith, came with his batteau to the rescue, and took on board the Lieutenant, Bombadier, Engell, and one cannonier and nine sailors remained with me; and these, added to my own force of 10 cannoniers, 1 drummer, 1 Sergeant, 1 boy and 10 sailors—in all 48 persons, came near upsetting my little boat, which was so overloaded that it could hardly move. In what a predicament was I? Every moment I was in danger of drowning with all on board, and in the company, too, of those I had just rescued and who had been already half lost![46]

During that same incident one well-aimed shot from an American vessel killed one of the men serving the single cannon on Dufais's vessel. Once the shot passed through the cannoneer it tore off the leg of another seaman before driving through the bulwark of the vessel.[47]

Two detachments of Indians and one hundred Canadians under the commands of Captain Christopher Carleton (nephew of General Carleton) and Colonel Simon Fraser, respectively, added musketry to the storm of shot that fell upon the American fleet from the British gunboats. Both groups landed their canoes on Valcour Island and the New York shoreline to the west of the Americans. Although they continued to fire upon the Americans throughout the day, their fire proved more annoying than destructive.[48]

Very late in the afternoon, Lieutenant John Schank finally managed to bring the *Inflexible* up before the American line. The crew of the ship-rigged vessel fired broadside after broadside into the American fleet. According to one historian, the sheer power of the *Inflexible*'s eighteen 12-pounders all but silenced the American cannons.[49]

The British gunboats maintained their fire until dusk, or just about five o'clock, when Pringle made the signal for recall. The vessels pulled back out of range and anchored in a confining semicircle to the south of the Americans. About one hour later the gondola *Philadelphia*, "hulled in so many Places," sank to the bottom.[50]

By the end of the battle the *Congress* had been hulled twelve times, with seven of these shot hitting below the waterline. The mainmast was damaged in two places and the yard in one. The situation was more serious on the *Washington*: the galley's first lieutenant was dead and Captain John Thatcher and his master wounded. The newly built galley had been hulled at least as many times as the *Congress*; its mainmast was "Shot thro" and was taking on water.[51] All the officers on the *New York*, except Captain Lee, died in the battle. Arnold later estimated that sixty Americans had been killed or wounded during the day. Without doubt, Dr. Stephen McCrea had had his hands full on the *Enterprise*. Jahiel Stewart wrote, "I beleve we had a great many cilld and I was abord of the hospitele sloop and they brought the wounded abord of us the Doctors Cut off great many legs and arm and See Seven men threw overbord that died with their wounds while I was abord."[52]

The British also suffered a number of casualties. Specifically, Lieutenant John Enys mentioned that one midshipman (presumably on the *Thunderer*) was wounded, and "5 or 6 Men and a Drummer Killed and one wounded on board a Gun Boat."[53] Several British soldiers also drowned as an indirect result of the American fire directed at the gunboats. Digby noted in his journal that the British losses were very close to that of the Americans': "about 60 men killed and wounded."[54] Rather than relying on a hospital vessel, the British transported the wounded back to their northern lines, where they had established a field hospital. J. F. Wasmus, a German company surgeon stationed at Point au Fer, related that on October 12 "A batteau arrived on which there were an Engl. officer, 8 Engl. soldiers and one Hesse-Hanau Artilleryman . . . one arm and 2 legs were amputated."[55]

The American casualty rate of approximately 10 percent was probably due almost entirely to fire from the British gunboats. Hadden noted that at the beginning of the battle the gunboats were supplied with "80 rounds of Ammunition, 30 of which were Case Shot." Just before their recall late that afternoon, each vessel needed to be resupplied with ammunition.[56] It seems probable, therefore, that the British gunboats alone may have fired well over one thousand rounds of solid shot.

The Americans, for their part, had also fired a large number of shot during the day. Benedict Arnold wrote that nearly three-fourths of the ammunition had been expended when the firing ceased that evening. He admitted to General Gates that the battle "suffered much for want of Seamen & Gunners." Evidently, he felt that the cannons could have been more accurately served because Arnold was "obliged . . . to Point Most of the Guns on board the Congress," which he felt he did with "good execution."[57] Captain George Pausch argued that the American fire was skillfully aimed because most of the British vessels had to be "well mended and patched up with boards and stoppers."[58]

At dusk, just after Thomas Pringle ordered his fleet to form in a semicircle south of the channel between Valcour Island and the mainland, General Carleton ordered the *Royal Savage* burned. Native Americans stationed on the island carried out the task. Shortly afterward, the powder supply on board the *Royal Savage* blew up and carried away the upper part of the vessel. The fire continued to burn all night before the lower hull finally settled into the water off the island. James Hadden considered "this [act of burning] an unnecessary measure as she might at a more leisure moment have been got off, or at all events her stores saved, and in her present position no use cou'd be made of her by the Enemy."[59]

At seven o'clock, Arnold summoned all his officers onboard the *Congress* for a council of war: there would be no surrender; they would make their escape during the night. Remarkably, the Americans did just that. Although there has been much speculation as to whether the American retreat was to the north or to the south, it is apparent that the American vessels slipped south, between the British fleet and the New York shoreline.[60] With the *Trumbull* in the lead, and a hooded lantern in the stern of each vessel, the fleet carefully passed single file "with so much secrecy that we went through them entirely undiscovered."[61] Jahiel Stewart described his escape on the *Enterprise* that night: "we histed Sails & put our oars & maid all the Speed we Could and they did not give us one gun nor we Did not fier one at them. . . . Did not Recive any Damage to our Sloop nor men so we got threw the fleet verrey Safe but we Run a ground but got off without much Diffelculte and we Sailed all Night and Roade so we thought we was Safe."[62] As one researcher has noted, the burning of the *Royal Savage* provided the perfect distraction.[63]

According to the British reports, some part of the American fleet was still visible at daylight. The British attempted to pursue them but, as the wind "was hard against them," they were forced back. Apparently, the *Thunderer* was in danger of sinking because "her lee boards [were] giving way which made heel so much as to let some water into her lower part." The *Inflexible* was also having some unspecified difficulty with the weather and was reported to be in danger as well. Later that evening, a British tender acting as a scout vessel spotted the fleet for the second time that day.[64]

When later asked to explain how the Americans escaped, Pringle merely said that his attempt to cut off their retreat was "frustrated by the extreme obscurity of the night."[65] A year later three of the other ship captains, John Schank, John Starke, and Edward Longcroft, charged Pringle with negligence. In an "open letter to Captain Pringle" they charged that "the fleet was not brought to anchor as near as possible to the rebels, for the MARIA weighd and run out above half a mile from the place where you had anchored her before as did the Carleton still farther, and the Inflexible was ordered by you to anchor near the Maria not to make the line too extensive. By which means the rear of the British line was at least one mile from the western shore, and the van beyond the small island at the southern end of Valcour. From this disposition, Sir, and not from the extreme obscurity of the night as you are pleased to say, the rebels escaped."[66]

Hadden placed the blame for the American escape on Pringle's positioning of the gunboats. In support of his own detachment, and in praise of Benedict Arnold, he wrote: "The Enemy finding their force diminsh'd and the rest so severely handled by little more than ⅓ the British Fleet determin'd to withdraw towards Crown Point, and passing thro. our Fleet about 10 o'clock at Night effected it undiscover'd; this, the former position of the Gun Boats wou'd probably have prevented. All the Enemies Vessels used Oars & on this occasion were muffled. This retreat did great honor to Gen'l Arnold who acted as Admiral to the Rebel Fleet on this occasion."[67]

Off Schuyler Island, about eight miles to the south of Valcour, some of the American fleet anchored to effect repairs. Arnold wrote to Gates: "Most of the fleet is underway to Leeward and beating up. As soon as our leaks are stopp'd the whole fleet will make the utmost dispatch to Crown Point, where I beg you will send ammunition & your further orders for us. On the whole, I think we have had a fortunate escape."[68]

During the stop, the Americans discovered the gondola *Providence* was so badly damaged that they removed the equipment and scuttled her. The *Trumbull*, being in the lead, sailed past Schuyler Island and on to Ligonier Point before anchoring to wait for the fleet, to stop their own leaks, and to secure the mainmast that had been split in two.[69] The *New Jersey* "was taking water" and apparently ran aground. With the weight of the water in the vessel it could not be moved.[70] According to Lieutenant Enys, a party of Canadians following the British found and took the vessel on the thirteenth.[71] For an unspecified reason, the crew of the cutter *Lee* also abandoned their vessel on the New York shoreline, allowing the British another easy capture.[72]

Unfortunately for the Americans, the wind changed direction on the afternoon of October 12 and blew directly from the south. Consequently, the ten remaining vessels, suffering from varying degrees of damage, became widely separated during the next twenty-four-hour period. The *Trumbull, Revenge, Enterprise,* and *New York* were well ahead of the *Washington,* the *Congress,* and the four remaining gondolas when they spotted the British ships following in their wake.

On the morning of October 13, Henry Sewall, thirty miles away at Fort Ticonderoga, noted in his diary that he "Heard a cannonading down the lake."[73] Most likely, these were the three guns fired twice in succession at Crown Point to signal the enemy's advance.[74] About that same time, Captain Pringle claimed he "saw 11 sail of their fleet making off to Crown Point, who, after a chace of seven hours, I came up with in the *Maria,* having the *Carleton* and *Inflexible* a small distance astern; the rest of the fleet almost out of sight."[75] When it became clear that the British were gaining on the Americans, Arnold sent an order to the *Enterprise* urging the hospital sloop to make all speed to Ticonderoga.[76] This was accomplished by ordering three men to each oar so that headway could be made against the wind.

At 9:00 A.M. Arnold instructed Colonel Edward Wigglesworth "to lie by for the fleet," which the *Trumbull* did by "stretching across the lake." Apparently, the two other vessels with Wigglesworth were too far away from Arnold to regroup. At this point, Wigglesworth "thought it [his] duty to make sail and endeavor to save the Trumbull galley if possible" by double-manning the oars, and throwing the ballast overboard to escape the British fleet.[77]

When the British closed within range, they began to fire on the *Washington* and the *Congress.*[78] "My vessel was so torn to pieces that it was almost impossible to keep her above water," Waterbury later explained to Gates. "It began to grow calm and I knew the next wind would be north and the enemy could spread so much sail and our vessel was so much torn and dull I thought best to put my wounded men into the boats and send them to Ticonderoga and row my galley ashore and blow her up."[79] As the *Inflexible* gained on the *Washington,* Waterbury sent an officer to Arnold's flagship for permission to destroy the vessel. Arnold refused and ordered Waterbury "to push forward to Split Rock, where he would draw the fleet in a line, and engage them again." When Waterbury reached Split Rock, he found the other vessels still fleeing and the *Washington* "left . . . in the rear to fall into the enemy's hands."[80]

Wigglesworth recorded that the first shots of the second engagement occurred at 10:00 A.M.[81] Pringle noted that the real battle, however, "began at twelve o'clock, and lasted two hours."[82] The three British vessels surrounded the *Washington* about five miles below Split Rock. According to Waterbury, the *Washington* "was so Shatored She Was Not able to Bare fiering"; he was forced to surrender without firing one gun.[83]

It is evident from a British prisoner list that most of the *Philadelphia*'s crew transferred to the *Washington* after the loss of their vessel at Valcour Island.[84] The journal of Jeduthan Baldwin records that just before Waterbury's surrender, Captain Benjamin Rue (of the gondola *Philadelphia*) and sixteen of his men escaped and later reached Fort Ticonderoga.[85] Rue and his followers left the galley in a bateau and fled to shore unmolested by the British.

Following Waterbury's surrender, the British were ready to turn their full attention toward the *Congress*, which was following the eastern shoreline. British firepower tore to pieces the vessel's rigging and sails, and grapeshot killed the first lieutenant and three others. The battle settled into a running chase, during which time Arnold sailed his vessel nearly nine miles from Split Rock to present-day Panton, Vermont.[86]

To keep his ships from falling into British hands, Benedict Arnold steered for tiny Ferris Bay, just ten miles north of Crown Point on the eastern shore of the lake, and ran his flagship and the four remaining gondolas into the bay until they were aground. With flags still flying in defiance of his British pursuers, he ordered the cannons dumped overboard and his vessels destroyed.[87] It is believed that Arnold intentionally choose Ferris Bay because of his familiarity with the anchorage. Arnold had stopped there on August 31 and knew both the area and the landowner, Squire Ferris.[88] The *Congress*'s sergeant of the marines, James Cushing, later told General James Wilkinson that "[Arnold] set [the ships] on fire, but ordered the colours not be struck, and as they grounded, the marines were directed to jump overboard, with their arms and accoutrements, to ascend a bank about twenty-five feet elevation, and form a line for the defense of their vessels and flags against the enemy, Arnold being the last man who debarked. The enemy did not venture into the cove, but kept up a distant cannonade until our vessels were burnt to the water's edge."[89]

Dr. Robert Knox's letter claimed that "Mr. Arnold run five ships ashore, and remained on the beach till he set fire to them, burning the wounded and sick in them."[90] The director of the Lake Champlain Maritime Museum, Arthur Cohn, defends Arnold, contending that the American commander feared spending the time to remove the dead from the vessels and that it was these dead that Knox saw and believed to have been only wounded. Arnold had just left a battle and had little time or reason to drop the bodies overboard, as Jahiel Stewart had earlier observed on the hospital sloop.[91]

Three weeks later, when the British soldiers returned to Canada, Lieutenant Digby visited the scene of the second battle. The soldiers with him referred to the area as "Destruction Bay" in reference to the American defeat and the burned vessels.[92] Several American dead still floating on the water were promptly buried by the British soldiers.

The remaining sailors of Arnold's flotilla, approximately two hundred in number, followed a bridle path to Crown Point, ten miles away. After narrowly avoiding an Indian ambush the tired men reached the undermanned fort. The *Trumbull, Enterprise, Revenge,* and *New York* were there to meet them, along with the *Liberty,* which had just recently sailed down from Ticonderoga with supplies.[93] Arnold quickly convinced Colonel Thomas Hartley that it would be impossible to hold the fort against the advancing British. Hartley and his garrison of the Sixth Pennsylvania Regiment, together with Arnold's survivors, burned all the buildings and retreated to Ticonderoga.

The next morning General Guy Carleton's soldiers took possession of Crown Point and Windmill Point (present-day Chimney Point) on the opposite side of the lake. Pringle sailed the fleet to the southern end of Lake Champlain and anchored within three miles of Fort Ticonderoga, where to the surprise of the Americans, several British rowboats came up under a flag of truce and delivered up General David Waterbury, the entire crew of the *Washington,* and the remaining eighteen of the *Philadelphia.*

Colonel John Trumbull, one of Arnold's senior officers, described the British treatment of the captured Americans: "When the action was over, Carleton gave orders to the surgeons of his own troops to treat the wounded prisoners with the same care as they did his own men. He then ordered that all the prisoners should be immediately brought aboard his ship, where he first treated them to a drink of grog, and then spoke kindly to them, praised the bravery of their conduct, regretted that it had not been displayed in the service of their lawful Sovereign, and offered to send them home."[94]

Carleton was true to his word. According to William Briggs, one of the *Washington*'s captured crewmen, "the wounded [were] taken great care of, all discharged upon their parole, and guarded thro' the woods by some soldiers, lest they shall fall in with the Indians, who were there in great numbers."[95] Apparently, the generous treatment on the part of Carleton "made such an impression on the captives, and they were so loud in their praise of him, that it was thought dangerous to allow them to mingle with the others."[96] Horatio Gates immediately ordered them sent home.

On October 14 Carleton wrote to Lord George Germain, British secretary of state for the American colonies, that winter was not far away and that any further action would have to wait until spring.[97] Lieutenant Digby's journal entry for the same day explained that Carleton had to contend with other logistical problems beyond that of the lateness of the season:

> Their force then at Ticonderoga, about 14 miles, was said to be 20,000, and it was thought from the lateness of the season and many other reasons, but this, the one most material, that it would be but a vain attempt to besiege it that year, we having but a small part of the army on that side of the lake; viz, the first Brigade and our Advanced corps. The remainder of the army not having battows ready to remove from St Johns, and Isle-aux-Noix, from whence it was thought by the advice of the engineers who were consulted respecting works, &c., that the enemy must return to winter in Canada, they not being then able to throw up lines for above 1300 men, and even then, we should have no place to cover our troops from the very severe cold shortly expected to set in.[98]

Americans at Fort Ticonderoga and Mount Independence were fully expecting a British attack, however, and had begun to increase fortifications. General Philip Schuyler ordered more militia to Ticonderoga to strengthen the nine thousand– to ten thousand–man force. The Americans built redoubts on both sides of the lake armed with a twenty-gun battery and a four-gun battery on Mount Independence. They placed a log boom across the lake to prevent the advance of the British warships past the Jersey redoubt and constructed a floating footbridge that would connect Fort Ticonderoga to Mount Independence.[99]

Carleton made the decision to return to Canada by October 20. Within a couple of days, he proposed building another ship the size of the *Inflexible* for a campaign in 1777. On October 24 General Burgoyne returned to Canada aboard the captured galley *Washington*, while his advance troops, who had been ordered down from Point au Fer on October 14, remained at Crown Point and made one probe toward Ticonderoga. British gunboats, numbering between three and five, trailed by thirteen to fifteen other craft, appeared at Three Mile Point, where British troops landed. The galley *Trumbull*, anchored safely behind the log boom, opened fire when the first gunboat came within range. One shot hit the gunboat, killing one man and wounding another. At sunset the British retreated to Crown Point, and Colonel Trumbull correctly surmised that their "appearance [at Fort Ticonderoga and Mount Independence] was indeed formidable, and the season so far advanced . . . that the enemy withdrew without making any attack."[100]

By November 3 scouting reports reached Ticonderoga that the British had left Crown Point. General Horatio Gates dismissed the militia at Ticonderoga and moved most of the regular troops south via Lake George and the Hudson River to New Jersey, where General Howe had driven Washington's army into retreat. Colonel Anthony Wayne temporarily became commandant of Fort Ticonderoga and Mount Independence for the winter. Wayne also supervised the remnants of Arnold's fleet and the galley *Gates*, which was completed after the battle.

In early November, Maria Carleton joined her husband in Montreal. She carried with her a proclamation of knighthood for the governor general of Canada; Carleton was now Sir Guy Carleton. In June the British cabinet had recommended to George III that Carleton, for his successful defense of Quebec, be made a Knight of the Bath.[101]

Arnold was also lauded for his courage and leadership skills following the Battle of Valcour Island. Horatio Gates wrote to Jonathan Trumbull, and he described Arnold as an excellent officer in a letter to the Connecticut governor shortly after the battle.[102] The praise was not universal, however. Russell Bellico notes that "Richard Henry Lee, a member of the Continental Congress, wrote Thomas Jefferson criticizing Arnold as a man 'fiery, hot, and impetuous, but without discretion,' who failed to obtain proper intelligence and retire when faced with a superior force."[103]

The noted naval historian Alfred Thayer Mahan agreed with Arnold's decision to remain in the channel believing that a "retreat before square-rigged sailing vessels having a fair wind, by a heterogeneous force like [the Americans], of unequal speeds and batteries, could only result in disaster." Mahan thought it better that Arnold fought from a "steady, well-ordered position, developing the utmost fire." He further stated that "the correctness of Arnold's decision not to chance a retreat was shown in the [results of his] retreat of two days later," whereby the fleet was essentially separated and lost. Gardner W. Allen expressed the same opinion believing "that a retreat would have been demoralizing and disastrous."[104]

Benedict Arnold, although rash and reckless, had bought the Americans valuable time—time for raising the regiments that in 1777 met and overwhelmed General John Burgoyne's invading armies at Saratoga. The largest contribution of the small American navy on Lake Champlain was that simply by its presence the British advance was delayed until it was too late.[105]

In 1776 Arthur St. Clair eloquently summed up the events on Lake Champlain when he wrote: "We have this satisfaction that our People tho' unsuccessful behaved with the greatest Intrepidity in general and he that looks for uninterrupted Good Fortune will certainly reckon without his Host. . . . We shall yet see an End of these troublesome Scenes, and tell our Stories over to our Children With the Pleasure that old Men have in reflecting upon the Scenes of their more vigorous life."[106]

Chapter 6

SALVAGING

THE PHILADELPHIA

'

The *Philadelphia* was raised from the bottom of Lake Champlain on August 9, 1935. The recovery of this historic vessel by Lorenzo F. Hagglund was considered a remarkable feat for the time, and both Hagglund and his partner, J. Ruppert Schalk, received high praise from the local community. The festive atmosphere that surrounded the project led the *Burlington Daily News* to print a special historical tabloid to satisfy the eager public's curiosity about the vessel and its salvagers.[1] The newspaper even enlisted a descendent of Benedict Arnold to provide a solemn commentary on the exploits of his tarnished ancestor in the Champlain Valley. For a brief time, the project received national attention with the release of newsreel footage.

The recovery of the *Philadelphia* was, however, purely a salvage operation; the science of nautical archaeology had not yet developed. Although the experienced salvagers carefully raised the vessel without apparent damage, no accurate site plan was made. The hull was meticulously searched for artifacts, but only a very limited effort was made to search the area surrounding the wreck for artifacts that might have scattered when the vessel sank. The ultimate fate of the *Philadelphia* and its associated artifacts, however, has been far better than many other historic wrecks raised from Lake Champlain in later years.

The idea of raising the *Philadelphia* began in 1917 when Lorenzo Hagglund arrived at Plattsburgh, New York, for overseas military training. Only three months short of graduation from Lehigh University, the twenty-three-year-old New York State native enlisted in military service when the United States entered World War I in 1917.[2] An avid history buff, Hagglund became intrigued with the local accounts of sunken Revolutionary War vessels at nearby Valcour Island. Undoubtedly, he heard stories from the local residents who could still remember seeing the charred hull of the *Royal Savage* during periods of low water.[3] When Hagglund's officers training course ended, he left the Champlain Valley for service in Europe, but with the hope that he would someday return and search for the wrecks.[4]

After the war ended, Hagglund was employed by Merritt, Chapman, and Scott, a New York marine salvage corporation.[5] While in the corporation's employ, he learned how to dive and trained other divers. Later, he became the operations manager for the company's subsidiary, the Underwater Cutting Company, for which he perfected an underwater cutting torch.

In the summer of 1932 the experienced marine engineer returned to Plattsburgh for a short family vacation. Hagglund spent most of that vacation trying to find the wreck of the *Royal Savage*. At first, he tried to learn the position from local residents; when that failed he relied on the more traditional divers' method of using circle searches.[6] Using this technique, he found cannon balls, bar shot, and grapeshot: a small portion of the hundreds that had been fired on October 11, 1776, at the Battle of Valcour Island. On the final day of his vacation, Hagglund discovered the wreck of the *Royal Savage* approximately 150 feet offshore from the southwestern tip of Valcour Island in twenty feet of water.

Before beginning his search, Hagglund attempted to interest government agencies in the salvage of Arnold's fleet in Lake Champlain or the British vessels scuttled at Yorktown in 1781.[7] With the discovery of the *Royal Savage*, he made one more attempt but met with no success. Undeterred, Hagglund returned to Valcour Island in 1934 to raise the remains of the vessel, financing the venture himself.

Before lifting the hull, Hagglund removed by hand all the sediment that had accumulated in the vessel and the mud that lay some distance on each side of the vessel. Each bucketful was washed for associated artifacts. With this method, he found several pewter spoons (one marked "1776"), grapeshot, cannon balls, and the fragmented remains of an iron pot that he attributed to the explosion of the vessel's powder stores shortly after British general Guy Carleton ordered the vessel burned.[8]

With the aid of twenty-two empty tar drums, Hagglund raised the surviving lower portion of the hull to the surface. The hull remains were disassembled and tagged in anticipation that they could later be reassembled and appropriately displayed.[9] Unfortunately, the timbers remained virtually untouched and untreated for the next fifty years while lying in storage in various garages in New York State. In the mid-1990s Lorenzo Hagglund's son, Hudson, sold the remaining pieces of the *Royal Savage* to a small, private Pennsylvania museum.[10]

After this first success at Valcour Island, Hagglund decided to search for the *Philadelphia*. During the fall of 1934 he began exploring the historical record for clues to the position of the gondola. A few months later, Hagglund began to collaborate with J. Ruppert Schalk of Rhinebeck, New York, a nephew and heir of Colonel Jacob Ruppert, New York brewery magnate and owner of the New York Yankees.[11] After Hagglund raised the *Royal Savage*, Schalk, a Lake Champlain enthusiast, became interested in the salvage operation and offered to aid the project. Throughout the winter the two men studied the written histories of the battle and the later events of 1776 and 1777 in an attempt to disprove local rumor that the British had raised the gondola after the battle. Encouraged by their research, Schalk agreed to provide the funding and the use of his yacht *Linwood* for the project. The pair assembled a salvage team and went to Valcour Island in July, 1935, to search for the *Philadelphia*.[12]

In company with Swedish-born William Lilja, a veteran diver of twenty-three years' experience, the crew began searching the channel between Valcour Island and the New York shore with grapnel irons (fig. 6.1).[13] In much the same manner as modern nautical archaeologists conduct underwater surveys, Hagglund relied on triangulation to mark the various underwater sites.[14] By placing a series of stakes along the New York shoreline and Valcour Island he ensured that all areas of the channel could be systematically searched in an efficient manner. Once an object was detected by the grapnel hook, Hagglund marked the site with a buoy and triangulated its position from the stakes with a range finder. Over a period of two weeks the salvage team located a variety of objects, including stumps, a discarded metal rowboat, anchors, and trees. On August 1, after a series of these disappointing finds, Hagglund replaced the grapnel hooks with a chain sweep. Late that afternoon, the sweep hung up on an object in midchannel bringing the slowly moving *Linwood* to a dead stop. The next morning Lilja descended in his hard hat to find the obstruction. When Lilja returned to the surface he informed the crew of the project's diving scow *Old Eli* that he had found a "fish house with a stove," Hagglund's predetermined code that was to be used until the *Philadelphia*'s condition was determined.[15] When it was later reported that the vessel mounted three guns and had a single mast still standing, Hagglund was positive they had found the *Philadelphia*. Lilja made a quick sketch of the wreck, which depicted the general shape of the vessel and the position of the three guns (fig. 6.2). After discussing the wreck and the labor that would be involved in raising it, Hagglund estimated it would take "three day's hard work to get the guns and a week to secure the hull."[16]

The *Philadelphia* was found sitting upright on the bottom, fifty-seven feet below the lake's surface, approximately three hundred yards south of Valcour Island.[17] Hagglund described the appearance of the sunken vessel in "A Page from the Past: The Story of the Continental Gondola *Philadelphia*."[18] Based on a series of dives, Hagglund provided a tour of the sunken vessel, beginning at the stern: "Here there is a brown shadow in front of us. We advance toward it and it takes shape. It is the hull of a vessel. Before us on the bottom, partly buried in the mud, lies the rudder. The tiller is gone, probably drifted away when she sank. Her stern is sharp and as we walk along her side, her gunwale is under our armpits."[19]

In testimony to the excellent preservation afforded shipwrecks by the cold, dark waters of Lake Champlain, the *Philadelphia* was in a remarkable state of completeness after 159 years. Thole pins for use with the vessel's long ash sweeps were still socketed in place in the port and starboard caprails along with several three-foot-high stanchions that had been used to support the gondola's awning. In the mud alongside the hull lay the remains of the fascines that the Americans had cut near Windmill Point in September, 1776,

Fig. 6.1. The
Philadelphia's
1935 salvage
team: from left to
right, J. Rupert
Schalk, William
Lilja, and Lorenzo
Hagglund.
Photograph
courtesy of the
Smithsonian
Institution,
NMAH/AFH.

where two men had been killed and seven wounded during a British ambush.[20] Originally, the bundles of saplings had been secured to the gondola's bulwarks in an attempt to protect the forty-four-man crew from sniper fire.

Surprisingly, the *Philadelphia*'s lower mast was still standing upright, reaching up to within ten feet of the surface. Two spars, the twenty-seven-foot-long main yard and the twenty-foot-long topsail yard, lay athwartship over the vessel's rails. They most likely had dropped straight down on the hull when their securing halyards and lines eventually deteriorated.

Hagglund reported that on the starboard side of the vessel, near the bow and "just above the mud line there [was] a hole in her side through the outer planking, a shattered rib and the inner planking."[21] This was the first of the three areas on the hull damaged by British cannon fire during the seven-hour battle on October 11, 1776. On the port side, a few feet aft of the stem, was evidence that a second British shot had bored through both the outer and inner three-inch, white oak planking. Another four feet farther down was the third damaged area. The cause of the damage was unmistakable, a 24-pound cannon ball was still lodged in the planking.

The *Philadelphia*'s starboard bower anchor was resting upright in the mud just under its cathead. Although waterworn, the two-piece oak stock was still pinned together at the upper portion of the shank. Just forward of the cathead was a lead-lined hawsehole with the wear of the anchor rope clearly visible. On the port side, the vessel's second bower anchor rested just under the second cathead.

At the center of the bow, the muzzle of the 12-pounder bow gun projected over the stem. Much to the divers' surprise, one end of a double-headed bar shot was found protruding from the end of the barrel. Hagglund correctly surmised that when the *Philadelphia* sank bow first, "the bar shot slid forward and half out of the muzzle, where, as one end dropped, its own leverage clamped it in position."[22]

After inspecting the outside of the hull, the divers boarded the vessel over the stern. On the port and the starboard sides of the stern deck were wooden lockers that had served as both benches and storage compartments aboard the cramped vessel. Over time, the sides had broken and fallen inward and were covered with an inch of mud. Among the few visible remains were an unbroken china cup and what Hagglund identified as a medicine bottle with

Fig. 6.2. *William*
Lilja's underwater
sketch of the
Philadelphia.
Courtesy of the
Smithsonian
Institution,
NMAH/AFH.

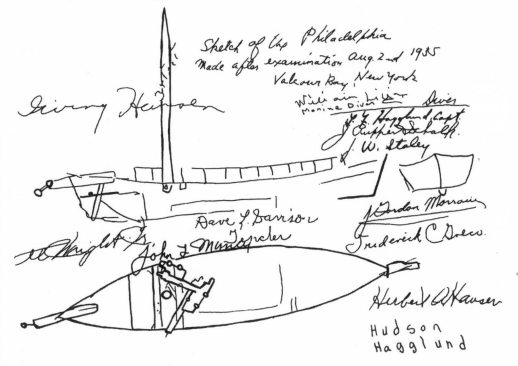

its contents intact. Seemingly out of place on this hurriedly built lake vessel, but true to naval tradition, were the remains of a broken sandglass. Other artifacts scattered about in the stern included leather shoes, shoe buckles, and a wooden gauge calibrated for both 9- and 12-pound shot.[23]

In the aft cockpit, thirteen feet forward of the stern knee, an iron swivel gun and its broken yoke were found resting on the ceiling. Later examination showed that this swivel gun, shaped like a small cannon, fired a ¾-pound ball. The barrel was marked with the British broad arrow suggesting that it was a captured piece or one taken out of stores at Fort Ticonderoga. In total, places for eight swivel guns had been fixed for use in the caprail. The other swivel guns were probably removed by the crew just before the vessel sank.[24]

On the midship deck, an area measuring approximately 12 by 14 feet, two 9-pounder cannons complete with their wooden carriages lay overturned. The starboard gun was out of position and jammed against the carriage of the port 9-pounder. Hagglund speculated that the position of the guns was not attributable to the sinking but was evidence that the *Philadelphia*'s crew had attempted to off-load the cannons prior to the vessel's sinking. Alternately, he suggested that their placement may have resulted from an unsuccessful attempt by the British to salvage the guns after the battle.[25] Typical of guns cast nearly a century before the start of the Revolution, "these guns," Hagglund wrote, "[were] of cast iron with trunnions low and cast of a piece with the gun."[26] Just forward of the touch hole, Hagglund stated that the letters *HP* were clearly visible on the barrels. The wooden gun carriages were fashioned from oak and ran on four solid wooden wheels, or trucks. The four trucks of one gun were still held in place by the linchpins on the wooden axles, but two wheels from the other gun had been broken off and were lost. Although the breech ropes were missing, the tackle blocks necessary for firing and reloading operations remained in place.

Just aft of the port waist gun, a pile of fifty-five 9-pound iron round shot was stacked between two of the gunboat's knees. In the same area, the divers located an iron shot gauge and a crumpled lead sheet that probably served as an apron for one of the guns. Between the two knees just forward of the port gun was a brick hearth. Still in place, a long-handled iron frying pan half eaten away by corrosion rested on the iron grating of the fireplace. Nearby, a cast-iron cooking kettle was found, from which Hagglund recovered a single bone.

In the forward cockpit a variety of artifacts were found, including a pot containing pitch and a horsehair brush, a musket stock, single and double blocks with sheaves and pins, axes, spades, an adze, a wooden canteen, a leather bullet pouch, bayonets, musket balls, and small tools. Underneath the foredeck was the cook's supply of wood for the fireplace and one of the craft's twelve ash sweeps. Later, when the silt was removed from the boat, the salvagers found one of the fatal projectiles: a 24-pound shot marked with the British broad arrow.

Fastened along each side of the bow was a curved wooden shot garland for holding round shot in a convenient position to the 12-pounder bow gun. Both garlands were empty except for a single 12-pound shot resting in the starboard rack. Scattered on the deck were what Hagglund identified as pieces of a human arm bone, several teeth, and part of a skull.[27] Lying with the bones were several uniform buttons, each bearing the number of the Twenty-Sixth British Regiment.

SALVAGING THE HULL

Salvage of the vessel began with the retrieval of the visible artifacts and the three cannons (fig. 6.3). Supplied with air by a crew of eager Boy Scouts drafted for pumping duty from nearby Camp Penn on Valcour Island, William Lilja set about recovering the guns. Lorenzo Hagglund's empty tar drums, which had been used the year before to raise the timbers of the *Royal Savage*, were similarly employed to remove the cannons from the vessel. By rigging a boom onto the stern of the *Linwood*, the salvagers lifted the guns off the hull and eventually moved them into shallow water near Seton's Wharf on Valcour Island.

At 9:30 on the morning of August 9, Hagglund took final bearings on the *Philadelphia*'s location from the lighthouse on Valcour Island, the bridge over Salmon River, and Day's Point. At 12:30 P.M., the Cashman derrick-lighter no. 3, the tallest floating derrick on the lake, arrived at the site in tow of the tug *Osceola* to lift the vessel to the surface.[28] To raise the *Philadelphia*, Lilja cut three holes through the mud underneath the hull with a high-pressure water

Fig. 6.3. The Philadelphia's cannons on the deck of the Cashman *lighter. Photograph courtesy of the Smithsonian Institution, NMAH/AFH.*

jet. Next, three rope slings were placed under the hull, one at midships and the others at bow and stern. The free ends of the slings were brought to the surface and attached to a hook suspended from the derrick's steel cables. To prevent the boat from being crushed during the lift, Lilja placed three logs across the gunwales to act as spreaders between the rope slings. When tension was applied to the cables and the *Philadelphia* began to take on a slight list, Lilja removed the mud from the bottom of the hull with the water jet and lessened the suction of the lake's bottom on the fragile hull. The hull pulled free of the sediments in which it had rested for 159 years, and the derrick crew continued to lift the vessel. To ensure that the gondola would be raised parallel to the lighter, Lilja attached an additional line on the bow to prevent twisting. The derrick slowly raised the hull to the surface and at 2:30 that afternoon the tip of the mast broke the surface of the water to the cheers of the many onlookers.

When about six feet of the mast was exposed, Schalk halted the operation so that Frederick Greco, the youngest member of the salvage crew, could attach a replica colonial flag to its tip. The mast proved so slippery that Greco was unable to climb it, necessitating the extension of a long plank from the *Linwood* so that the thirteen-striped flag could be nailed to the mast.

Once the hull broke the surface, Stephen M. Driscoll, collector of customs at St. Albans, Vermont, asked the crowd to join in a minute of silent prayer. The solemn ceremony was followed by three volleys to honor the fallen Revolutionary War heroes. Once the fanfare ended, and the salvagers were properly introduced to the crowd, the *Philadelphia* was towed to shallower water near Valcour Island.[29]

The *Burlington Daily News* reported that the raising of the *Philadelphia* was performed in what was very like a holiday atmosphere, with a large crowd of onlookers in "36 craft ranging from rowboats to palatial cabin cruisers and yachts."[30] The enthusiastic crowd created a considerable traffic problem. One overeager visitor seeking a close-up view even threw a sharp boat hook into the starboard bulwark of the *Philadelphia*. Hagglund solved the problem created by enthusiastic spectators by towing the vessel into shallow water near the shore. The day's events were captured on both still and movie cameras. A short film made by Horace Eldred of the University of Vermont's Fleming Museum has been preserved and is regularly shown at the *Philadelphia* exhibit in the National Museum of American History.

With the vessel safely raised and secured, a large piece of canvas was used to wrap the hull so that the water could be pumped out and the interior searched (fig. 6.4). All the mud from the vessel was sifted through screens. It was by this process, as well as one by which salvagers groped in the mud with their hands, that most of the artifacts were recovered. According to records kept at the Smithsonian Institution more than seven hundred objects were found on the gondola.[31]

A local Vermont legend asserts that the salvagers also recovered several bottles of rum from the deck of the *Philadelphia*. Supposedly, the liquor was not part of the original ration provided to the crew of the gondola but the remains of a jettison of illegal cargo smuggled from Canada during U.S. Prohibition.[32]

Once the gondola was raised, the question arose of what to do with it. Schalk and Hagglund reportedly assembled the crew the night before the recovery to take a vote on the ultimate disposition of the gondola. According to J. W. Staley, the first man to go on board the sunken gondola in Valcour Bay following her discovery in 1935, a unanimous decision was made to send the vessel to the

Fig. 6.4. The Philadelphia soon after it was raised in 1935. Photograph courtesy of the Smithsonian Institution, NMAH/AFH.

Smithsonian Institution.[33] For unspecified reasons, the *Philadelphia* did not make the trip to Washington, D.C., for another twenty-five years. Shortly after its recovery, Hagglund and Schalk offered the gondola to the state of Vermont, provided that a suitable museum building could be found to contain it. Initially it was suggested that a stone building be constructed on the campus of the University of Vermont for the vessel's permanent housing. In anticipation of this possibility the *Philadelphia* was placed in storage for the winter at Shelburne Harbor, Vermont.

In the spring of 1936, Hagglund received a letter from the University of Vermont stating that the necessary funds for the building could not be raised. In response, Hagglund declared that the *"Philadelphia* is part of American History. As such, it belongs to all the American people. Why not show it to them and let it tell its story."[34] Therefore, on July 3, 1936, the *Philadelphia* became a floating tourist attraction. Hagglund placed the gondola on a barge and towed the temporary historical museum to Burlington, Vermont.

Between 1936 and 1941, the barge and its historic cargo toured

Lake Champlain and the Hudson River Valley.[35] Lengthy stopovers were made at several historic places at which the *Philadelphia* had originally called, including Whitehall (modern-day Skenesborough), Fort Ticonderoga, and Crown Point, New York. Hagglund also sent the *Philadelphia* through the Hudson River Valley, making stops as far south as Albany and Long Island, New York. In his words, the gondola was "sometimes towed by tug boats, sometimes by launches; and sometimes, when the wind blew adversely, towing the towboat; arriving at her ports of call when wind and weather permitted and sometimes arriving at unscheduled ports, and glad to make them."[36] For the price of a fifty-cent admission ticket visitors boarded the gunboat and examined Hagglund's collection of Revolutionary War artifacts, including those raised from the *Royal Savage*. Hagglund's commercial enterprise also included the sale of a historical pamphlet, souvenir postcards, and miniature lead-cast replica cannons.

Maritime historian and naval architect Howard Chapelle examined the *Philadelphia* in 1939 and recommended that it be brought to the Smithsonian Institution for treatment and preservation. Frank Taylor, curator, Division of Engineering, rejected this plan in a memorandum: "War vessels are outside the scope of the [Smithsonian's] watercraft collection. It appears to be a relic for some public agency to acquire and preserve, but I understand that it would take about $40,000 to buy it and erect a suitable building for it at the site."[37]

During World War II, Hagglund returned to military service, attaining the rank of lieutenant colonel, and he later served with the Red Cross office in Germany.[38] When Hagglund returned to the Champlain Valley in 1948, he offered the gondola to the U.S. Navy but was told that the navy was not interested in an "Army boat."[39]

After the war Hagglund also attempted to locate other vessels from Arnold's fleet. Between 1951 and 1953 he made exploratory dives at Schuyler Island and Ligonier Point in search of the other lost gondolas.[40] Unsuccessful in finding the *Providence*, Hagglund took his search to Arnold's Bay where four other gondolas were known to have been burned on October 13, 1776. These wrecks had been visible during periods of low water since at least 1849.[41] All four gondolas and the *Congress* had been visited numerous times by souvenir hunters in the intervening hundred years. Russell Bellico notes that local tradition had it that "three of the gondolas were dragged out of the water with teams of horses during the nineteenth century and cut up for souvenirs."[42] Pieces left by the scavengers eventually rotted away, and one hull was reported to have burned on the shore of Arnold's Bay.[43]

In 1952 Hagglund raised the last gondola from the bay. Reported to be nearly identical in construction to the *Philadelphia*, the remarkably well-preserved vessel was towed to the New York shore. Two years later, the flat-bottomed hull was set alongside the remains of the early nineteenth-century steamer *Vermont* near Ausable Chasm, New York.[44] Hagglund had used his empty oil drums to assist the Lake Champlain Associates (LCA) in raising the 1809 steamer in 1953. The LCA made plans to build an exhibition hall to display the new gondola, the *Royal Savage*, the *Vermont*, and the *Philadelphia*, but efforts to secure the building funds through the sale of common stock were unsuccessful. The gondola was eventually abandoned in the woods and after years of neglect and vandalism by souvenir hunters the last remaining pieces were removed to make way for a new campground in 1973.[45]

Concerned for the future of the *Philadelphia* and its long-term care, Hagglund again contacted the Smithsonian Institution in 1959.[46] According to Hagglund, "local public agencies [had] shown no interest in it, although private entities, such as Shelburne Village, Shelburne, Vermont, and the Fort Ticonderoga Museum at Fort Ticonderoga, New York, had expressed interest in the gondola." Hagglund added that although he had substantial offers from individuals interested in purchasing the vessel, he preferred "to see it preserved under public auspices."[47]

Hagglund wrote a letter to Frank Taylor, director of the Smithsonian's Museum of History and Technology (MHT), offering to donate the vessel to the Smithsonian Institution. His only stipulation was that he be reimbursed for his expenses in recovering and preserving the boat. He believed that a figure of "30 to 50 thousand dollars would be fair," but would leave it up to the MHT to suggest the actual figure.[48] In response to Hagglund's letter, Taylor wrote a memo recommending that the MHT purchase and exhibit the vessel.[49] Fourteen years earlier Howard Chapelle, the

Smithsonian's naval architecture expert, had appraised the gondola and placed a value of $25,000 to $30,000 on the vessel and its associated artifacts. Taylor believed the museum "would be justified in paying up to $40,000." Accordingly, the MHT informed Hagglund that his figure was within a reasonable range for discussion.

The MHT's first step in acquiring the *Philadelphia* was to authenticate the vessel and its equipment. In addition to a thorough inventory of the objects, the museum wanted to make a careful investigation into the ownership of the boat.[50] Hagglund assured the Smithsonian that none of the volunteers who had assisted in raising the gunboat had a claim or was making a claim.[51] And while New York State had once sent a truck to take the gunboat away, nothing came of the event. Around 1945 the New York State Attorney General's Office investigated the state's claim to the *Philadelphia* but found that it had no apparent rights to the vessel.[52]

Since neither Hagglund nor the MHT wanted the transaction to appear as an outright sale, an attorney representing the Smithsonian Institution thought it best to obtain a deed of gift. Simultaneously, the museum would offer to reimburse Hagglund for his expenses.[53] In 1960 the MHT wrote a formal agreement of transfer between the two parties. Before the document could be signed and a final inventory of the objects made, Colonel Hagglund died.

A short time later, the MHT received a letter from Hagglund's attorney indicating that the city of Philadelphia was trying to raise money to purchase the gunboat from the Hagglund estate.[54] According to Peter Schaufler, Philadelphia city planner, Hagglund had begun negotiations with the Philadelphia Museum some years before. The city was planning to feature the gunboat in a comprehensive exhibit of historic vessels in its newly renovated downtown waterfront.[55] Schaufler argued that the *Philadelphia* with its "unique significance and associated name would be directly affiliated with Independence Hall from which the philosophy of freedom underlying the Revolution was first declared."[56] To this end, the city offered $60,000 in municipal bonds for the *Philadelphia*.

Colonel Hagglund's will stipulated, however, that the *Philadelphia* would be given to the Smithsonian Institution provided his surviving heirs agreed. Ultimately, Gladys Hagglund contacted the MHT and indicated that she felt it was her husband's wish for the

Philadelphia to go to the Smithsonian. She deeded the vessel to the museum under the original terms her husband had negotiated, namely $40,000 to be paid over a period of four years.

Once the Smithsonian's acquisition of the *Philadelphia* became public, a number of editorials and letters appeared in newspapers concerning its movement from New York to Washington, D.C. The village of Whitehall, New York (formerly Skenesborough), had attempted to purchase the vessel from Hagglund several years earlier. At the time of Whitehall's bicentennial celebration in 1959, the village conducted lengthy negotiations with him in an effort to have the gunboat returned to Whitehall as a permanent exhibit. Whitehall's bicentennial committee hoped to make the vessel "the keystone of a permanent display," stressing Whitehall's claim as the "Birthplace of the U.S. Navy."[57] According to the *Whitehall Times*, "what the Bicentennial committee desired and what Colonel Hagglund wanted were poles apart; the committee felt that it was an impossibility to meet the terms offered by the Colonel, and he in turn felt that he had an attraction which deserved better treatment than could be accorded him here."[58]

After the transfer, residents of Whitehall attempted unsuccessfully to persuade the Smithsonian to leave the gondola in New York.[59] The owner of the Fort Ticonderoga Museum, John H. G. Pell, was equally unsuccessful in his effort to have the vessel left in his museum's care.[60]

When it became evident that the *Philadelphia* would be taken from New York, Senator Kenneth B. Keating and Representative Carleton J. King wrote the Smithsonian and asked that the *Philadelphia* exhibit include "mention of the local interest in the Lake Champlain area in the restoration and display of important relics of the Revolution." The MHT assured the two legislators the exhibit not only would do that but also would "emphasize to visitors from all sections of the country the importance of New York State in winning the Revolutionary War."[61]

According to the *Whitehall Times*, the village's only consolation was that if it "couldn't have the boat, the Smithsonian was the next best place for it." "In the long run," the editorial continued, "probably more people will learn through the Smithsonian exhibit that the first U.S. Fleet was built at Skenesborough, than would have had the *Philadelphia* been returned to Whitehall."[62] In a move to replace the unobtainable *Philadelphia*, Whitehallers recovered the *Ticonderoga*, one of Captain Thomas Macdonough's warships at the Battle of Plattsburgh, War of 1812, from East Bay and moved it to the area south of Skenesborough Museum in 1958.[63]

CONSERVATION OF THE PHILADELPHIA

The *Whitehall Times* concluded in the end that Hagglund had made little attempt toward preserving or restoring the vessel: "the 25 years above water took a far heavier toll than the 159 years on the bottom of the lake."[64] In Hagglund's defense, treatment techniques for waterlogged wood were barely known in 1935 and still relatively new in 1960. The first attempts to preserve archaeological waterlogged wood began in Denmark in the middle of the nineteenth century. Wooden objects were boiled in a supersaturated solution of alum (potassium aluminum sulphate, $KAl[SO_4]_2$) for two hours. While not an ideal method, the technique was fairly successful if the treated wood was allowed to absorb as much linseed oil as possible following the treatment. Drawbacks to the treatment involved penetration problems and a tendency for the interiors of wooden objects to collapse. Between 1900 and 1950 there were few technical improvements in the treatment of waterlogged wood.[65] Later methods included impregnation with glycerol, embedment in paraffin wax, and treatment with creosote and linseed oil. The creosote–linseed oil treatment was a simple approach and only proved effective for ship timbers that were very sound to begin with. The Viking ship burial (c.e. 800) at Oseberg, Norway, was successfully treated by this method following its recovery in 1904.[66]

The development of polyethylene glycol (PEG) as a conservation process was the first simple and reliable method for treating waterlogged wood.[67] In practice, the excess water in wood is removed and the wood cells are "bulked" in one operation. Typically, the treatment involves cleaning to remove all dirt on the surface of the object and placing it in a ventilated vat in which the temperature is gradually increased until, after a period of days to weeks, it has reached 60 to 70 degrees C (140°–158°F). During this time the PEG percentage of the solution increases as the solvent (water or alcohol) evaporates or as increments of PEG are added. In the process, the wax slowly diffuses into the wood, displacing the water.

Although first synthesized in 1859, PEG was not commercially produced until Union Carbide began doing so in 1939. In 1956 the first suggestion of using PEG for archaeological wood was published. One scientist noted that the success of PEG as a treatment was due to the fact that it is completely soluble in water in all proportions and, therefore, can totally replace water in the cell wall of wood.[68] In specific applications to "archaeological" wood it was found that optimum results were achieved by raising the temperature and concentration slowly by gradual evaporation of water until the wood specimens were immersed in pure molten PEG at 70 degrees C (158°F).

Before the MHT moved the *Philadelphia* from New York, Smithsonian researcher Mendel Peterson contacted the National Park Service Preservation Laboratories for recommendations on treating the desiccated wood. The National Park Service recommended the application of Carbowax (polyethylene glycol). Further research by the Smithsonian indicated that the Forest Products Laboratories at Madison, Wisconsin, was using a 50 percent solution of Carbowax 1000 and water.[69] Because the Smithsonian was using a heavier molecular weight, that is, Carbowax 1500, it was thought best to use a 30 percent solution (based on weight) to insure adequate penetration.

The gondola had completely dried out many years earlier, and the MHT decided to apply the PEG by gently brushing it onto the moistened wood rather than using the more costly and time-consuming immersion approach. Due to the poor ventilation in Hagglund's shed, the PEG was applied with a spray rig, rather than by brush as had been originally planned. By doing so, the surface of the wood was not disturbed and it was possible to spray many interior areas not accessible with a brush. According to Peterson, the vessel was definitely more limber following two applications of PEG, "relieving the ship's somewhat dried-out appearance."[70] At the time, the treatment appeared to have been successful.

The MHT prepared the *Philadelphia* for shipping in June, 1961. After skidding the gondola nearly half a mile overland to the edge of Lake Champlain at Essex, New York, workmen constructed a wooden crate around the vessel (fig. 6.5).[71] The vessel was then slowly moved to the water's edge and over a specially built ramp to a barge. The Smithsonian paid Lake Industries $8,100 to transfer the *Philadelphia* to Albany via the Lake Champlain–Hudson River Canal.[72] At Albany the gondola was swung on board the U.S. Coast Guard buoy tender *Firebush* for transport to Washington, D.C., where through the generous assistance of the U.S. Navy she found temporary berth at the Naval Weapons Plant.[73] Four years later, the *Philadelphia*, still encased in its wooden crate, was raised by derricks and slid along a track into its third-floor berth in the new National Museum of American History (fig. 6.6). With the opening of the Halls of the Armed Forces in the new museum, the *Philadelphia* entered upon yet another chapter in her long and inspiring career, surrounded by several hundred artifacts recovered from her resting place in Valcour Bay.[74]

In 2001 the *Philadelphia* had been on exhibit at the Smithsonian Institution for almost four decades. Although the hull timbers were treated with PEG in 1961, the wood bulking treatment proved to be too minimal to be effective. Consequently, many of her timbers have split and cupped, indicating that the wood has failed on a cellular level. It is also feared that corrosion of the vessel's iron fittings have further fragmented the wood from within. Access to the interior of the vessel for cleaning purposes is now prohibited. The *Philadelphia's*

Fig. 6.5. After crating the Philadelphia, *the Museum of History and Technology sent the vessel to Washington, D.C., for preservation, documentation, and permanent display. Photograph courtesy of the Smithsonian Institution, NMAH/AFH.*

Fig. 6.6. The Philadelphia being placed into the newly constructed National Museum of History and Technology (now the National Museum of American History). Photograph courtesy of the Smithsonian Institution, NMAH/AFH.

conservation problems are further complicated by the fact that the Smithsonian Institution applied Gentol 101 (liquid nylon) to the wood in an attempt to seal in the PEG in the 1960s.[75] The liquid nylon has probably become insoluble and may hamper further efforts to introduce other preservative materials into the wood. Unfortunately, the Smithsonian Institution does not have the specialized conservation staff needed to assess and address the problem. The museum's conservators are seeking funding to determine: (1) the degree to which PEG and soluble nylon penetrated; (2) the extent to which soluble nylon has become insoluble; and (3) the phases of metal and corrosion products present in the iron fasteners.[76] A recent Navy Legacy grant proposal designed to bring in a team of conservation consultants to the National Museum of American History (NMAH) was not funded. Because the Smithsonian considers the *Philadelphia* a premier attraction for the museum, the conservation staff plans to submit its proposal to other agencies.

Chapter 7

CONSTRUCTING
THE PHILADELPHIA

ollowing the Smithsonian Institution's acquisition of the
gondola *Philadelphia* in 1961, Howard P. Hoffman (museum
specialist, Division of Naval History, National Museum of
History and Technology) researched and surveyed the hull. The
results of his work, *A Graphic Presentation of the Continental Gondola* Philadelphia, *American Gunboat of 1776*, are presented in a set
of plans consisting of sixteen sheets.

Rather than produce a graphic record of the hull in its present
state, Hoffman's objective was to develop a set of detailed plans
that represented the *Philadelphia* as it was fitted out in 1776.[1] In
addition to providing a brief history of the northern campaign on
Lake Champlain in 1776, the comprehensive plans detail almost
every aspect concerning the *Philadelphia*'s construction and outfitting and include a well-researched reconstruction of the vessel's
rigging and sail plan. Other sheets provide reconstructed elements
for missing, but necessary, equipment relating to the vessel's armament, cooking facilities, and awning. The contemporary fabrication of sails, fittings, and ammunition was also researched and illustrated.

To record the *Philadelphia*'s lines and structure, Hoffman and
museum specialist Harold Ellis laid out predetermined station lines
on the floor beneath the gondola and set up a transit to act as a
horizontal datum plane from which vertical measurements of the

hull could be taken.[2] Two scribed vertical supports positioned on either side of the vessel and a sliding arm between enabled Hoffman to lift the water lines. Measurements and data derived from this method were used to develop the lines drawing and determine the location of structural members. Existing hull fittings in the form of spars, blocks, and deadeyes provided additional information about the *Philadelphia*'s rig.

To test the development of the preliminary plans, Hoffman built a model of the fully outfitted gondola at a scale of 1 inch to 1 foot.[3] The model was subsequently placed on display next to the original hull so that visitors to the museum could see the *Philadelphia* as she would have looked before the Battle of Valcour Island.

The *Philadelphia*'s overall length measured 53 feet, 2 inches.[4] Extreme breadth from outside planking to outside planking measured 15 feet, 2 inches. Depth at midships, from bottom to rail, was 4 feet. The *Philadelphia*'s armament consisted of one 12-pounder mounted on a slide carriage in the bow and two broadside 9-pounders; the rail was fitted for 8 swivel guns, of which one ¾-pounder was recovered. Hoffman calculated a full-load displacement of 29 tons, a figure that accounts for the weight of the arms, crew, and stores. In a freshwater body such as Lake Champlain, the *Philadelphia* would have had a full-load draft of 1 foot, 11½ inches.

The carpenters at Skenesborough built the *Philadelphia* and the other seven gondolas on fixed-timber platforms called stocks.[5] Hoffman suggested that to facilitate the construction and launching of the gondolas these stocks were approximately the same size and width as the hull's flat bottoms, raised to a convenient working height, and probably sloped toward the water.[6] The first step in the construction sequence at Skenesborough was to lay the gondola's bottom planking on the platform and saw it to the proper double-ended contour.[7] The planking served as a foundation to which floors, frames, stem, and sternpost were attached. Throughout this construction progress the *Philadelphia* remained in an upright position.[8]

BOTTOM PLANKING

The *Philadelphia* is completely flat-bottomed with no keel or keel plank present. Eleven strakes of 2-inch-thick white oak laid side by side comprise the gondola's bottom (fig. 7.1).[9] Individual strakes

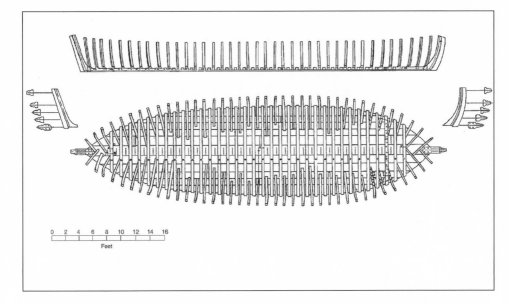

vary in width between 10 and 17 inches and, with the exception of the central strake, are composed of two to four planks. The center strake consists of a single plank 48 feet, 10½ inches in length. Planks in the other runs are connected, where necessary, with simple butt joints. To secure the joints, butt blocks made of 1½-inch-thick white oak were fastened over exposed plank butts after the framing was installed.

Hoffman proposed that once the planks were positioned and temporarily fastened, the basic outline of the hull's bottom, with a maximum breadth of roughly 12 feet, 1½ inches, was scribed onto the surface and cut out. At the same time, the position of posts, floor timbers, and frames could have been marked.[10]

To facilitate draining the vessel of water during construction, a 2¾-inch-diameter hole was drilled through one of the bottom planks about 4 feet forward of the sternpost.[11] Because the hole would have become inaccessible once the aft deck was added, Hoffman suggested that the shipwrights inserted a wooden stopper from underneath before launching the vessel.

Fig. 7.1. Bottom planking and framing structure. Courtesy of the Smithsonian Institution, NMAH/AFH, Howard P. Hoffman, A Graphic Presentation of the Continental Gondola *Philadelphia*: American Gunboat of 1776 *(Washington, D.C.: Smithsonian Institution, 1982), sheet 4.*

STEM

The heel of the *Philadelphia*'s one-piece curved stem is flat-scarfed to the center bottom plank with four 1-inch-diameter treenails.

The outboard portion of the white oak stem is set flush with the lower face of the bottom planking. Sided dimension remains a constant 10 inches on the post's after face. On its forward face, the stem decreases from a sided dimension of 6½ inches at the base to 2½ inches at the top. Molded dimension at the top is 11¾ inches and at the bottom 2 feet, 2 inches.

To allow the muzzle of the 12-pound bow chaser to clear the stem, it later became necessary to trim the stem and a portion of the uppermost strakes a few inches below the existing sheer. As modified, the post's maximum height is approximately 4 feet, 9½ inches. In addition to securing the plank ends, the post is also used to anchor the mainstay eyebolt and the bow breast hook.

STERNPOST

The *Philadelphia*'s straight sternpost is also of white oak. Like the stem, it is fastened to the center bottom plank with four 1-inch-diameter treenails. Sided dimension is constant at 9½ inches inboard of the rabbet and 7 inches outboard, decreasing to 3 inches on the post's after face. Width in the rabbet is approximately 5 inches. The top of the sternpost is molded approximately 10¾ inches. Maximum fore and aft dimension, 2 feet, 1 inch, occurs at heel. The post's maximum height is 4 feet, 11½ inches. To support the gondola's rudder, two holes were drilled through the post for the placement of eyebolt-type gudgeons that are secured with rings and forelocks.[12] A third forelock bolt positioned about halfway up the post is used to fasten the stern breast hook.

When it came time to place the fore- and aftermost cant frames, the inboard heels of both the stem and sternpost were trimmed so the frames could occupy their proper positions. Similarly, the top of the sternpost was also trimmed to allow proper clearance for the vessel's tiller.

FLOORS

Thirty-four white oak floors are positioned across the bottom planking of the *Philadelphia*. Each floor is straight, 4 inches molded, and 4 to 5 inches sided. Spacing is approximately 15 inches between centers. Two rectangular limber holes, approximately 1 inch by 2 inches, are present in each timber, one on each side of the vessel's centerline.

Floors are attached to the bottom planking with 1-inch-diameter white oak treenails. All treenails are octagonal and none are wedged. Two treenails are placed at every floor/bottom plank interface. To reduce the possibility of splitting the timbers, treenail locations are staggered along the length of the floor. After installation, the ends of each timber were beveled to match the outer contour dictated by the frames and chine. The presence of nails and nail holes indicates that before drilling the holes for the treenails, the *Philadelphia* shipwrights temporarily secured the floors in place by toenailing.

FRAMES

The frames of the *Philadelphia* would properly be called "standing knees," because they are not attached to floor timbers. These 39 pairs of frame knees are set perpendicular to the outer hull contour (90 degrees off the chine) instead of being fastened to the floor timbers. This method of ship construction saved a tremendous amount of time that otherwise would have been spent in beveling the frames to match the hull contour.[13]

This type of construction—a flat-bottomed, double-ended hull with standing knees instead of attached frame timbers—is similar in form to a scaled-up bateau. The simple design of the bateau had been in use in North America for more than a century before the *Philadelphia*'s construction and continued to be employed by both the American colonists and the British.

All the *Philadelphia*'s frames appear to have been hewn from natural-growth timbers of white oak (in other words, the cut of the knee matches the grain of the wood) and have the same molded dimension of 3¼ inches at the top, increasing to 4¼ inches directly above the chine, and decreasing back to 3½ inches along their horizontal bottom sections. Sided dimensions vary from 2½ to 4½ inches. Frame knee spacing is the same as for the floors, approximately 15 inches between centers.[14] The Smithsonian survey determined that the side contours of the frames were developed from a series of radii. On both sides of the vessel, frames 13 to 30 have identical contours, indicating that they were mass-produced from an existing template. Hoffman calculated that if the other seven gondolas were similarly constructed, a tremendous amount of manpower would have been saved by not beveling the 624 frames needed for all the vessels.[15]

The upper arms of every *Philadelphia* frame were probably cut slightly longer than necessary. After the planking and ceiling were added, the tops of the frames were simply trimmed off to match the sheer defined by the planking. Nails and nail holes also indicate that the floors were temporarily secured in position by toenailing and then, like the floor timbers, frames were tightly secured to bottom planking with unwedged treenails driven into 1-inch-diameter holes. Staggering of treenail fasteners was impractical due to the small-sided dimension of the frames.

One pair of frames was erected between every two floors with the exception of three pairs that were placed at either end of the hull beyond the last floors. In many cases, it was necessary to saw the lower arms of frames to the proper angle to butt against the floors.

KEELSON

The full length of the keelson was not accessible for examination, but Hoffman suggested that this internal reinforcing timber is made of two pieces scarfed together amidships. The white oak keelson has a molded height of 5⅞ inches and a sided dimension of 8¼ inches.[16] The 48-foot-11-inch-long timber rests on the upper surface of each floor and is toenailed to the stem and sternpost (fig. 7.2). To further secure the timber, ten iron bolts were driven through drilled holes into the floors and central bottom plank at approximately 5-foot intervals. The ends of the bolts are flush with the upper face of the keelson and the lower face of the central bottom plank.

A mast step is located approximately one-third of the vessel's length (18 feet, 8¼ inches) aft of the stem. It consists of a 12-by-3½-inch mortise cut 4 inches deep into the keelson's upper surface. A ½-inch-square iron rod formed into the shape of a staple was found driven into the upper surface of the keelson a few inches aft of the mast step. Hoffman suggested that it secured the mainyard tie tackle.

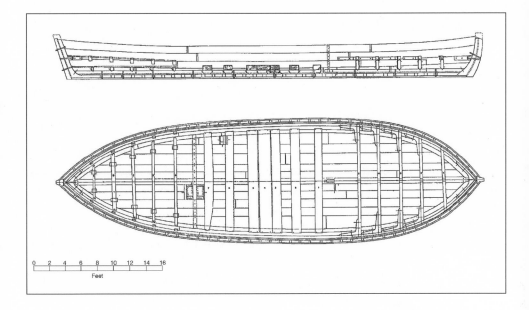

0 2 4 6 8 10 12 14 16
Feet

PLANKING

The *Philadelphia* is planked with five 1½-inch-thick white oak strakes
(fig. 7.3). The lowermost strake is spiked directly to the outside
edges of the bottom planking; the latter had already been beveled
flush with the outer face of the frames. Individual strakes are composed of three to four planks that butt each other on the center of
a frame. The planks are fastened to every frame with a minimum of
four iron nails. Strake ends are secured in their rabbets with seven
or eight nails driven into the stem or sternpost. The edges of the
planks are beveled, probably to receive caulking material.[17]

WALES

The *Philadelphia* has one rectangular wale 3 inches thick and 4½ inches
wide running directly below the sheer strake. On each side of the
vessel, the reinforcing member is made from two pieces of white oak
fastened by a simple flat scarf over a span of four frames.[18] The wale
is attached to the vessel with one spike at every frame position. Three
iron nails and one spike are used to secure the timber to the stem
and sternpost. Hoffman noted that the 1-inch-diameter bolts for the
midship deck knees also pass through the wales.[19]

*Fig. 7.2.
Additional
structural details.
Courtesy of the
Smithsonian
Institution,
NMAH/AFH,
Howard P.
Hoffman,* A
Graphic
Presentation of
the Continental
Gondola
Philadelphia:
American
Gunboat of 1776
*(Washington,
D.C.:
Smithsonian
Institution, 1982),
sheet 5.*

CEILING

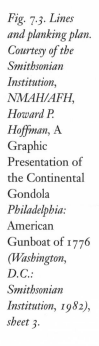

*Fig. 7.3. Lines
and planking plan.
Courtesy of the
Smithsonian
Institution,
NMAH/AFH,
Howard P.
Hoffman*, A
Graphic
Presentation of
the Continental
Gondola
Philadelphia:
American
Gunboat of 1776
*(Washington,
D.C.:
Smithsonian
Institution, 1982),
sheet 3.*

The *Philadelphia* has two types of internal planking or ceiling, side ceiling and what Hoffman referred to as flooring (see fig. 7.2). After the keelson was installed, 1½-inch-thick ceiling was laid over the rectangular floor timbers in a fore and aft direction.[20] Floor ceiling is white oak of varying width (10 to 18 inches). The planks closest to the centerline of the vessel butt against the keelson, and the outboard planks are beveled to fit around the frames. The ceiling is attached to each floor timber with two or three iron nails. A well area, approximately 2 feet, 5½ inches by 1 foot, 9½ inches was created in the stern by cutting out a rectangular portion of the flooring on each side of the twenty-fifth floor timber. Hoffman suggested that a bailing cover may have been present but was not recovered; he theorizes that it floated away when the vessel sank.

Side ceiling is also fashioned from white oak, but ¼ inch thinner than the flooring. Four ceiling strakes of varying width (10 to 12 inches) are present on both sides of the vessel. The uppermost ceiling plank is placed at the same height as the corresponding external plank, effectively covering the frames up to their tops. The lowermost ceiling plank sits directly on the flooring. Side ceiling is secured with three nails at every frame position. The ends of every strake are beveled to butt against the stem and sternpost and are fastened to each post with seven or eight nails in a staggered pattern.[21]

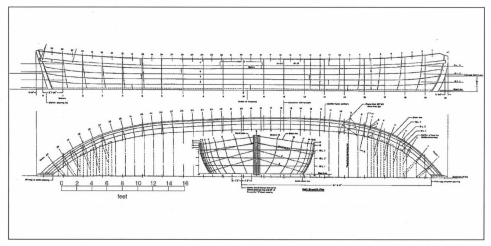

A series of rectangular cutouts (five on each side) in the side ceiling indicates that the afterdeck may have been located in a more elevated position. Hoffman suggested that a higher deck may have been installed with the idea of placing an additional cannon in the stern of the vessel.[22] Historical documents indicate that Benedict Arnold ordered a mortar platform installed in the stern of the *Philadelphia* just before the vessel was launched.[23] The Skenesborough builders would have been faced with two choices: raising the existing afterdeck or installing a new platform above it. After the mortar blew apart during its first test firing at Ticonderoga, the platform was either removed or lowered to its original position. Stone ballast weighing 3,375 pounds was then placed underneath the afterdeck to counteract the weight of the bow gun.

Once the ceiling and planking were nailed, the carpenters strengthened the hull by driving twenty-nine through bolts of ⅝-inch diameter into the hull through its sides. The bolts were then passed through the ceiling, frames, and exterior planking. To secure the bolts, washers were placed underneath the heads, and the outboard ends were hammered flat to fit flush with the face of the exterior hull planking.

BREAST HOOKS

One breast hook of naturally curved white oak is placed at each end of the vessel. Both are approximately 5½ inches thick and positioned about halfway up the stem and sternpost. The bow breast hook has an arm length of approximately 3 feet; the opposite member spans a distance of 2 feet. Forelock bolts secure these timbers to the stem and sternpost, and nails fasten them to the ceiling.

THE DECKS

The *Philadelphia* has three decks: the afterdeck, midship deck, and forward deck (fig. 7.4). The afterdeck may have been lowered after the gondola was sent to Fort Ticonderoga. The midship deck sits at approximately the same level as the lowered afterdeck, but the forward deck is placed at a higher level to permit the 12-pounder bow gun to fire over the stem of the vessel. Five white oak deck beams of varying sided dimension (3 to 5 inches) and 5¼ inches in

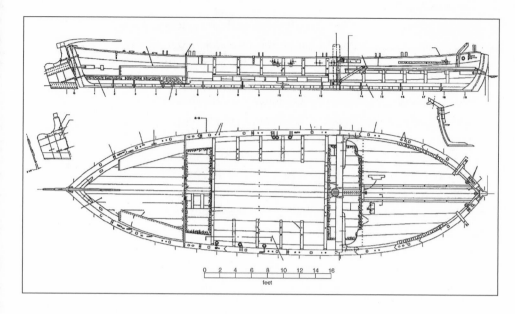

Fig. 7.4. Complete structural assembly. Courtesy of the Smithsonian Institution, NMAH/AFH, Howard P. Hoffman, A Graphic Presentation of the Continental Gondola *Philadelphia:* American Gunboat of 1776 *(Washington, D.C.: Smithsonian Institution, 1982), sheet 6.*

molded dimension rest on the keelson to support the afterdeck planking. The straight beams are toenailed to the keelson and ceiling. The ends of the beams are trimmed to fit the contour of the ceiling. Additional support is provided by placing two 4¼-inch-thick blocks or pillars between the lower surface of each beam and the flooring.

The midship deck is supported by seven beams, 11 inches molded and between 6¾ inches to 18 inches in sided dimension. Unlike the other deck beams, these are fashioned from straight lengths of white pine. The beams rest on top of the floor timbers and are notched on their undersides to fit around the keelson. The outboard ends are trimmed to fit the contour of the ceiling. Like the other beams, they are secured in place by toenailing to the floor and ceiling.

Five straight white oak timbers support the forward deck. The timbers are sided 3 to 5½ inches and molded 5¼ inches. Partial support is provided by placing the ends of the beams through cutouts in the ceiling. Additional support is provided by toenailing 4-by-5-inch pillars to the keelson and lower surface of each beam. Eight lodging knees (four to a side), cut from natural-growth timbers, provide additional support for the forward deck. One 4-inch-thick knee is attached to the aft face of each forward deck beam, except the beam farthest forward. The lodging knees are attached to both the beams and ceiling with wrought iron nails.

Deck planking was milled from white oak. On both the fore- and afterdecks, the planking is 1¼ inches thick, and the midship deck planking is made from 2-inch-thick planking. The increase in thickness of the midship deck was justified as it held the two 9-pounder cannons. Because the planking of the foredeck was not used to support the weight of the 12-pounder bow gun, it too was thinner. In all three cases deck planking is fitted to the ceiling and secured to the deck beams with iron nails. On the forward deck the planking butts up against the slide carriage tracks of the 12-pounder. Coaming is present only on the midship deck and consists of two pieces that scarf into two deck knees. The white oak coaming is bolted through the deck and into the beams.

Originally six white oak standing knees were placed on each side of the midship deck. These timbers were intended to reinforce the sides of the hull against the force of breeching when each 9-pounder recoiled. Cut from natural-growth wood, the supporting timbers were bolted through the hull and wale. Nails were used to fasten the timbers to the deck and ceiling. The presence of bent bolts and empty bolt holes in the deck planking indicate that two of these knees had to be removed for the correct placement and efficient operation of the two 9-pounder guns that were installed at Fort Ticonderoga. To ensure sufficient space for each to recoil and for the gun crews to load and aim each weapon, the guns were not mounted directly opposite one another.

Upon completion, the afterdeck ran forward of the sternpost 13 feet, 6 inches. Both the midship and forward decks are 14 feet, 9 inches long. The two outermost planks of the forward deck are situated so that they extend to cover lodging knees placed at the intersection of its aftermost beam and the ceiling planking. By this design, two cockpit areas were created between the three separate deck areas. The aft cockpit provides access to the bailing well in the bilges, and the forward cockpit allows access to the storage area under the forward deck.

CAPRAIL

Once the planking and ceiling had been installed and the upper frame arms cut off even with the sheer, the white oak caprail was added. The 1½-inch-molded by 8-inch-sided covering plank is fastened to the top edges of the upper strake and ceiling with iron nails, spaced approximately 1 foot apart.[24] To fit the contour of the vessel, the caprail is fashioned from five individual pieces on the port side of the vessel and six pieces on the starboard side that butt together in V-shaped joints.

The Skenesborough carpenters pierced the caprail along its length so that catheads, swivel gun mounting brackets, awning and bow rail stanchions, thole pins, bitts (timber heads), and eyebolts could be installed. The caprail also serves to support seven cleats on its upper face.

RUDDER

The *Philadelphia*'s "barn door" rudder is made from three pieces of white oak fastened both with wood battens and iron bolts.[25] The three rudder planks are edge-fastened by two ½-inch-diameter iron bolts across each of the two plank seams. Two 1-inch-thick battens are fitted in mortises cut into the starboard sides of the rudder planks so they can support the structure and sit flush with the rudder's surface. These battens are secured with a series of clenched iron nails. Two pintles are strapped to the rudder and held in place by nails. A 1-inch-diameter pin is welded to the front of each strap for placement in the eyebolt gudgeons bolted through the sternpost.

The forwardmost rudder timber extends approximately 6 inches above the sternpost and terminates in a tenon for the tiller. The *Philadelphia*'s original tiller was not recovered in 1935. Hoffman suggested that the original tiller would have projected approximately 6 feet forward, terminating in a rounded handle. Just above the upper pintle, a ⅝-inch-diameter hole in the rudder indicates that a rudder pendant may have been attached to prevent the rudder from lifting up and off of the gudgeons.

AWNING STRUCTURE, BOW RAILS, AND FASCINES

The *Philadelphia* was fitted with a canvas awning for the protection of the crew. Only a few pieces of the awning's beams and stanchions were recovered in 1935. As evidenced by rectangular openings in the caprail, a total of fourteen stanchions supported the gondola's awning (fig. 7.5). Awning stanchions were approximately

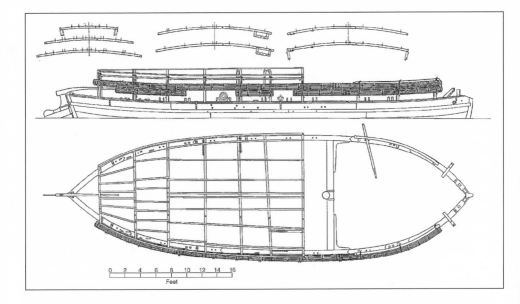

4 feet in length and probably cut from 3-inch-square white pine stock. Surviving pieces show that the lowermost 10-inch section of the stanchion was inserted into a rectangular cutout in the caprail between the inner and outer planking and secured by three iron nails driven through the ceiling. The tops of the stanchions were shaped into a tenon to fit rectangular mortises (1¼ inches square and 3 inches deep) in the ends of the awning beams. Stanchions were spaced between 4 and 5 feet and provided support for an awning that would have covered the entire midship deck and most of the aft deck. Hoffman suggested that the two end awning stanchions on each side of the hull would have been fitted with a small cleat for securing awning pendants and lashings.

Three awning beams were recovered in 1935. Fabricated from 3-inch white oak stock, the end of each member is fitted with a mortise to receive an awning beam. To ensure that water would drain off the awning, the beams are curved so that their centers are positioned approximately 10 inches higher than their outboard ends. The length of the seven awning beams was made to suit the breadth of the hull at the corresponding stanchion positions. No awning battens were recovered. Nail holes in the awning beams allowed Hoffman to reconstruct the position of awning battens that would have provided additional support for the canvas cover. Hoffman suggested that the battens were made from 1-inch-by-2-inch stock.

Fig. 7.5. Awning structure, bow rails, and fascines. Courtesy of the Smithsonian Institution, NMAH/AFH, Howard P. Hoffman, A Graphic Presentation of the Continental Gondola Philadelphia: American Gunboat of 1776 (Washington, D.C.: Smithsonian Institution, 1982), sheet 7.

Battens were attached to the upper surface of the awning beams or to the outer face of the stanchions with one iron nail at each position.

Hoffman proposed that the builders of the *Philadelphia* could have placed a set of racks on the port side of the vessel underneath the third and fourth awning beams to store rammers, sponges, ladles, and worms for the 9- and 12-pounder cannons, thus alleviating overcrowding on the vessel's decks. Similarly, an additional storage rack may have been attached to the starboard side of the vessel between the first two awning beams to store the same equipment for the swivel guns. This position would also serve to hold the handspikes for the 9-pounders.

Six additional stanchions were placed into rectangular cutouts in the bow caprail to support the bow railing. Like the awning stanchions, these members were placed between the inner and outer planking and secured with three nails driven in from the outer planking. The upper ends of the stanchions projected up from the caprail for a height of approximately 2 feet, 4 inches and terminated in a tenon designed to fit a mortise in the white oak rails. Bow rails were cut from 2½-by-3½-inch white oak stock. A notch on the aft end of each rail suggests that an additional section of railing may have extended across the bow deck. The section, which appears impractical aboard such a cramped vessel, was either lost or never installed.

Historical documents indicate that the gondolas were fitted with fascines (bundles of saplings) to protect the crew from sniper fire.[26] Hoffman proposed a practical arrangement of 9-inch-diameter bundles of various lengths that would have provided some protection to the crew but would not interfere with the rigging or the operation of the sweeps, swivels, or broadside cannons. Presumably, the fascine bundles were secured to the rail and awning stanchions with rope lashings.

OTHER HULL FITTINGS

Two lockers that could also serve as seats were on the aft deck. Hagglund recovered the two wooden top pieces (2½ inches thick) and other fragments that appeared to be ends and fronts of the lockers. Hoffman's reconstruction indicates that the lockers were toenailed to the deck and ceiling.

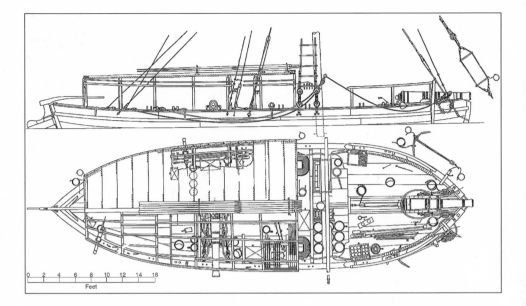

Fig. 7.6. General arrangement, lower rigging, and ordnance. Courtesy of the Smithsonian Institution, NMAH/AFH, Howard P. Hoffman, A Graphic Presentation of the Continental Gondola *Philadelphia:* American Gunboat of 1776 *(Washington, D.C.: Smithsonian Institution, 1982),* sheet 8.

The carriage for the *Philadelphia*'s 12-pounder was designed without trucks or axletrees; the gun was designed to recoil on wooden tracks (fig. 7.6). These tracks, 5⅞ inches thick, extend the full length of the deck and are bolted to the deck beams. A T-shaped timber is situated at the end of the tracks and is braced against the mainmast with a 3-inch-square timber. The backstop of the track is also used to secure the eyebolt for the 12-pounder intackle.

One curved shot garland is nailed to the topmost ceiling plank in the bow on each side of the 12-pounder. Fashioned from white oak, the 2⅝-by-4½-inch timbers have a number of semiglobular cavities gouged out to a depth of 1½ inches to hold the 4.4-inch-diameter round shot for the 12-pounder. The port rack is designed to hold fourteen shot and the starboard rack thirteen.

A white oak cathead is located on each side of the bow. Before placement, the rail was notched flush with the ceiling and the timber placed parallel with a frame. Each cathead is secured in place with nails driven through the timber and ceiling. The upper arms of the catheads angle out and have a 1-inch-diameter hole to secure the anchor stopper rope. Just forward of the catheads is a pair of mooring bitts positioned much as the rail and awning stanchions were by inserting them through the caprail and next to a frame.

The *Philadelphia*'s uppermost strakes of exterior planking and ceiling are pierced in a number of places for other hull fittings. On each side of the stem, just forward of the catheads, is a lead-lined hawse pipe 3½ inches in diameter. The pipe is made from ⅛-inch sheet lead that had been rolled into a tubular shape, hammered outward into a 1¼-inch flange on both inboard and outboard sides of the hull, then secured with nails.

Places for four eyebolts are located on each side of the midship deck. The eyebolts were obviously used with rings to secure the side tackles and breeching ropes for the 9-pounder cannons. Additional eyebolts and rings in the same area served to anchor the main backstays. One other pair of eyebolts, located just forward of the hawse pipes, was similarly used for the 12-pounder breeching ropes. Four pairs of holes present in the upper strake and ceiling just aft of the mainmast most likely served to secure deadeye straps, which in turn secured the lanyards and main shrouds.

Places for eight swivel gun brackets are on the caprail. Before the wrought iron straps of the brackets were attached to the hull it was necessary to notch the caprail flush with the planking and ceiling. The brackets rest directly on the caprail and are fastened to the interior and exterior planking with three iron nails per side. A 1⅝-inch-diameter hole was chiseled or drilled through the caprail for the insertion of the swivel gun yokes.

Additional square openings in the caprail mark the position of thole pins. Both the port and starboard side of the vessel are fitted for seven positions. Considering the positions of the 9-pounders and the close quarters in the stern, however, Hoffman proposed that four of these locations would have proved impractical for manipulating the long sweeps. He suggests that ten sweeps and two spares would be sufficient and practical for propelling the vessel and depicts a reconstructed sweep storage rack nailed over the canvas and the two center awning battens.

The caprail also serves to anchor eyebolts for the vessel's braces and sheets. Two eyebolts on each side of the stern are driven through the caprail and into the top of frames. A pair of elliptical holes in the caprail on each side of the vessel led Hoffman to believe that bitts were originally located in this position and served to belay the tacks. Similar openings in the rail near the aft cockpit may have contained other bitts to belay the mainsheets. Although few cleats

· were recovered with the vessel, nail holes and markings on the rail indicate that four were present on the starboard side and three on the port side. The cleats likely served to belay the main- and topsail braces and topsail halyard.

MASTS, YARDS, AND RIGGING

Remnants of the *Philadelphia*'s rig recovered in 1935 include the white pine mainmast, square sail boom, and topsail yard. Hagglund also located the white oak crosstrees, pin rack, and pins. Four blocks of different sizes were also recovered, but it is unclear if these were designed for rigging or for cannon breeching. One wooden sheave and three wooden deadeyes were also found but their locations were not recorded.

The *Philadelphia*'s 35-foot-11-inch-long mainmast was found sitting upright in the vessel.[27] Maximum diameter of the mast is 10½ inches just above the heel tenon. The heel of the mast is cut into a rectangular tenon 3½ inches wide and 10½ inches long. As positioned in the mast step, *Philadelphia*'s mast rakes aft 1 inch for every 3 feet of its height.[28] A wood shim placed on the aft side of the mast heel ensures correct alignment. To support the mast, a 10-inch-wide mast partner is placed athwartships on the forward face of the mast. The timber protrudes through the ceiling on the starboard side of the vessel but only butts up against the ceiling on the port side.[29] Two lodging knees, 4½ inches molded, are attached to the forward face of the mast partner and ceiling with iron nails. The mast is secured to the partner by an iron mast ring that is fastened to the partner with four ⅞-inch-diameter bolts. Near its top, the mast becomes octagonal in shape with an 8⅜-inch-diameter sheave in the center of the hounds for the tye of the main yard. Above the hounds, the mast is circular in cross section and tapers to 5 inches in diameter.

The *Philadelphia*'s square sail boom, 27 feet, 6 inches in length, is 5 inches in diameter at its center, decreasing to 2 inches at its tip. The topsail yard is shorter at 20 feet, 2 inches with a maximum diameter of 4⁵⁄₁₆ inches tapering to 1¾ inches at the outboard ends. Hoffman reconstructed a cleat position for each of the three spars for use in tying off the topsail sheet pendant, clew pendant, and clew line respectively.

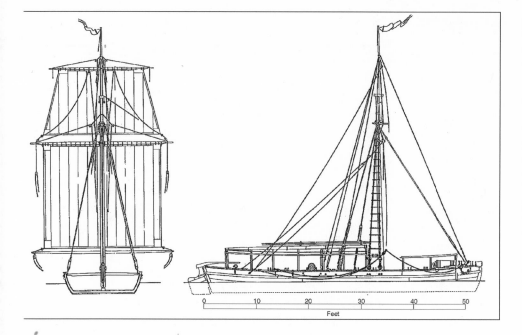

0   10   20   30   40   50
Feet

Fig. 7.7. Profile and sail plan. Courtesy of the Smithsonian Institution, NMAH/AFH, Howard P. Hoffman, A Graphic Presentation of the Continental Gondola Philadelphia: American Gunboat of 1776 *(Washington, D.C.: Smithsonian Institution, 1982),* sheet 1.

The final plan of the *Philadelphia*'s reconstructed spars, sails, and rigging is based mainly on these surviving rigging elements recorded with the hull. Existing deadeye strap holes, cleats, and eyebolts allow further inferences about the overall rig. To complete the rig and sail plan, Hoffman consulted contemporary records and sketches. In the end, he details "a practical rig suitable for service on Lake Champlain."[30] The *Philadelphia*'s sail plan is shown in figure 7.7. The Smithsonian Institution's plans also provide tables detailing the size of cordage and blocks needed for the restoration of the *Philadelphia*'s standing, running rigging, sails, ordnance, anchors, and other miscellaneous lines.

PAINT

Aside from some traces of red paint on one of the *Philadelphia*'s tompions, the gondola appears to have been unpainted. During the Smithsonian survey it was determined that the hull retained some traces of linseed oil. It is likely, however, that the linseed oil was applied by Hagglund as a preservative when the gondola was under his care.

TOOL MARKS

In the 1980s William A. Bayreuther III, a graduate student from
Texas A&M University's Nautical Archaeology Program, surveyed
the *Philadelphia*'s hull for the presence of tool marks that could provide other clues to the gondola's construction. Bayreuther concluded
that a variety of cutting implements were employed throughout
the three-week construction process. These included the adze,
broadax, drill, crosscut saw, and chisel. Markings on the less-eroded
planks suggest that they were cut with a water-powered up-and-
down sash saw with regularly patterned teeth. Significantly,
Bayreuther found no evidence for the less-regular angled tooth
marks indicative of a pit saw. He concluded that Philip Skene's mills
satisfactorily supplied the carpenters with oak planking.[31]

It is generally assumed that the *Philadelphia* and the other seven
Skenesborough gondolas were based on a design made by Benedict
Arnold on May 2, 1776.[32] The specifications detailed by Arnold
are similar, but not identical, to those of the extant *Philadelphia*.
For whatever reasons, the New York carpenters engaged by
Schuyler either modified Arnold's plans or adopted their own. The
end result was a vessel similar in size, simpler to construct, and
somewhat smaller in scantlings. Simplicity in design was particularly
important considering the short amount of time available to the
Americans in the summer and fall of 1776. Equally important, the
simple construction process allowed carpenters who were unfamiliar with building ships to help construct the hulls under the supervision of shipwrights.

Chapter 8

THE PHILADELPHIA
ARTIFACT COLLECTION

The *Philadelphia* artifact collection comprises a wide variety of materials and provides an idea of the equipment and supplies carried on a naval craft of this size and period. This chapter describes some of the more significant finds and, where possible, provides information on distribution and quantity. Unfortunately, some items were either unavailable for examination or had been lost. Information about these items is based solely on written or photographic evidence.

A minimum of 767 objects were found with the *Philadelphia*. This number was determined by comparing the number of artifacts described in Lorenzo Hagglund's report of the salvage project with an accession list and Polaroid photographs kept at the Smithsonian Institution's National Museum of American History (see appendix). Many of these artifacts, including the cannons and shot, were removed from the hull before it was raised. The remainder were recovered by washing and screening the mud that had accumulated in the hull during its 159-year immersion. Undoubtedly, a number of artifacts, particularly those associated with the vessel's rigging and awning were lost; they either floated away or dropped outside the hull after the gondola sank. Due to poor visibility and a muddy bottom, the salvagers did not search the area outside the hull to any extent.

The tools that underwater archaeologists rely on today—such as scuba, metal detectors, magnetometers, and side-scan sonar—

were not available to Hagglund's salvage team. Much to its credit, however, Hagglund's salvage team diligently searched and apparently kept everything found onboard the vessel. The recovery of coal cinders, dropped in the hull by passing steamboats, was even recorded. Because the project was a salvage operation and not conducted using modern archaeological practices, no accurate map of the artifacts' exact locations within the hull exists. Fortunately, Hagglund's reports provide a general location for many artifact positions. Except for a few missing items, some of which may have been given away at the time of the salvage, the artifacts are now with the Smithsonian Institution. The majority of these are displayed either next to or onboard the *Philadelphia*. Visitors entering the Armed Forces History wing on the third floor of the NMAH encounter the hull of the vessel resting on the floor, its mainmast alongside. A much shortened replica mast has been installed to fit underneath the museum's ceiling. The *Philadelphia*'s cannons are onboard in their original locations, but rest upon unobtrusive iron supports instead of the fragile hull. The brick fireplace has been reassembled and is displayed in the position in which Hagglund reported finding it. Much of the *Philadelphia*'s original equipment is also exhibited on the vessel, including the iron kettles and shot.

ARMAMENTS

The largest category of artifacts recovered from the hull was armaments, the foremost being the three cannons and their wooden carriages. The *Philadelphia*'s main battery consisted of one 12-pounder on a slide in the bow and two 9-pounders mounted amidships (figs. 8.1 and 8.2).

The tube of the *Philadelphia*'s cast-iron 12-pounder has an overall length of 8 feet, 6½ inches, measured from the base ring to the end of the muzzle.[1] A knoblike cascabel projects 10 inches from the rear of the base ring (see fig. A.1). Forward of the base ring is the ½-inch-diameter touch hole, first reinforce astragal, paired first and second reinforce rings, and the muzzle astragal. Caliber, or bore, is 5 inches. Trunnions are set approximately one-half caliber below the centerline axis at a distance of 3 feet, 7½ inches forward of the base ring. Distance between the trunnions is 2 feet, 1 inch. A raised *F* is present on the end of each trunnion. The only other marking on

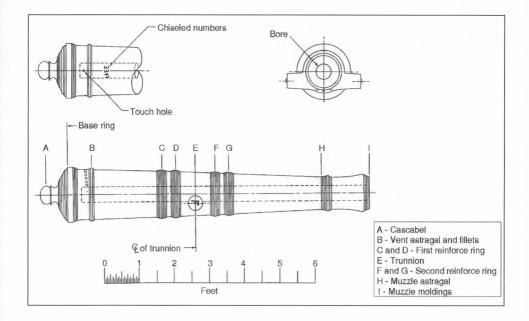

Chiseled numbers

Bore

334

Touch hole

Base ring

A   B   C D E F G   H   I

℄ of trunnion

0   1   2   3   4   5   6
Feet

A - Cascabel
B - Vent astragal and fillets
C and D - First reinforce ring
E - Trunnion
F and G - Second reinforce ring
H - Muzzle astragal
I - Muzzle moldings

Fig. 8.1. Twelve-pounder bow gun. After Howard P. Hoffman, A Graphic Presentation of the Continental Gondola Philadelphia: American Gunboat of 1776 (Washington, D.C.: Smithsonian Institution, 1982), sheet 14.

the cannon is a crudely chiseled weight stamp on the top surface forward of the touch hole (see fig. A.2). There are four numbers: the first three digits are *334* and the last appears to be a *3*. This figure of 3,343 pounds compares well with the present weight of the cast-iron tube at 3,490 pounds.

In length and weight, this cannon tube matches the standards established by the English Board of Ordnance of 1764.[2] The fact that the bore is slightly oversized at 5 inches suggests an earlier casting date, however. According to Hoffman, the standard bore for 12-pounders of the period was 4.7 inches.[3] Criteria established by the Board of Ordnance maintained that a bore of 4.63 inches diameter should be used. Considering that the *Philadelphia's* round shot for the 12-pounder were 4.4 inches in diameter, the cannons may have been rather inaccurate at anything other than short range due to excessive windage.

Another clue to an early casting date is the fact that the trunnions are not set on the centerline of the piece but are located approximately one-half caliber below. Although this position improved vision to the side and reduced recoil by producing downward pressure on the breech, it placed greater stresses on the carriage. By 1750 English artillerists were maintaining that trunnions should be located on the axis of the bore.[4]

Research at the Smithsonian Institution concluded that this gun is a "finbanker," cast at Finspong, Sweden, as much as a hundred years earlier.[5] A similar cannon mounted on a conventional naval carriage is depicted in the *Guide to the Royal Danish Arsenal Museum*. This cannon was recovered in 1909 from the wreck of the *Enigheden*, a Danish 66-gun, line-of-battle ship that sank in the southern channel at Kalmar, Sweden, in 1679. Like the *Philadelphia's* 12-pounder, this cannon has the letter *F* on the end of each trunnion. *Finbankere* were Dutch and Swedish export articles and were sold in large quantities to the Danish navy.[6]

The tube of the 12-pounder is mounted in the bow of the *Philadelphia* on a slide carriage. The unusual carriage has no trucks or axletrees but is designed with notches, or cutouts, in the outboard bottom section of the carriage's cheeks (side pieces) so it can be positioned on two wooden tracks bolted to the forward deck beams. Through careful placement of the tracks or by allowing clearance in the design of the carriage, the 12-pounder can move without restriction along the tracks. The simple design saved time that otherwise would have been spent manufacturing the carriage's axletrees and trucks. However, the entire gondola has to be turned in order to train the weapon.

Fig. 8.2. Example of 9-pounder waist gun. After Howard P. Hoffman, A Graphic Presentation of the Continental Gondola Philadelphia: American Gunboat of 1776 (Washington, D.C.: Smithsonian Institution, 1982), sheet 14.

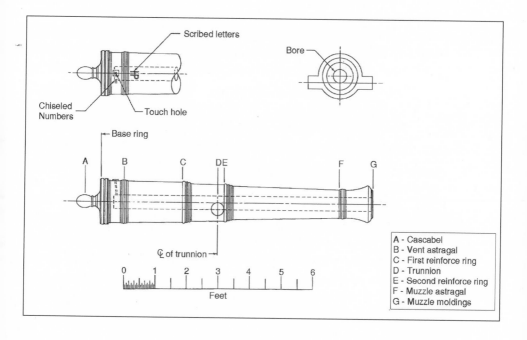

Scribed letters

Bore

Chiseled Numbers

Touch hole

Base ring

A   B   C   DE   F   G

℄ of trunnion

0 1 2 3 4 5 6
Feet

A - Cascabel
B - Vent astragal
C - First reinforce ring
D - Trunnion
E - Second reinforce ring
F - Muzzle astragal
G - Muzzle moldings

Hagglund noted that the recoil from the 12-pounder must have carried it well inboard since the back stop of the carriage tracks is reinforced with a brace set against the mast.[7] In later periods, slide carriages sat upon inclined skids. The incline reduced the recoil and allowed the gun to be heaved back into position more easily.[8]

The *Philadelphia*'s two cast-iron 9-pounders are nearly identical (see fig. A.3). The starboard gun weighs 2,195 pounds; the port gun weighs just 5 pounds less. Each gun is 7 feet, 9 inches long from the base ring to the muzzle. Forward of the base ring is a ½-inch-diameter touch hole, first reinforce astragal, first and second reinforce rings, and muzzle astragal. Like the 12-pounder, these guns have an oversized bore of 4½ inches for the placement of the 4-inch-diameter balls they were designed to fire. Distance between the 4½-inch-diameter trunnions is 1 foot, 10 inches. The letters *HP* are scribed on the top surface of each cannon just forward of the touch hole (see fig. A.4). The roman numeral *VII* is also scribed on the port gun just to the right of the touch hole. The design of these guns indicates that they are also of Swedish origin and were probably cast during the late seventeenth century.[9]

The carriages for the 9-pounder tubes are virtually identical to the ordinary British design of the period. The standard published work of the period for gun carriage design was the English artillerist John Muller's *Treatise of Artillery* published in 1757. According to Spencer C. Tucker, "Muller was a professor of fortification and artillery at Woolwich, known for his advocacy of lighter guns and the use of cast iron rather than bronze in their fabrication. While the so-called Muller system was never officially adopted in the Royal Navy, his book with its illustrations and calculations for determining the dimensions of carriages was certainly known in the American colonies at the time of the Revolutionary War."[10]

The chief difference between the *Philadelphia*'s carriages and Muller's carriage is in the size of the trucks and a variation in placing the iron work.[11] Muller proposed a dimension of 4 bore diameters for the size of the fore trucks and 3½ for the hind.[12] The five surviving trucks on the *Philadelphia*'s 9-pounder carriages are approximately 13 inches in diameter (2.88 bore diameters) for the both the fore and the hind (see fig. A.5).

Three corroded carriage rings, one with an attached eyebolt, are exhibited next to the *Philadelphia* (see fig. A.6). Seven keys for the carriage trunnion plates were also recovered in various shapes and degrees of preservation (see fig. A.7). Only six were actually needed, however. The iron keys are roughly L-shaped and possess a hole in the wider end for the attachment of a lanyard.

To date no historical document has been found that specifically states where these three cannons or the other cannons on Arnold's fleet were obtained. It is generally assumed that they were taken from stores at Fort Ticonderoga. When the Americans captured the British fort in May, 1775, 58 guns (42 cannons and 16 mortars and howitzers) were inventoried.[13] Approximately half of these were sent to the Continental army outside Boston. Some of the latter were apparently returned to the lakes, carried with the army to Canada in early 1776, and eventually transported back to Fort Ticonderoga following the American retreat.[14]

Alternately, some of the *Philadelphia*'s cannons could have been taken from Crown Point. Colonel Thomas Hartley wrote to General Horatio Gates to lament the possible loss of more cannons to the fleet: "I understood General Arnold has wrote to you for the guns I have here. It is well known to your Honour that we had the greatest search after them. We spent much time and labour in digging them from under the ruins of wood earth, where they lay long, and might have remained there had it not been for us."[15]

These were evidently older cannons, probably left over from the French and Indian War. Following the Battle of Valcour Island, British troops occupied the deserted American outpost at Crown Point. German company surgeon J. F. Wasmus wrote that "Among the enemy cannons found at Crown Point, one came upon several cannons quite carefully inscribed AUGUST WILHELM H.Z.B.U.L. and the rest. How did those ever get here?" Braunschweig troops had fought as British allies against the French in Europe during the Seven Years' War. It is possible that these cannons had been captured by the French and later installed at Fort St. Frédéric. The inscription refers to August Wilhelm (1715–81), the Duke of Braunschweig-Bevern, one of the outstanding soldiers in the army of Frederick the Great (Herzog zu Braunschweig und Lüneburg).[16]

Certainly, the supply of cannons at Fort Ticonderoga and Crown Point was not plentiful enough to adequately supply both the posts and the fleet. Arnold informed Schuyler of this situation in July and suggested that an attempt be made to find cannons in other colonies.[17] One of the reasons for the shortage of cannons in the American colonies was that British policy did not allow for their manufacture. The few cannons available to the Americans at the outbreak of the revolution consisted of "a motley collection of every sort and caliber." According to Spencer C. Tucker, the Americans had three choices: cast the cannons themselves; capture guns from the British; or secure cannons from other foreign sources, chiefly France.[18] His research suggests that all three eventually proved to be viable solutions. For the *Philadelphia* and the rest of Arnold's fleet, however, the chief source of cannons seems to have been the stores at Fort Ticonderoga.

Although the *Philadelphia*'s caprail is pierced in eight places for swivel gun brackets, only one swivel gun was recovered. Hagglund reported finding the cast-iron gun and its broken yoke in the bottom of the aft cockpit. In form, the swivel is a small-bore cannon, 2 feet, 11¼ inches in length as measured from the base ring (see figs. A.8 and A.9).[19] A flat-ended cascabel projects back 3⅜ inches from the base ring. No monkey tail or other handle is present. Forward of the touch hole, the swivel tube is marked with a weight stamp of *1-1-23* indicating one British (or long) hundredweight of 112 pounds, one quarter-hundredweight of 28 pounds, and 23 additional pounds for an original casting weight of 163 pounds (see fig. A.10). An additional mark in the form of a broad arrow denotes that the weapon was originally property of the British Crown. The size of the bore (1⅞ inches) indicates that the gun would have fired a ¾-pound iron ball, 1¾ inches in diameter.

A broken iron yoke was found resting beside the swivel (see fig. A.11). The Y-shaped pivot was designed to retain the swivel's trunnions in iron rings. The lower end of the yoke terminates in a cylindrical pivot that would have rested in one of the eight sockets placed in the *Philadelphia*'s rail. Clearly, the yoke broke at the junction of the two arms and the swivel either fell, or was deposited, into the aft cockpit along with its broken yoke. The missing arm was not recovered. The fact that no other swivels were found suggests that they were either not present or were off-loaded before the vessel sank.

During the Revolutionary War period swivels were even less standardized than cannons. They ranged in size from a heavy musket to a small cannon.[20] In their fixed mounts, swivels could not sustain great recoil and so had to be limited in size. They were usually of the heavier, cannon-type, and the loose shot they fired were effective against personnel at close range. In general, they varied from 34 to 36 inches in length, from 1½ to 1¾ inches in bore, and threw shot weighing ½ to ¾ of a pound. Swivels were particularly favored for early colonial merchant vessels and were also popular onboard vessels patrolling the Great Lakes.[21]

Although the *Philadelphia* and the other gondolas were supposed to have been armed with eight swivel guns, it is not known how many were actually placed on the vessels. Richard Varick attempted to procure swivel guns from the ironworks at Salisbury, Connecticut, and the "Furnaces and Bloomerys at Livingston Manor."[22] Apparently Varick was successful to some degree because Gates wrote Arnold on September 12 to inform him that swivels were being sent forward.[23] Considering the presence of the broad arrow on the one surviving swivel, it seems probable that this gun was taken from naval supplies captured at St. Jean or from one of the British vessels taken by the Americans on the St. Lawrence River. Alternately, swivels might have been taken from stocks at Ticonderoga. British ships from the French and Indian War were heavily armed with swivels. The investigation of one of these, the sloop *Boscawen*, produced a total of 22 swivel guns.[24]

One wrought iron ring gauge was recovered from the gondola (see fig. A.12). Although Hagglund reported finding the gauge on the midship deck next to the port 9-pounder, its dimensions suggest it would have been more suitable to the 12-pounder. The inner dimension of the ring is $4\frac{7}{16}$ inches, which would have just allowed a 12-pound round shot ($4\frac{13}{32}$ diameter) to pass through.[25] More unusual was Hagglund's find of a wooden double shot gauge, for both 12- and 9-pounder shot resting on the aft deck (see fig. A.13). Fashioned from white ash, the wooden board has an overall length of 2 feet, ¼ inch and a width of 6⅞ inches that tapers down to 6⅜ inches. Two holes are present: a $4\frac{15}{16}$-inch-diameter hole and a $4\frac{5}{16}$-inch hole. Although simply made, the wooden gauge could effectively separate the main battery shot. In order to protect the gauge from splitting, three battens made from $\frac{5}{16}$-inch-thick white ash were nailed to one surface. The center batten was missing when recovered, but like the two that remain, it was nailed to the gauge with four small nails.

The NMAH accession list does not include an apron among its inventory of the *Philadelphia* artifacts, although Hagglund reported finding a crumpled lead apron next to the port 9-pounder. Amazingly, wooden tompions were found for all three cannons despite their tendency to float when not in use. Two smaller tompions, nearly identical in size, are appropriate for the 9-pounders; they include a drilled center hole, which was once presumably threaded with a knotted cord to aid in removal from the muzzles (see fig. A.14). Each example retains traces of red paint on its outward faces. The larger tompion for the 12-pounder is approximately twice as long and lacks a center rope hole.

Very few gunners' tools were recovered with the *Philadelphia*. One rammer head fabricated from white ash was found and is appropriate for the 12-pounder.[26] The surviving head is tapered, 4⅜ inches in diameter and length. According to Tucker, the length of the head should have been 1½ times the diameter of the cannon's bore, in this case 7½ inches.[27] Fragments of wood inside the hole indicate that a wooden handle was originally attached. Hoffman's reconstructed rammer positions the head at one end of an ash handle, with a sponge at the other. Contemporary literature suggests that the turned wooden sponge would have been covered with a sheep skin, wool side out.

A wrought iron worm for the ¾-pound swivel was found in an unspecified location (see fig. A.15). Like the rammer head, the wooden handle is missing but presumably was made of ash and attached to the worm with a single nail through the sleeve of the worm. Overall length is 6 inches with a diameter of 1⅜ inches.[28] Hoffman suggested that a copper ladle may have been positioned at the other end of the tool.

SHOT

Two bar shot were recovered with the gondola (see fig. A.16). One bar shot suitable in size for use with the 9-pounders has a present weight of 7 pounds, 2 ounces.[29] Hoffman calculated an original weight of exactly 8 pounds. The two shot hemispheres have a diameter of 3.85 inches and were connected with a ¾-inch-square wrought iron bar. The 10⅞-inch-long connecting bar was inset into the two hemispheres to a depth of ¾ inches. The single 12-pounder-sized bar shot was found protruding from the muzzle of the bow gun, having slid forward and wedged itself in the tube after the Philadelphia sank. Identical to the 9-pounder bar shot, but manufactured on a larger scale, the 12-pounder-sized bar shot had cast iron hemispheres of 4.85 inch diameter connected with an ¹¹⁄₁₆-inch-square wrought iron bar set in to a depth of 1 inch. The present weight of the shot is 16 pounds with a calculated original weight of 16 pounds, 7 ounces.

According to Hagglund's 1936 report, fifty-five 9-pound round shot were recovered. Eleven of them may have been lost or given away as souvenirs because the NMAH accession papers only list forty-four.[30] The shot pile was found between the two knees just forward of the port 9-pounder. Other than some casting marks and sprue traces, the round shot are unmarked. Average diameter is 4 inches.

Only two 12-pound round shot were found, indicating that this cannon may have seen more service than *Philadelphia*'s two 9-pounders during the battle at Valcour Island. One 12-pound shot was found resting in the shot garland in the bow and the other under the forward deck. Average diameter of the 12-pound round shot is 4¹³⁄₃₂ inches.[31] Neither is marked.

Three other round shot were found aboard the vessel: a 24-pounder, 6-pounder, and 4-pounder. The 24-pound shot is credited with sinking the *Philadelphia*. The shot, marked with the British broad arrow, was found lodged in the hull planking on the port side of the vessel.[32] Because the *Philadelphia* did not mount any 4- or 6-pounder guns, these shot may have been fired into the *Philadelphia;* the vessel exhibits evidence of having been hulled in two other places. Both the *Maria* and the *Carleton* had batteries consisting of 6-pounders. Alternately, the two shot could have been carried aboard in error.

One grapeshot canister and its white oak sabot are included in the *Philadelphia* collection, and both are remarkably well preserved (see figs. A.17 and A.18). Although not originally accessioned with the rest of the collection, the tinplate cylinder was later donated by Lorenzo Hagglund's son. This artifact was recovered from one of the 9-pounder cannons in 1935. Upon recovery, the cannon was found to have been loaded with the canister of shot, a 9-pound ball, and three thick wads and powder.[33] The canister as originally assembled contained eighty-four ⅞-inch-diameter shot arranged in six layers, fourteen 1½-ounce shot per layer, giving a total weight of shot of 7 pounds, 12 ounces. Although no canisters or wooden sabots suitable in size for the 12-pounder were found, a cluster of ten 1-inch-diameter iron shot recovered suggests that canisters may have been used by this cannon.

The Smithsonian collection also includes 108 grapeshot of two other sizes. A handwritten note by Hagglund indicated that a total of 116 grapeshot were recovered in 1935.[34] The majority of these are 1¾ inches in diameter and served as shot for the swivel guns. Alternately, Hoffman suggested that this size shot could have been used in the fabrication of canvas-covered grapeshot clusters for the 9-pounders. No wooden spindles or bottoms were recovered from the wreck that would indicate that complete stands of grapeshot were actually in use, however. Other grapeshot in this group are 1 15⁄16 inches in diameter, suggesting that the 12-pounder bow gun may have fired grapeshot as well.

Four pieces of iron langrage were also recovered with the *Philadelphia*. Each appears to have been cut from crudely formed iron rod or bar stock (see fig. A.19). Like grapeshot, langrage could have been fired in preloaded canisters or simply packed into the cannons. Langrage was effective only at short ranges, not exceeding 300 to 500 yards, due to the rapid dispersion and lightness of the cylinder's contents. At short range, canister shot was more effective than any other projectile, including grape.[35]

SMALL ARMS

A badly eroded wooden musket stock lacking any of its original hardware was found on the bottom of the forward cockpit (see fig. A.20). Due to its incomplete preservation, it is difficult to identify the type, but the weapon appears similar to contemporary Brown Bess or French Charleville muskets. Although no mention is made in Hagglund's salvage reports or in the NMAH accession list, a Polaroid photograph on file at the Smithsonian Institution indicates that fragments of this same gun and several others were also recovered (see figs. A.21 and A.22). Four trigger guards (presumably brass) are depicted in the photograph along with some other concreted gun fragments. This photograph and one other brass trigger guard fragment included in the collection suggest that at least five muskets or similar weapons may have been left behind by the *Philadelphia*'s crew.

Trigger guards on regulation British muskets were consistently of brass after 1720, and up to about 1775 possessed a terminal nipple at both ends and had one screw hole just behind the loop of the guard.[36] Around 1775 the guard was shortened, the nipples were removed, and a second screw hole was added close to the end of the tail. Both styles of guard were drilled through the fore edge of the loop to receive a sling swivel.

Two of the *Philadelphia*'s trigger guards are complete and, although they are shown only from the side in photographs, do not appear to have nipples on either end. Only one has been drilled through the fore edge of the loop to receive a sling. Two other trigger guards are depicted in the photograph but are still concreted to musket firing assemblies. One is obviously broken at the beginning of the tail. The second possesses a screw opening in the end of the tail similar to that of the later style of the Brown Bess musket. The fifth trigger guard is also fragmented, having broken across screw openings at either end (see fig. A.23). Its overall shape does not resemble either model of the Brown Bess.

Other gun fragments in the Polaroid photograph appear to be a very simple key plate (probably brass), a wooden ramrod fragment, and two gun barrel fragments. Five wooden ramrod fragments are displayed at the NMAH (see fig. A.24). The fragments have undergone considerable shrinkage and distortion due to a lack of conservation following their recovery in 1935. These same fragments were found in association with several ramrod thimbles (see figs. A.25 and A.26). Two brass thimbles (or pipes) fashioned from sheet brass with the ends drawn up into a pierced strip for attachment to the stock are included in the collection. In style, these appear similar to ones found on either the Brown Bess model 1 (long land musket, introduced about 1727), or the Brown Bess model 2 (short land musket, introduced about 1740).[37] The British and the Americans used both these weapons during the Revolution. Two brass rear ramrod thimbles were also found. The first example has two fastening holes, approximately ⅛ inch in diameter. The second is similar, but only possesses one fastening hole. More unusual was Hagglund's find of one fragmented rear ramrod thimble fashioned from iron (see fig. A.27). The length of the surviving tail is 4¾ inches.

The remains of nine bayonets are included in the *Philadelphia* artifact collection (see fig. A.28). Each is badly corroded, making exact identification difficult. The bayonets were found in the forward cockpit and appear to represent several different types. Surviving blade lengths vary from 4 inches to 16¾ inches. In most cases, the blades appear to be triangular in cross section, fullered on two sides. Only two fragments retain portions of their sockets.

Bayonets are usually identified on the basis of the length and shape of the blades, shanks, and sockets. Three bayonets in the *Philadelphia* collection have blade lengths of nearly 16¾ inches, the standard for the British Brown Bess musket.[38] Only one retains a portion of the socket, however. This bayonet has suffered some additional damage since 1935 but appears to have had a 4-inch socket with a rear reinforcing collar. In all respects, this bayonet is identical to the British standard type. One other bayonet has a 3-inch socket. Because the mounting slot in the thin-walled socket is fragmented, it is difficult to identify precisely; however it is similar in design to the French 1763 model.[39] Alternately, the bayonet may be an American copy of the French model. Most of the other bayonets include portions of the shanks, but these appear to have many variants in both feature and design. Any or all them could be American copies of either British or French styles. None appear to have the flat, swordlike blades associated with German bayonets or pre-1750 British models.[40]

Included in the same cluster as the other gun parts were eight gun flints (see fig. A.29). All are honey-colored and possess rounded ends suggesting that they are of the common French type. One other interesting find associated with the small arms is a wooden cartridge box (see fig. A.30). Although the box is heavily eroded, it appears to have been designed to hold seventeen or eighteen paper tubes of powder and shot (cartouches). The leather pouch in which it would have been carried was recovered, but its present location is unknown.[41]

One iron musket ball (½-inch-diameter), four lead musket balls (11⁄16-inch-diameter), two lead musket balls (⅝-inch-diameter), and

349 lead buckshot (⅜-inch-diameter) were recovered from the forward cockpit (see fig. A.31) Conceivably, buckshot could have been fired from any of the weapons aboard the vessel including the cannons, swivels, or small arms. Small arms charged with the combination of "ball and buck" were especially lethal weapons when fired at short ranges.

The varied types of firearm furniture and bayonets, as well as the sizes of small arms shot, together suggest that a mixed collection of weapons was aboard the vessel. Presumably, these were the personal arms of the soldiers who were drafted to serve in the *Philadelphia*. According to Harold L. Peterson, "variety was the word for the firearms of the Continental soldier." Even though America possessed a large number of British small arms at the outbreak of the Revolution, there were not nearly enough to supply the entire army. The individual colonies and Congress were forced to turn to American gunsmiths to make up for the shortage. The majority of the *Philadelphia*'s crew was drafted from the New Hampshire militia stationed at Fort Ticonderoga. New Hampshire did not let a specific contract for arms but periodically collected money and sent out agents to procure firearms from wherever they were available. Just how serviceable these weapons were is open to debate. George Washington wrote to the colony in 1777 to inquire about purchasing muskets for the Continental troops. By way of reply, the Committee of Safety wrote: "fire arms cannot be procured from us that can be depended upon."[42] The committee added that they had practically run out of unreliable firearms.

IRON FASTENERS

The majority of the *Philadelphia*'s wrought iron nails, spikes, and bolts remain in the hull in their original positions, and only eighteen loose nails and spikes are included in the collection (see fig. A.32). Preserved lengths range from 2 1⁄16 inches to 7 13⁄16 inches. The heads and shanks are corroded, but all have square shanks that taper down to a flat or chiseled point. On most, the four corners of the head angle downward into a characteristic rose head shape. During the survey of the vessel, Hoffman determined that the majority of these fasteners fell into four categories of original length: 3½, 4¼, 5½, and 9¾ inches.[43]

One other very large fastener (13¾ inches long) displayed at the NMAH is labeled as a timbering spike (see fig. A.33). The shank is round in cross section (1¾ inches in diameter) but tapers down to a corroded point. The original position of the round-headed fastener was not determined. Three iron eye spikes, between 7¼ inches and 9¼ inches in overall length, were recovered from an unspecified location. These were presumably used to secure tarpaulins and light lines.

TOOLS

Four axes were recovered from the forward cockpit of the *Philadelphia* (see figs. A.34 and A.35). Two of these retain a portion of their wooden handles. Each ax blade is of a different type. Carl P. Russell wrote: "For nearly a century after the American ax was perfected, older ax types lacking niceties of balance continued to be manufactured in America as well as in Europe. These various forms, intermediate between the typical European ax and the distinctive American product, found use along with the better tool to which they had given origin, and it is not unusual for the archeologist and historian to uncover specimens in one site that are representative of all stages in the development of the American ax. A good example of this overlapping is seen in the axes from the recovered hull of the Continental gondola *Philadelphia*, which was sunk in 1776."[44]

One of the *Philadelphia*'s axes is of the "French" ax type and does not possess any poll (see example A in fig. A.34). Two others have been described as an "intermediate" ax type and show some development of a counterbalancing poll (see examples B and C in fig. A.34). The last example can be called "a full-fledged American ax" (see example D in fig. A.34). All these types were used by the Continental fighters who manned the *Philadelphia*.[45]

A large wooden mallet was also found in the forward cockpit (see fig. A.36). It has been presumed that this mallet was used for serving (or wrapping) the vessel's rigging with spun yarn as protection against chafing, although it does not exhibit the distinctive groove down the center of the mallet head. The mallet may also have been used to assemble and disassemble staved containers or to hammer in wooden plugs that would stop leaks made by enemy round shot. Two (or possibly three) wooden plugs of a size appropriate to fill a hole from 9- or 12-pounder-sized shot were also recovered in 1935 (see fig. A.37).

A round brush with horsehair bristles, approximately 10 inches in overall length, was found in association with a dish shaped from sheet lead (see figs. A.38 and A.39). Both the dish and the brush retains traces of pitch. Pitch may have been used along with caulking on the *Philadelphia*'s seams. Another possible use of pitch aboard Arnold's vessels was in the manufacture of a medicine used to treat impetigo (see p. 133)

Based on Hagglund's report, it appears that at least two spades were recovered. In a 1935 photograph, one of the salvagers is seen holding a spade complete with wooden handle (see fig. A.40). The blade of this spade appears much shorter, broken, or extremely corroded when the photograph is compared to a second spade, which is exhibited at the NMAH. The latter spade is 15 inches long (including the 3½-inch handle socket); the blade is 11½ inches long, 7¾ wide at the forward end, and 8½ inches wide near the handle (see fig. A.41). As originally manufactured, the spade was probably made by hammering a flat sheet of iron over a form. The end result strengthened the blade by producing a supporting arch down the center and a socket in which a 1¾-inch-diameter wooden handle could be inserted.

Other tools, most of which were probably recovered from the forward cockpit, include an iron file approximately 12 inches long (see fig. A.42) and two iron fascine knives (see fig. A.43). The two knives, essentially a type of billhook, were probably used to cut the saplings that were bundled and secured to the bulwarks of the gondola as fascines.[46] One fascine blade is stamped with the letter *H* (see fig. A.44). At least one auger and one chisel were also recovered from the forward cockpit. One other tool mentioned in Hagglund's account, but not included in the NMAH accession list, is an iron adze head. The artifact, clearly depicted in a 1935 photograph, is approximately 12 inches long with a blade width of about 4 inches (see fig. A.45). One broken grindstone was also recovered. As pictured in a 1935 photograph, this object appears to have been approximately 12 inches in diameter and 4 inches thick (see fig. A.46). A hole is present in the center and a wedgelike section is missing from the circumference.

Four wood rigging blocks were included in the *Philadelphia* collection when accessioned by the Smithsonian Institution.[47] These include one 12-inch double block, one 10-inch single block, one 10-inch double block (see fig. A.47), and one 8½-inch single block. In each case, the shells are made of white ash and all sheaves, except for the 8½-inch single block, are fashioned from lignum vitae. The smaller block's sheave is made of hop-hornbeam. Pins for the three larger blocks are made of lignum vitae, and the smaller block has a white ash pin. Unfortunately, Hagglund did not indicate where the blocks were found. Other than the 8½-inch single block, Hoffman made no use of these blocks in the *Philadelphia*'s reconstruction.

Three wooden deadeyes of several sizes were also found in 1935. One of these was obviously converted from a sheave (see fig. A.48). One 7-inch deadeye made of white ash was chosen as the model for reconstruction. In total, eight such deadeyes were needed to secure the *Philadelphia*'s lanyards and shrouds.[48]

Hooks served a variety of purposes onboard the *Philadelphia*. Hoffman noted that a total of sixteen would be needed for gun tackles, main backstay, forestay, and the pendants used to secure the anchor flukes.[49] The NMAH collection includes nine iron hooks, one of which includes both a rope thimble and a clevis (see figs. A.49 and A.50). One hook was found with a fragment of parceled rope wrapped around a thimble. Thimbles were used in conjunction with many of the hooks and appear to have been hand-forged for four sizes of rope diameters: ⅝, 13⁄16, 1⅛, and 1¾ inches.

ANCHORS

Two anchors were recovered with the *Philadelphia*. Both were in their original stowed positions before the vessel sank. Eventually, their securing lines deteriorated and the anchors fell into the mud alongside the hull. Just below the starboard cathead was an anchor marked *320*. Apparently, this number bears no relation to the anchor's original weight since its present weight, including the stock is only 112 pounds.[50] The anchor's two-piece, white oak stock is also in remarkably good condition. Sixteen white oak treenails are placed in ¾-inch-diameter holes staggered along the length of the stock. An 8-inch-diameter ring made from ¾-inch wrought iron is looped through the eye at the top of the shank. This anchor has a unique removable locking pin in the stock. Once the pin is disengaged from a nut on the shank, the stock can be rotated in the same plane as the arms, a feature that would simplify stowage onboard the vessel. Cutouts in the stock allow for a smooth rotation around the nut. Two white oak wedges driven from underneath the stock and alongside the shank prevent any further movement once the stock is locked into position.

The port anchor was also found underneath its corresponding cathead. It is slightly larger in both weight and length than its starboard companion and lacks the rotating feature of the starboard anchor stock (see fig. A.51). The stamped number *129* on the anchor's crown closely matches its present weight of 134 pounds.[51] This stock is also made from two pieces of white oak. Eight 1-inch-diameter white oak treenails secure the two timbers. An 8-inch-diameter ring, identical to the other anchor, is found at the anchor's eye.

SWEEPS

Hagglund found the remains of two sweeps underneath the forward deck. Both sweeps are made of white ash and, together, provided enough details for Hoffman to reconstruct their original dimensions. Overall length was approximately 20 feet, 6 inches. Handles were approximately 11 inches long and 1½ inches in diameter. Forward, the sweep becomes 3 inches square in cross section in the area of the loom and transitions to a 3-inch-diameter round cross section at the body. The last 6 feet of the sweep is occupied by a blade 4 inches wide and ⅝ inches thick. Hoffman noted that this width is approximately 2 inches narrower than what was normally used during the period.[52]

NAVIGATIONAL EQUIPMENT

During the examination of the stern lockers, Hagglund found the remains of a broken sandglass (see fig. A.52). As originally assembled, the sandglass was mounted between two wooden disks that were separated by five dowels.[53] The deteriorated remains of the wooden frame are not included in the NMAH collection but are depicted in Hagglund's account of the salvage. Testing at the Smithsonian Institution on the "log glass" as reassembled by Hagglund revealed that it was designed to measure 28-second intervals and could possibly have been used with a log reel.[54] Considering the short duration of measurement, the only useful function of the glass would have been in determining the vessel's speed.

One pair of iron navigational dividers was also found onboard the vessel (see fig. A.53). Since the parent material is iron, the tool is badly corroded, and one arm has a surviving length of half the other arm. Overall length was approximately 6⅛ inches. Like the sandglass, the usefulness of this tool aboard the gondola is problematic. The vessels were not provided with charts of Lake Champlain, and Arnold sailed without one. Gates eventually sent one to the fleet.[55] It seems plausible that these two items belonged to Captain Rue and were retained from navigational equipment belonging to the schooner he captained on the St. Lawrence River in April or May, 1775.

FIREPLACE AND COOKING UTENSILS

According to Hagglund, the fireplace was located on the port side of the hull between the two knees just aft of the forward cockpit (see fig. A.54). Char marks found on the underside of the mast partner suggest, however, that the true position may have been in the well.[56] When examined at the Smithsonian Institution, the red clay bricks still retained traces of the original mortar that cemented the fireplace together.

An iron cooking kettle was found sitting in the vessel's fireplace. The outer flared rim is broken along most of the circumference except in the two areas where the triangular-shaped lugged handles attach to the rim and body (see figs. A.55 and A.56). Three legs support the bottom of the kettle. Approximately one-half of the kettle's bail survived the long immersion in the lake. Next to the kettle was a long-handled iron skillet (see fig. A.57). Although half the pan's outer rim has corroded away, its outer diameter originally measured 13 inches.[57] A hole in the socket end of the handle suggests that this pan could have been used with a wooden extension. Undoubtedly, these two vessels were used in food preparation. In close association with these two objects was a heavy wooden chopping block (see fig. A.54).

A smaller iron kettle or pot was recovered from the forward cockpit (see figs. A.58 and A.59). Although this container could have been used in food preparation, it was found to contain traces of ochre, which may attest to the use of paint on the vessel. The only traces of paint found on the vessel, however, were a red coating on the end of the 9-pounder tompions. It is possible that these utensils were obtained from the Salisbury Iron Works, as were some of the fleet's swivel guns.[58]

PERSONAL POSSESSIONS

Eight pewter buttons, two brass buttons, and one wooden button back were recovered from the *Philadelphia* (see fig. A.60). Two pewter buttons, found on the foredeck, bear the number 26. Hagglund correctly determined that these were British buttons of the Twenty-Sixth Regiment. Although seemingly out of place aboard an American vessel, their presence is easily explained by the fact that in December, 1775, General Montgomery captured Montreal and with it a quantity of uniforms belonging to the Seventh and Twenty-Sixth British Regiments.[59] Afterward, Montgomery distributed clothing to Arnold's corps, which had just arrived in Quebec after an extremely difficult trek across Maine.

Plain-faced buttons, brass buttons, and several of the pewter buttons found aboard the *Philadelphia* were worn in all nations, by military personnel and civilians alike.[60] Star and script button motifs found on the *Philadelphia* are common finds from Revolutionary War land sites.

Five complete spoons, one spoon bowl, and one spoon handle were found in various places in the *Philadelphia*'s hull (see fig. A.61). All were made of pewter. Incredibly, one spoon was found resting on the caprail of the vessel after it was brought to the surface.[61] Three spoon bowls were scratched with their owner's initials. The letters *P.H.S.*, *I.M.*, and *L.P.* are present. Two sets of initials may correspond to names of *Philadelphia* crewmen. *P.H.S.* may refer to to Peter Stephens. Considering that *I* sometimes stands for *J*, *I.M.* may represent James Mars, John Mills, Jacob Murrel, or one of the two crewmen named James McIntire. No crew members had the initials *L.P.*

Eight shoe and knee buckles were found scattered on the aft deck among some leather shoe remains (see fig. A.62). One example is a brass shoe buckle complete with chape and tongue. Buckles of this type were used with shoes possessing two straps. The shoe's lower strap would be secured by the chape and the upper strap fastened over the lower by the tongue.[62] The *Philadelphia* artifact collection also includes three silver shoe or knee buckle frames, all rectangular but with rounded corners. Two have some decoration in the form of ridges or raised circles. One other example is a highly decorated silver shoe buckle. The frame is oval and approximately two-thirds complete. The high quality and fine decoration on most of these buckles suggest that they were lost by the gondola's officers. The one brass example recovered may typify the quality and shoe style worn by the sailors and marines.

A white ceramic cup found in one of the stern lockers is purportedly the crew's grog cup (see fig. A.63). The glazed surface is crazed and discolored in a fine network of cracks due to its long immersion in Lake Champlain. The vessel appears to be creamware. The surface is undecorated except for a fine scallop pattern underneath the rim.

Two other ceramic fragments were also recovered. One of them is a base sherd from what was probably another cup and the other is a body sherd, likely from the same vessel (see fig. A.64). Like the intact cup, the surfaces of the fragments are similar in fabric and are also discolored and crazed.

Twenty-five leather shoe fragments, representing several pairs of shoes, were found in the stern of the vessel in the lockers or on the deck. One pair of men's shoes with wooden pegged heels has been reconstructed and is on display at the NMAH (see fig. A.65). No textiles were reported to have been found with the *Philadelphia* nor are any listed on the Smithsonian accession list. One textile fragment, however, was documented at the Smithsonian Institution by a Polaroid photograph (see fig. A.66). The coarse fabric appears to be canvas and is shaped like a sash or the remnant of a man's jerkin.

Hagglund mentioned finding a wooden canteen in the forward cockpit in his 1936 report.[63] The item is also included in a list of artifacts he provided to the Smithsonian Institution shortly before his death. The canteen is not displayed, and the accession list is notated with a question mark beside it. Similarly, a pair of officer's cuff links were also reported to have been found in 1935 but are no longer included in the collection.

MISCELLANEOUS FINDS

Two wrought iron strap hinges believed to have come from the gunner's chest are included in the *Philadelphia* collection (see fig. A.67). The first example has three fastener holes present and the partial remains of a fourth at the broken loop on the end. The second example is smaller in length and has openings for two fasteners. One other metallic object, a small brass rod approximately 2 inches long and bent into a U-shape, may have served as a sailor's belt hook (see fig. A.68).

Hagglund's salvage crew recovered seven pieces of sulfur intermixed with the other bilge debris (see fig. A.69). The cylindrical shape of the sulfur fragments suggests that they may have been carried aboard in paper tubes, a common practice in the eighteenth-century. Although it has been suggested that the sulfur was used onboard the vessel as a fumigant, it was most likely used as a medicinal.[64] During the Revolutionary War an ailment known as impetigo, and referred to by soldiers as "the itch," was often described in contemporary journals. This bacterial infection was a common and troublesome disorder, very contagious and easily spread by contact. Affected areas included the hands, especially between the fingers, and the infection caused the person to break out in itchy vesicles that were easily ruptured by scratching. Continued scratching produced a "disgustful crust" that further developed into pustules and ulcers.[65]

Two methods could be employed to stop the spread of the disease: frequent washing of the body and frequent changes of linen. Alternately, the clothing could be scented with brimstone (burned sulfur) before being worn. Those stricken with the ailment could be bathed in water impregnated with sulfur and a lard-based ointment.

That the crew members of the *Philadelphia* may have been suffering from impetigo infection is borne out in the journal of Bayze Wells, who wrote "Monday 16th Septr . . . about Six P. M. Mr Tiffany and I Bathd for the Itch with Brimstone tallow and tar mix together and Lay in our Cloaths." Wells makes two other references to the ailment and was forced to continue his "baths" for the next two nights.[66]

In amongst the other items in the stern lockers was a small, filled medicine bottle. Like several other objects salvaged in 1935, this artifact is not included in the Smithsonian collection. According to Hagglund's 1936 report, an analysis of the original substance revealed an oleoresin of copaiba (derived from the leaves of a South American tree of the genus *Copaifera*) flavored with several essential oils—oil of thyme being the most characteristic of the flavors. References to copaiba from the 1800s indicate that it was regarded as a panacea with varied medicinal uses.[67]

Three human teeth were found lying loose on the forward deck. The roots have been stained black following their long immersion and several caries are visible on each (see fig. A.70). All appear to be molars.[68] According to Hagglund's original report and contemporary newspaper accounts, there were also "several pieces of the bones of an arm . . . and a part of a skull" next to the teeth.[69] Only one bone is included in the Smithsonian collection, however. It is an animal bone that was found inside the iron kettle (see fig. A.71). The three teeth are the only human remains included in the Smithsonian collection.

One wooden cleat is included on the NMAH accession sheet (see fig. A.36). Although badly eroded, its original dimensions were reconstructed by Leon Hope, one of the original salvagers of the *Philadelphia*. Distance between the arms is 13½ inches. Width at the base is 4¾ inches and the thickness is 1½ inches. This specimen is larger than any cleat reconstructed by Hoffman for use on the *Philadelphia*'s caprail. Therefore, this particular cleat may have served to secure the main yard lift.

Among the other wood fragments found on the *Philadelphia* were pieces of northern white cedar that were obviously the remains of half and quarter barrels.[70] One small wooden artifact, previously unidentified, may be a plug for a powder horn (see fig. A.72). A similar item was recovered from the *Boscawen*.[71] The only other wooden fragments mentioned by Hagglund were pieces of firewood for the cook's stove discovered under the forward deck.

The last artifact discovery on the *Philadelphia* occurred during the cleaning and recording operations at the Smithsonian in the late 1960s. Fragments of chalk were discovered underneath the decks and ceiling.[72] These had probably been left by the *Philadelphia*'s carpenters and were used to mark the locations of floors, deck beams, or other timbers.

For the most part, the *Philadelphia*'s artifact collection is typical of the assemblage to be expected from a gunboat of this type and period. Only a few artifacts, such as the navigational tools and the British military buttons, appear out of place. The collection reflects the difficulties the Americans encountered in outfitting their hastily built fleet. The cannons were old, indicating the shortage of guns at Fort Ticonderoga. Artifacts such as the bayonets and ax heads are varied in style, indicating that they may have been obtained from a variety of sources. A deadeye was fabricated from a sheave, suggesting adaptation by the shipwrights and a shortage of time in outfitting the fleet. Personal items such as spoons, buttons, and buckles indicate that the crew carried many of their individual possessions and varied in uniform and outfitting.

Chapter 9

THE CREW OF
THE PHILADELPHIA

W hen it came time to man the *Philadelphia* and the rest
of the hurriedly built fleet in July, 1776, Benedict
Arnold looked to the ranks of the Northern Army
for experienced sailors. Out of the thousands of soldiers assembled
at Fort Ticonderoga, only 70 volunteered for the duty. Undoubtedly, there were many more men at Ticonderoga with maritime
skills, but none volunteered. Arnold understood the reason for the
soldiers' caution. He reported to Philip Schuyler that "there is no
prospect of [their] making reprisals on the Lake, but rather Fa-
tigue & Danger."[1] No matter how uncomfortable the soldiers were
at the fort they were a lot better off behind stone walls than sailing on the open lake. There was not even the temptation of prize
money; the only reward for those who signed up was the usual
monthly pay.[2]

Arnold wanted to send to Connecticut for seamen but feared
that the sailors would turn down Congress's established rate of 48
shillings and accept nothing less than the "Common Premium"
and $10.00 per month. He suggested to Schuyler that sailors might
be found in the army at New York but insisted that "by no means"
would soldiers or landsmen answer the call.[3]

Later that July, the call for seamen and marines to man the fleet
arrived in the maritime seaports, but it soon became apparent that
luring experienced seamen and marines from the healthier and

potentially more profitable privateering fleets would be difficult, if not impossible. Consequently, Congress was forced to order drafts from the Northern Army stationed at Fort Ticonderoga.[4] Drafted out of the various regiments on August 7 were 300 officers and soldiers.[5] Half the draftees were to serve as seamen and the other half as marines. The draftees received $1.00 a month above their regular pay.[6]

At Arnold's request, Schuyler wrote Connecticut governor Trumbull on July 31 requesting an additional 300 men to augment the numbers already drafted.[7] Captains Seth Warner, David Hawley, and Frederick Chapel each raised a company of seamen, but only after they had been assured their men would receive higher wages than those paid to the sailors already in service. Bounties increased from $7.50 to $15.00, and an additional premium of $2.50 went to every man who provided his own musket, cartridge box, blanket, and knapsack. Wages increased to $6.00 a month for seamen, $15.00 a month for lieutenants, and $24.00 a month for captains. The sailors were to receive the premium and the first month's wages before they began their march.[8]

In fear that a British invasion could come at any time, Arnold ordered his small flotilla (which then consisted of only ten vessels) to sail from Crown Point on August 24.[9] Still short of his complement of seamen and marines, Arnold drafted into temporary service a detachment of troops from Colonel Thomas Hartley's force at Crown Point. As replacements for the troops, and to appease an irate Hartley, Horatio Gates sent 70 men from Ticonderoga. Several days later, Arnold wrote Gates from Buttonmold Bay that he needed an additional 74 men to man the vessels.[10] Gates ordered 33 soldiers drafted from Colonel Asa Whitcomb's Sixth Massachusetts Regiment to serve as marines and the same number of soldiers from Colonel Samuel Brewer's Massachusetts Militia Regiment to serve as seamen.[11]

The fifteen American vessels that eventually assembled and fought at Valcour Island were designed for 800 sailors and marines. Arnold specified that 80 crewmen be onboard each galley, 45 men on each of the eight gondolas, 50 sailors and marines on both the schooner *Royal Savage* and the hospital sloop *Enterprise*, 65 crewmen on the cutter *Lee*, and 35 men onboard the smaller schooner *Revenge*. It is doubtful that Arnold ever enjoyed the desired complement of seamen. As late as October 1 he requested 100 sailors and marines ("no land lubbers") to fill his quota.[12] Only one day before the Battle of Valcour Island, Arnold wrote to Gates: "I am much surprised so little attention is paid to us by the good people below. I should have imagined two hundred seamen could have been sent us in three or four months, after they were so pressingly wrote for."[13] The promise of bonuses and high wages was not enough to attract experienced sailors and gunners to serve with Arnold on Lake Champlain. By contrast, the British fleet was adequately staffed by veterans and officers of the Royal Navy, as well as a large number of other British and German troops.[14]

With the fortuitous discovery of the *Philadelphia*'s original payroll in 1973, the names of her American crew became known.[15] Although the gondola was designed to be manned with a crew of 45, only 44 men actually served onboard the *Philadelphia* (table 9.1).

The *Philadelphia*'s captain, Benjamin Rue, was unknown for many years because pioneering archivist Peter Force mistakenly spelled his name as "Benjamin Rice" in the *American Archives, Fifth Series*.[16] Once the error was detected, the captain became known to twentieth-century researchers. Rue began his military career in Bucks County, Pennsylvania, as a private in Bristol Company, one of eight companies organized into the First Battalion of the Pennsylvania Line on October 12, 1775.[17] Rue quickly rose to orderly sergeant of the company. Additional promotions followed, and Rue became ensign in Captain Willet's company in November, 1775. After Colonel John Philip de Hass took command of the First Battalion on February 22, 1776, he dispatched several companies, including that of Benjamin Rue, to Canada to join the Northern Campaign. Rue's company marched from Philadelphia to New York City where the men boarded a sloop for Albany. From there Rue traveled with his company up the Hudson River to Fort Edwards and on to Fort William Henry (Fort George). Thereafter, the Bristol Company crossed Lake George by bateaux, marched the short distance to Fort Ticonderoga, and traveled down Lake Champlain to Montreal by watercraft. Sometime between April 15 and May 1, 1775, Rue assumed the command of a schooner on the St. Lawrence River, a position he held until the American retreat from Canada.[18] After the evacuation, Rue followed the army back to Ticonderoga

TABLE 9.1

Payroll of Captain Benjamin Rue's Crew belonging to the gondola Philadelphia from the time they entered service to October 16, 1776, inclusive

Officers & Privates Names	When Entered the Service	Time in the Service	Wages per Month [mos./days]	Total Amount of Wages	What amount each pr. after [deductions] remains to receive	Money Due
Benjamin Rue, Captain	August 1	2 16	£9–12–0	£24–6–5	————	£24–6–5
Johnathan Blake, Lieutenant	Dto 16	2 ——	6	12	————	12
Joseph Bettys, Mate	Dto 1	2 16	2–10–0	11–3–0	5–1–4	6–6–8 x
Ezekiah Budthomas, Boatswain	Dto 1	2 16	2–10–0	11–8–0	5–1–4	6–6–8
George Berry, Boatswain's Mate	Dto 6	2 11	2–16–	6–12–6	4–12–8	4–17–10
James McIntire, Gunner	Dto 6	2 11	2–10–0	10–13–0	4–12–8	5–18–4 x
James McIntire, Gunner's Mate	Dto Dto	2 11	3–4–0	7–11–0	4–12–8	2–16–10 x
Thomas Savage, Sargent	Dto Dto	2 9	2–16–0	8–10	4–12–0	1–16–10 x
Joseph Chace, Dto	Dto 16	2 ——		5–12	4	1–12
Michael Chapter, Corporal	Dto Dto	2 ——	52 ——	5–2	4	1–4
Moses Stephens, Dto	Dto ——	2 ——		5–2	4	1–4
Robert Avery, Private	Dto 1	2 16	28 ——	6–1–7	5–1–4	1–0–3
George Walton, Dto	Dto 6	2 11		5–13–7	4–12–8	1–10–12
Henry Provose, Dto	Dto ——	2 11		5–13–7	4–14–8	0–18–10
John Walls, Dto	Dto Dto	2 11		5–13–7	4–14–8	0–18–10 x
Jacob Row, Dto	Dto 13	2 3		5–0–9	4–4	0–16–9
William Sebastern, Dto	Dto 9	2 7		5–7–1	4–9–4	0–17–9
Edward Thomas, Dto	Dto 12	2 2		2–19–2	4–2–8	0–16–0
James Stewart, Dto	Dto 15	2 1		2–17–2	4–1–4	—16–8
John Leach, Dto	Dto 15	2 1		2–19–7	4–1–4	—16–8
Josiah Berry, Dto	Dto 16	2 0		2–16	4	—16— x
Daniel Obrian, Marrean	Dto 6	2 11		5–13–7	4–14–8	—18–12 x

TABLE 9.1, *(continued)*

Officers & Privates Names	When Entered the Service	Time in the Service	Wages per Month [mos./days]	Total Amount of Wages	What amount each pr. after [deductions] remains to receive	Money Due
Richard Ward, Dto	Dto Dto	2 11	—	5 – 13 – 7	4 – 14 – 8	—— 18 —
Webster Simpson, Private	Dto 9	2 7	2 – 10 –	10 – 2 – 0	4 – 9	2 – 11 – x
Thomas Shepperd, Marrean	Dto 13	2 3	— 48 —	4 – 4	—	0 – 16 —
Samuel Harris, Dto	Dto Dto	2 3	—	5 – 0 – 9	4 – 4	0 – 16 – 0
Ephream Guile, Dto	Dto 16	2	—	2 – 16	4	0 – 16 – 0
Ephream Davis, Dto	Dto 16	2	—	2 – 16	4	0 – 16 – 0 x
John Davis, Dto	—— Dto	2		2 – 16	4	0 – 16 – 0 x
Silas Fox, Dto	—— Dto	2		2 – 16	4	0 – 16 – 0 x
Samuel Cook, Dto		2		2 – 16	4	0 – 16 – 0
Peter Stephens, Dto				2 – 16	4	0 – 16 – 0
Mattias Seales, Dto				2 – 16	4	0 – 16 – 0
John Mills, Dto				2 – 16	4	0 – 16 – 0 x
Thomas Hues, Dto				2 – 16	4	0 – 16 – 0 x
Jacob Murrel, Dto				2 – 16	4	0 – 16 – 0 x
Asa Barnam, Dto				2 – 16	4	0 – 16 – 0
James Mars, Dto				2 – 16	4	0 – 16 – 0 x
Samuel Heath, Dto				2 – 16	4	0 – 16 – 0
Amos Johnston, Dto				2 – 16	4	0 – 16 – 0 x
Daniel Whitworth, Dto				2 – 16	4	0 – 16 – 0 x
Samuel Smith, Dto				2 – 16	4	0 – 16 – 0
Benjamin Walker, Dto				2 – 16	4	0 – 16 – 0 x
Ebenezar Bailey, Dto				2 – 16	4	0 – 16 – 0

Source: After Philip K. Lundeberg, *The Gunboat* Philadelphia *and the Defense of Lake Champlain in* 1776, 48.

where he was promoted to second lieutenant on August 6, 1776.[19] Only twenty-one years old, Rue took command of the *Philadelphia* on August 1, 1776, one day after it arrived at Mount Independence for masting, rigging, and arming. In fitting out the *Philadelphia*, Rue had the help of Mate Joseph Bettys of New York, Boatswain Ezekiah Budthomas, and Private Robert Avery. Boatswain's Mate George Berry joined the crew on August 6, as did a gunner and gunner's mate (both named James McIntire), Sergeant Thomas Savage, three marines, and two additional privates.[20] Seven more marines and privates joined between the ninth and fifteenth of August. The remainder of the crew, including the lieutenant, Jonathan Blake, New York Regiment, joined the crew on the sixteenth, for a total complement of 44 men.[21]

The payroll designates most of the *Philadelphia*'s crew as either "privates" or "marreans." Here, the word "marrean" probably refers to the men whose duties were to act as sailors, while a private was supposed to fill the role of the traditional naval "marine." The payroll clearly delineates the wages of the men and the deductions charged against each person. The "marreans" and privates of the *Philadelphia* did not earn the higher wages guaranteed to the sailors from Connecticut, who later came to man the galleys. Furthermore, by the date of the final muster, October 16, 1776, almost three-fourths of the salary of the *Philadelphia*'s crewmen was consumed by unspecified deductions; the men may not even have been paid. Captain Rue did not receive his wages until 1784.[22]

Curiously, 18 crew members have an *X* in a column next to their names. The payroll unfortunately does not include a heading for the column notation. It has been suggested that the *X* represents a man whose life may have been lost during the battle. This does not seem to be the case because Mate Joseph Bettys, who has an *X* in the column next to his name, not only survived the battle but went on to fight for the British. The *X* may represent a man who was not present at the final muster but may have been taken prisoner by the British on October 13. There are 18 soldiers with an *X* next to their names, and 18 of the *Philadelphia* crewmen appear on a British prisoner list made after the Battle of Valcour Island. Only 5 names, however, match both lists. Virtually every crew member of the *Philadelphia* can be traced in the historical record to his original militia or Continental regiment. As seen in table 9.2, 27 of the *Philadelphia*'s crew probably were drafted from two New Hampshire regiments. Colonels Joshua Wingate and Isaac Wyman received orders "to furnish 12 Subalterns, 12 Serjeants, 12 Corporals, 5 Drums & 259 Privates to assist in manning the fleet."[23] Allowing some leeway for phonetic spellings and common names, the remainder of the crew can be traced to Massachusetts (which then included present-day Maine), Connecticut, and New York, with the exception of one man whose last name may have been badly misspelled phonetically: Ezekiah "Budthomas."

The New England militia regiments from which these men came did not receive a great deal of respect from the troops of the Northern Army when they began to arrive at Ticonderoga in August and September, 1776. Captain Persifer Frazer of Chester County, Pennsylvania, wrote upon the arrival of the New England troops: "I have not seen them yet but unless they are better than the greatest part of those that all have been here before them, they had better stay at home. No man was ever more disappointed respecting New Englanders in general than I have been. They are a set of dirty, low, griping, cowardly rascals. There are some few exceptions & very few. They may do well enough at home but every fresh man that comes here is so much loss to the army, as they will get sick with small pox or some lazy disorder & those that are seasoned must take care of them & by that means weaken the army."[24]

Arnold was of much the same opinion. He described the draftees from the regiments as "motley, a miserable Set"; the marines as "the Refuse of every Regiment, and the Seamen, few of them, ever wet with Salt Water."[25] This last charge, that they were landlubbers, may have been true for most of the men drafted from the units at Ticonderoga, although many of the *Philadelphia*'s crew probably had a great deal of inland water experience judging from their hometowns. Massachusetts, and especially New Hampshire, relied extensively on inland and tidal watercraft similar to Arnold's flat-bottomed gondolas. The indigenous Pitscataqua and Merrimac River gundalows and the Durham boat had long been used in these regions for the transport of bulk cargoes such as marsh hay and timber. These flat-bottomed craft of similar size and construction used the same means of propulsion as did the *Philadelphia*: sweeps and square sails set upon a single mast.

TABLE 9.2

Crew Members of the Continental Gondola *Philadelphia*

Name	Residence	Company	Regiment
Avery, Robert	—	—	
Bailey, Ebenezer	Bolton, Mass.	Captain Woods	Colonel Ward
Barnum, Asa	Dunbarton, N.H.	Captain William Barron	Colonel Isaac Wyman
Berry, George	Barrington, N.H.	Captain James Arnold	Colonel Joshua Wingate
Berry, Josiah	New Hampshire	Captain James Arnold	Colonel JoshuaWingate
Bettys, Joseph	Ballston Spa, N.Y.	Captain Ball	Colonel Wynkoop
Blake, Jonathan	New York	—	—
Budthomas, Ezekiah	—	—	—
Chace, Joseph	Massachusetts	Captain Gilman	Fourth
Chapter, Michael	Hampstead, N.H.	—	—
Cook, Samuel	New Hampshire	Captain James Shepherd	Colonel Isaac Wyman
Davis, Ephream	New Hampshire	Captain James Shepherd	Colonel Isaac Wyman
Davis, John	New Hampshire	Captain James Arnold	Colonel Joshua Wingate
Fox, Silas	Campton, N.H.	Captain James Shepherd	Colonel Isaac Wyman
Guile, Ephream	New Hampshire	Captain David Quinby	Colonel Joshua Wingate
Harris, Samuel	Amherst, N.H.	Captain James Shepherd	Colonel Isaac Wyman
Heath, Samuel	New Hampshire	Captain David Quinby	Colonel Joshua Wingate
Hues, Thomas	—	—	—
Johnston, Amos	—	—	—
Leach, John	New Hampshire	Captain Ebenezer Dearing	Colonel Pierce Long
Mars, James	Scarborough, Maine	Abraham Tyler	Colonel Edmund Phinney
McIntire, James	Portsmouth, N.H.	Captain James Arnold	Colonel Joshua Wingate
McIntire, James	Portsmouth, N.H.	Captain James Arnold	Colonel Joshua Wingate
Mills, John	Dunbarton, N.H.	Captain William Barron	Colonel Isaac Wyman
Murrel, Jacob	New Hampshire	Captain David Quinby	Colonel Joshua Wingate
Obrian, Daniel	New Hampshire	Captain James Arnold	Colonel Joshua Wingate
Provose, Henry	Boxford, Mass.	Captain Richard Peabody	Colonel Edward Wigglesworth
Row, Jacob	Haverhill, Mass.	Captain Timothy Eaton.	Colonel Edward Wigglesworth
Rue, Benjamin	Bucks County, Pa.	1st Pennsylvania	—
Savage, Thomas	Portsmouth, N.H.	Captain James Arnold	Colonel Joshua Wingate
Seales, Matthias	New Hampshire	Captain James Shepherd	Colonel Isaac Wyman
Sebastern, William	Pepperellborough, Mass.	—	—
Shepperd, Thomas	Biddeford, Maine	Captain Timothy Eaton	Colonel Edward Wigglesworth

Table 9.2 *(continued)*

Name	Residence	Company	Regiment
Simpson, Webster	York, Maine	—	Colonel Edward Wigglesworth
Smith, Samuel	Goffstown, N.H.	Captain William Barron	Colonel Isaac Wyman
Stephens, Moses	New Hampshire	Captain David Quinby	Colonel Joshua Wingate
Stephens, Peter	New Hampshire	Captain James Shepherd	Colonel Isaac Wyman
Stewart, James	New Hampshire	Captain James Arnold	Colonel Joshua Wingate
Thomas, Edward	Andover, Mass.	Captain Samuel Johnson	Colonel Edward Wigglesworth
Walker, Benjamin	Goffstown, N.H.	Captain William Barron	Colonel Isaac Wyman
Walls, John	New Hampshire	Captain James Arnold	Colonel Joshua Wingate
Walton, George	New Hampshire	Captain James Arnold	Colonel Joshua Wingate
Ward, Richard	Amherst, N.H.	Captain James Arnold	Colonel Joshua Wingate
Whitworth, Daniel	New Hampshire	Captain William Stilson	Colonel Isaac Wyman

Sources: Hammond, *The State of New Hampshire: Rolls of the Soldiers in the Revolutionary War, 1775, to May, 1777;* Secretary of the Commonwealth of Massachusetts. *Massachusetts Sailors and Soldiers of the Revolutiony War;* Lundeberg, *The Gurnboat* Philadelphia *and the Defense of Lake Champlain, 48–49.*

The historical record also preserves clues to what happened to the crew after the *Philadelphia* sank. Armed with a letter of commendation from Benedict Arnold, Benjamin Rue left Fort Ticonderoga on October 27 and returned to his home state of Pennsylvania.[26] Here he raised a company of artillery and served under General George Washington at the battles of Trenton and Princeton.[27] Later, he took command of the armed vessel *Firebrand* of the Pennsylvania State navy on the Delaware.[28] Rue's final federal service occurred when President Washington gave him command of a cutter for the newly formed Revenue Service.[29] The soldier's land bounty plan allowed him to settle in Ohio in the 1800s and establish a tavern near Fort Washington (present-day Cincinnati) and later, the Golden Lamb Tavern at Lebanon, Ohio. Rue was a colorful figure and popular host. He continued to dress in "small-clothes," the fashion of Revolutionary times.[30]

The federal government rejected his 1818 pension petition on the basis that he then possessed an estate of some three thousand dollars, an amount deemed too high to require the need for a federal pension.[31] Benjamin Rue died in 1820 in Lebanon, Ohio, and was buried with full military honors.

The gondola's second and third officers had far less patriotic careers than did Captain Rue. Lieutenant Jonathan Blake left the service in 1778. According to one historian, Blake was cashiered for "tearing and concealing a letter written by Colonel Kosciusko to Colonel Hay; absenting himself frequently without leave; employing in a clandestine manner several of his men upon his farm while he drew provisions for them from the public stores, and returning them present and fit for duty."[32] Mate Joseph Bettys, following his capture onboard the galley *Washington* on October 13, recruited for the Crown in Loyalist areas of New York, during which he was rumored to be involved in "ambuscades and arson incidents" that led New York State authorities to offer a reward for his capture.[33] He was captured near Albany in 1782, with ciphered documents in his boots. Bettys's actions after being captured may have been foretold in a letter that Cornelius Wynkoop wrote Horatio Gates: "I also send you one sailor [Bettys] out of my regiment down. I would be glad you would order hime *[sic]* on board immediately, or I am afraid he will run off and leave you."[34] Bettys joined the British army after the Battle of Valcour Island as an ensign in the Second Company of the King's Rangers, a regiment raised on May 1, 1779, that functioned until 1784. The company was very active in scouting and recruiting along the frontiers of New York, Lake Champlain, and Vermont. It participated in the capture of the American forts Anne and George and aided in a raid on Ballstown, New York (Joseph Bettys's hometown) that netted many rebel prisoners. The battalion also provided secret service agents (or spies) for the Crown forces in rebel territory.[35] It was on one of these expeditions near Albany, New York, that Joseph Bettys, disguised as a civilian, was captured with the ciphered documents hidden in his boots and then hung.[36]

At least thirty-two of the *Philadelphia's* forty-one remaining crew members can be accounted for. Following the *Philadelphia's* sinking, most boarded the galley *Washington* and became prisoners of the British when the galley's commander, General Waterbury, surrendered the ship to an overwhelming British force on October 13. Following the surrender of the galley *Washington*, the military service of the eighteen captured crew members ended, at least temporarily

TABLE 9.3

Philadelphia Crew Members Included in a List of American Prisoners

Robert Avery	Samuel Harris
George Berry	James Mars
Joseph Bettys	Jacob Murrel
Jonathan Blake	William Sebastern
Joseph Chace	Thomas Shepperd
Michael Chapter	James Stewart
Samuel Cook	Edward Thomas
Ephream Davis	George Walton
Ephream Gile [Guile]	Richard Ward

Source: Haldimand Papers, Special Collections, John C. Pace Library, University of West Florida, Pensacola.

(table 9.3). Governor Sir Guy Carleton released all the American prisoners on their own parole after they swore an oath "not to say or do anything that may be contrary to the interest of His Majesty's government"[37] Nine members of the *Philadelphia*'s crew are missing from the historical record. Presumably, these men were killed in the battle on the eleventh, or they may have boarded a vessel other than the *Washington*. Those wounded in the battle may have been carried aboard the fleet's hospital sloop (the *Enterprise*), which returned safely to Ticonderoga. Few of the *Philadelphia*'s crew filed for or received pensions. The Pension Act of 1818 required a minimum service of six months for qualification; the majority only served for four or five months before being taken prisoner by the British.

Chapter 10

THE PHILADELPHIA II

In 1989 the Lake Champlain Maritime Museum (LCMM) undertook the task of building a full-size replica of the gondola *Philadelphia*.[1] Founded in 1984 as the Basin Harbor Maritime Museum, the LCMM is located along the shores of Lake Champlain at Basin Harbor, Vermont. With steady yearly growth the museum has developed into a sizeable complex, housing small craft, workshops, boatbuilding activities, and exhibit areas to explore the lake's nautical history. As part of a series of ongoing projects, the museum has built replicas of several boat types that have seen use on Lake Champlain, Lake George, and other New England waterways. These reconstructions, based on archaeological evidence or modeled after surviving examples, educate the public and scholars alike on maritime construction, sailing, and boat-handling techniques.[2]

The LCMM utilized Howard Hoffman's detailed plans of the *Philadelphia* to assure an accurate reproduction, one that could be used to evaluate how the gondola was built, manned, sailed, and propelled by sweeps. The project celebrated the birth of the U.S. Navy at Whitehall, New York, in 1776 and coincided with the bicentennial of Vermont's admission into the Union as the fourteenth state in 1791.[3]

Construction of the *Philadelphia II* began as soon as a combined boat shed–exhibition hall was erected on the museum grounds. Like the gondola's original builders at Skenesborough, the Lake Champlain Maritime Museum had difficulty in securing timber for the replica. Much of the countryside of Vermont and New York has long been deforested, and it was necessary to scour the countryside for scattered stands of second-growth trees.[4] This was accomplished with the help of local farmers who provided the museum with modern milling equipment, and most important, their time.

The planks for the original *Philadelphia* were cut with a water-powered reciprocating saw in the captured mills of loyalist Philip Skene; the LCMM set up a portable sawmill and modified it to accept 30-foot logs.[5] A standing, 36-inch band saw and, on occasion, a chain saw replaced the Skenesborough shipwright's tools: the broadax, ship's saw, and adze (fig. 10.1). Project volunteers, however, were encouraged to learn to use the adze, drawblade, gimlet, and so on. More visible timbers such as the stem and sternpost were shaped with the traditional adze and hatchet, as were the mast, yards, and boom of the replica.

The *Philadelphia II* replica project required three years of effort because the museum had only three shipwrights. Their work was often intentionally interrupted by the educational program associated with the project. As part of that program, however, the museum relied on the help of numerous volunteers, including schoolchildren. In return, the apprenticeship program allowed participants the opportunity to learn traditional boatbuilding skills. The educational program also included temporary and permanent exhibits to interpret the Battle of Valcour Island and the eighteenth-century heritage of the Champlain Valley.[6]

Like the construction of the original *Philadelphia*, that of the replica started with a flat building frame. In contrast to the construction technique used at Skenesborough, the bottom of the *Philadelphia II* was built upside down. Floor timbers were laid out on raised stocks, and bottom planking was then laid over the floors and treenailed into them. Afterward, the bottom assembly was turned over. In 1990 the museum's shipwrights added the stem, sternpost, and frames to the *Philadelphia II*'s flat bottom.[7] After nine months of framing work, the 48-foot, 11-inch keelson was installed by joining two scarfed white oak timbers to the replica's floors with ten iron bolts. During the same building season, the museum also constructed a blacksmith's shop and forge so the gondola's ironwork could be manufactured on site in a traditional manner. An extremely popular display in itself, the shop fabricated almost all the iron hard-

Fig. 10.1. The Philadelphia II's boatbuilders, John Gritter and Bill Swartz, fabricate one of the replica's knees. Photograph courtesy of the Lake Champlain Maritime Museum.

ware needed for the vessel, including gudgeons, swivel gun socket straps, ring bolts for the cannon breeches, and hundreds of iron fasteners.

In 1991 planking of the vessel took place, a process that required nine weeks and was accomplished by planking inside and outside simultaneously (fig. 10.2). Considering the time constraints at Skenesborough and the speed with which the eight gondolas were originally built, all were probably built with green lumber. Because of the museum's difficulties in finding enough white oak timber, some of the replica's planks had to be stored for nearly a year before being incorporated into the vessel. The use of this seasoned wood required the employment of a steam box to make the lumber more pliable.[8] Once the vessel was planked, the services of an expert caulker were secured to teach the modern boatbuilders the nearly lost art of properly caulking a wooden vessel (fig. 10.3).[9]

The original *Philadelphia* was not built with any idea of lasting longer than would be necessary for the colonials to maintain control of the Lake Champlain invasion route. The LCMM, on the other hand, built the *Philadelphia II* to last at least twenty years. Protective modern paint and tar were used beneath the decks where it would not show. Use of other modern materials was addressed, especially in regard to the vessel's rigging. Natural fibers expand and contract in response to moisture, and the designers knew that

Fig. 10.2. Steam-bending the Philadelphia II's exterior planking into position. Photograph courtesy of the Lake Champlain Maritime Museum.

adjustments would be constant if the replica was rigged with natural-fiber rope. Ultimately, natural fibers were used for the running rigging where appearance was important. Synthetic fibers were chosen for the standing rigging and sails, providing greater strength and requiring less maintenance.[10]

The museum builders made only minor deviations from Howard Hoffman's plans. In the interest of safety, additional cleats were added fore and aft for towing and mooring.[11] To provide for more headroom, the awning beams were set about an inch higher than specified. A

Fig. 10.3. Caulking the Philadelphia II's seams with oakum. Photograph courtesy of the Lake Champlain Maritime Museum.

Fig. 10.4. The Philadelphia II's amidship and forward decks. Photograph courtesy of the Lake Champlain Maritime Museum.

Fig. 10.5. The Philadelphia II's classic "barn door" rudder. Photograph courtesy of the Lake Champlain Maritime Museum.

The Gondola
Philadelphia

Fig. 10.6. Arthur B. Cohn assisting in the Philadelphia II's *final rigging. Photograph courtesy of the Lake Champlain Maritime Museum.*

small change was also made to the topsail running rigging to ease dousing the sail from the deck.

With the final addition of the decks and the barn door rudder, the hull was completed and ready to be rigged in midsummer of 1991 and the vessel launched soon thereafter (figs. 10.4, 10.5, and 10.6). The standing and running rigging had been spliced and wormed, parceled, and served in the traditional manner; ash blocks with lignum vitae sheaves had been fashioned; and the mast, yards, and boom had been shaped from white pine. With the aid of a truck from a local power company the newly fashioned mast was stepped into the hull and the final rigging completed. One dozen ash oars, each 21 feet long, were placed aboard for propelling and maneuvering the *Philadelphia II*. On August 18, 1991, the *Philadelphia II* was launched into the waters of Basin Harbor to the cheers

Fig. 10.7. The Philadelphia II's launch day, August 18, 1991. Photograph courtesy of the Lake Champlain Maritime Museum.

of four thousand spectators (fig. 10.7). As Art Cohn, director of the project, stated, "The career of the *Philadelphia II* as a floating history exhibit had begun."[12]

In an attempt to visually authenticate the original vessel in every practical way, the museum was fortunate in having three large, replica concrete cannons donated to the project by the Rodney Hunt Company of Orange, Massachusetts (figs. 10.8 and 10.9).[13] Four cast-iron swivel guns were obtained from West Bend Replica, West Bend, Indiana. These are operational guns and were patterned directly from the swivel raised with the original *Philadelphia*.

To complete the appearance of authenticity, the *Philadelphia II* was equipped with a brick fireplace, shot garlands, storage lockers, assorted gunners' implements, and anchors. A canvas awning and sweep storage rack were added as indicated in Howard Hoffman's reconstruction of the original gondola.

EVALUATING THE REPLICA

Since 1991 there have been many opportunities to put the *Philadelphia II* through its "sea trials." During the summers of 1992 and 1993 the museum maintained a busy tour schedule that sent the *Philadelphia II* to many of the same historic places its namesake visited in 1776, including Whitehall (the former Skenesborough), Fort Ticonderoga, and Valcour Island.[14] Unlike the original, however, the *Philadelphia II* also traveled to the site of the 1776 British shipyard at St. Jean, Quebec, and passed by Fort Lennox on Isle aux Noix where many colonial soldiers died during the American retreat in early May and June, 1776.

A traveling historical exhibit and a mostly volunteer crew dressed in eighteenth-century apparel completed the "living reflection of Lake Champlain's vibrant history" during the *Philadelphia II*'s inaugural tour.[15] In 1992 alone, more than twelve thousand visitors stepped aboard the new replica. The crew, familiar with the vessel's place in history and the archaeology, answered questions concerning the Battle of Valcour Island, Colonel Lorenzo Hagglund's recovery of the original *Philadelphia* in 1935, and a myriad of others, such as where forty-four men might have found room to sleep on the crowded boat.

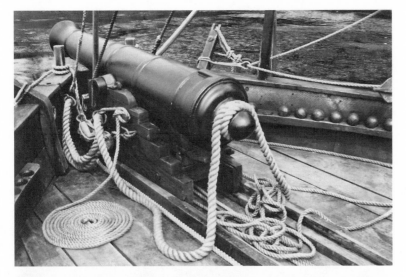

Fig. 10.8. Twelve-pounder replica cannon in slide carriage onboard the Philadelphia II. *Photograph by author.*

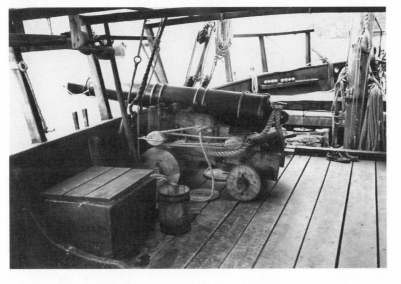

Fig. 10.9. The Philadelphia II's *port side 9-pounder concrete replica. Photograph by author.*

The gondola is primarily a rowing vessel. The square rig is designed for running before the wind only in relatively smooth waters. The rig is appropriate for the no-lateral-resistance hull. On Lake Champlain, 90 percent of the winds of any real strength generally blow north or south, so the vessel either has a fair wind and can run under sail or has the wind in its teeth and cannot sail anywhere.[16] According to Roger Taylor, captain of the *Philadelphia II*, sailing the new vessel with a fair wind is "a treat" (figs. 10.10 and 10.11).[17] The *Philadelphia II* can make three or four knots easily, but four is about the maximum. As an experiment, the replica's crew brought the vessel up as close to the wind as they could, approximately 90 or 10 degrees from the true wind; the *Philadelphia II* forged ahead very slowly and made about as much leeway as headway.[18] If the helmsman steered a course of 120 degrees off the true wind, the gondola made good a course approximately 150 degrees off the true wind. If it was sailed any closer, its performance decreased because the leeway increased so much.

Fig. 10.10. The Philadelphia II *under sail. Photograph courtesy of the Lake Champlain Maritime Museum.*

The gondola has very high initial stability with its wide flat bottom, beam, and great weight; however, it has also proven to be unmaneuverable at times. The *Philadelphia II*, with its heavy, shallow hull and with considerable windage in its rig, is very vulnerable to the wind when maneuvering under oars. In fact, the crew found it difficult to make progress sweeping against even a gentle breeze.

Fig. 10.11. Volunteers set the Philadelphia II's *topsail during "sea trials." Photograph courtesy of the Lake Champlain Maritime Museum.*

Fig. 10.12. The Philadelphia II *is extremely maneuverable under sweeps during calm conditions. Photograph courtesy of the Lake Champlain Maritime Museum.*

Once, when the *Philadelphia II*'s towboat ran out of fuel, the crew was forced to row the vessel two miles to windward. The volunteers "could well imagine the exhaustion of Arnold's seamen, as they worked to make slow and painful progress against the southerly wind on October 12 and 13, 1776, desperately trying to keep ahead of the pursuing British." If the wind was of any real strength, the *Philadelphia II* would travel with it, regardless of the direction the vessel was pointed.[19] On a calm day in 1992, however, the twelve oars, skillfully applied, propelled the vessel forward at a sustained speed of two and a half knots (fig. 10.12).[20]

Roger Taylor concluded that one reason why Arnold fought from moorings was that he realized how unmaneuverable the gondolas were, under oars, sail, or both. Essentially, the *Philadelphia* and its sister ships were floating gun platforms. The uncomplicated design was ideally suited to the colonials' immediate need of a gunboat that could be quickly assembled with only a minimum of men and materials.

Today the *Philadelphia II* is tied up at a harbor adjacent to the museum's grounds. Visitors to the museum unfamiliar with Lake Champlain's history often mistake the replica for the original. Reconstructions like the *Philadelphia II* provide archaeologists and historians with a unique opportunity to discuss and replicate the technology, problems, and solutions to the tasks that were faced by those who built, fought, and sailed the vessels.

Chapter 11

CONCLUSION

The strategic importance of Lake Champlain as an invasion corridor was well known to both the British and the Americans. In the early spring of 1776, when General Guy Carleton was poised to launch his offensive from Canada, the Americans loosely held control of the lake. Their deployment of the four vessels they had captured the year before effectively prevented the British advance. With only one avenue before them, the British began preparations to gain control of the lake in the late spring of 1776. Naval control of the lake was key to their strategy of separating the New England colonies from those in the south.

The Americans, lacking the wherewithal to build, arm, and man a fleet, were forced to increase their naval strength when they learned of the British shipbuilding efforts to the north. Philip Schuyler began by ordering the construction of gondolas at Skenesborough, New York. These small, flat-bottomed craft were well suited to the lake. With their shallow draft they could negotiate shoal water and land on nearly any shore. The simplicity of their design and construction enabled the carpenters at Skenesborough to build one every two or three weeks. Had there been no difficulties in obtaining iron and other materials, Schuyler's New York carpenters might have filled their quota by building one every week. That this was possible, even with what were probably inexperienced shipwrights and house carpenters, is evident in the *Philadelphia*'s construction.

The *Philadelphia*'s floors are merely straight timbers that do not mate with futtocks. This method of frame construction saved a tremendous amount of time by avoiding the labor-intensive tasks of drilling lateral bolt holes through the floors and futtocks and fitting the frame timbers tightly together, methods used in the contemporary bateau. Howard Hoffman's survey of the *Philadelphia* at the Smithsonian Institution determined that the independent side frames—essentially standing (or rising) knees—were mass-produced from one pattern. The use of single pattern frames in all eight gondolas saved the Americans valuable time. The flat-bottomed, hard-chined, transomless hull form did not require complicated shaping and bending of planks to conform to complex framing curves. By setting the frames perpendicular to the chine, there was no need to bevel their outside faces to accept the planking. Out of necessity, the hulls of all the Skenesborough vessels were built entirely of green timber.

Schuyler repeatedly requested that an experienced shipwright be sent to Skenesborough to oversee the gondola construction, but it does not appear that one arrived before the large influx of shipwrights from Pennsylvania, Connecticut, and Rhode Island. Following their arrival, Arnold turned the construction efforts to the larger and potentially more formidable galleys. It seems likely, therefore, that the model for the Skenesborough gondolas was adapted from the plan that Arnold drafted at Chambly on May 3, 1776. The elimination of the keel specified in Arnold's plan is puzzling. The addition of a keel would not have added a tremendous amount of time and effort to the overall construction. With the timber's addition, the vessel would undoubtedly have performed better under sail, because of the keel's natural tendency to resist lateral resistance and inhibit leeward movement.

Following the launching of the vessels, the next step in the assembly-line construction process occurred at Fort Ticonderoga. When it came time to arm and rig the *Philadelphia*, some modifications to the hull were necessary. In order to fit the cannons, two knees had to be removed from the midship deck for the proper placement of the 9-pounders, and the stem had to be cut down to allow for clearance of the 12-pounder bow gun. Likewise, the forestay had to be divided into two legs, and a spreader placed between, in order to keep the single stay from obstructing the gun. Once the final armament plan had been determined, stone ballast was added in the stern to counteract the weight of the bow gun.

Historical sources indicate that the gondolas and the other vessels in Benedict Arnold's fleet were rigged from supplies taken from vessels in New York and with locally manufactured blocks. Archaeological evidence of this is reflected in the variety of sizes of blocks, hooks, rings, and thimbles found with the *Philadelphia*.

Further examination of the *Philadelphia*'s artifact collection provides insights into the types of weapons and ammunition that could be obtained from the limited American supply line. Aside from missing swivels, which were probably off-loaded just before the vessel sank, the *Philadelphia* at its salvage was armed as historical documents specified. In fact, all but one of the colonial warships were armed and rigged in time for the Battle of Valcour Island, which reflects well on the logistical abilities of Arnold, Schuyler, and Schuyler's aide Richard Varick. Certainly, cooperation from merchants and sloop owners in New York helped, as did the participation of Connecticut's governor Trumbull. The presence of the broad arrow on the swivel gun and the finding of British uniform buttons confirm that the Americans also relied on captured supplies to meet their needs.

The *Philadelphia*'s small arms and personal possessions demonstrate that there was no standard uniform or weapons among the men who served aboard the gondola. The majority of the marines and privates on the vessel were drafted from New Hampshire militia units stationed at Fort Ticonderoga, and these men probably carried their own personal weapons aboard. Typical of colonial militia units, at least one man appears to have been wearing an overcoat captured from the British army. Ornate shoe and knee buckles may have been the personal possessions of officers aboard the small vessel. Other individuals left their personal marks behind in several initialed pewter spoons abandoned with the vessel.

Few of these crew members filed for or received federal pensions, but their names are still preserved in the historical record. The discovery of the vessel's final payroll confirmed the names of the forty-four men that served aboard. Nearly every member in this group can be traced to his original militia unit or state regiment.

The Smithsonian's display of the *Philadelphia* and its artifact collection have educated countless thousands of visitors on the importance and fragility of the small American flotilla on Lake

Champlain in 1776. This same story was also brought alive when the Lake Champlain Maritime Museum completed the construction of a full-size working replica in 1991. This vessel is patterned in exact detail to the original and provides a firsthand opportunity to evaluate eighteenth-century construction, sailing, and handling techniques.

Coinciding with a multiyear lakewide survey that began in 1996, a museum team under the direction of Arthur Cohn found the *Philadelphia*'s sister ship, another Skenesborough gondola, in June, 1997. An investigation of historical sources suggested that this vessel lay off, or near, Schuyler Island. According to Cohn, the vessel "is in an excellent state of preservation, sitting upright on the bottom, its mast still standing over fifty feet high and its large bow cannon still in place."[1]

Because the vessel lies in relatively deep water, the initial survey was conducted with the use of a remotely operated vehicle. Still photographs and digital video from the survey are being examined to aid in the development of a management plan for this significant archaeological site. A study is also being undertaken to determine the feasibility of installing a remote-controlled camera to provide visual images to the public and to help in monitoring the site.[2]

A lakewide underwater survey of Lake Champlain (in its fourth year in 2000) was prompted by the invasion of nonnative zebra and quagga mussels. That these mussels may encrust most of the lake's submerged historic shipwrecks poses another challenge to the long-term preservation of the gunboat find. On behalf of the U.S. Naval Historical Center, LCMM is developing a management plan that will serve as a guide for protecting and interpreting the site. LCMM is also collaborating with the U.S. Army, the Advisory Council on Historic Preservation, and the State Historic Preservation Offices of Vermont and New York to ensure that the plan is comprehensive.[3]

The museum is considering strategies for the gunboat's long-term preservation. Raising the gunboat necessitates expensive and lengthy conservation and the need for suitable long-term exhibit facilities. Using nautical archaeologists to record the gunboat in situ with photography and videography is technically feasible and relatively inexpensive. The latter strategy, combined with the possibility of limiting access to the site to experienced divers as an underwater historical preserve, will allow the resource to be shared with the public with minimal damage or disturbance.

The vessel was reexamined in October, 1998, and again in November, 1999. At that time, no zebra or quagga mussels were found anywhere on the wreck.[4] Video footage and still photographs were taken and will be used to form a preliminary plan of the site and assess the vessel's condition and integrity. Public input is also being considered. As of early 2001 a final decision by the museum and their collaborators was pending.

In 1999 the National Trust for Historic Preservation designated the gunboat as an official project of the presidential program Save America's Treasures. The program is part of the National Millennium Commemoration and seeks to protect America's threatened cultural resources.[5]

Now that this vessel has been discovered and partially surveyed, its scantlings and artifact assemblage can be compared to the *Philadelphia* to determine how similar the two gondolas were in terms of construction and armament. Parallels between this vessel, whose specific identity among the original Skenesborough gondolas has yet to be determined, and the *Philadelphia* are already evident in terms of overall appearance, size, and armament.[6] More intriguing, however, are the notable differences in construction details. A comparison of these two vessels will add much to our knowledge of the ships and the men that fought in the Battle of Valcour Island.

Senator Patrick Leahy of Vermont has remarked that both the *Philadelphia* and her sister gunboat symbolize "our heritage as the greatest democracy history has ever known."[7] Benedict Arnold, although later branded as a traitor to his country, played a crucial role in America's heritage of democracy.[8] Arnold was decidedly clever in choosing to anchor his small fleet of gondolas and galleys near Valcour Island. His nighttime retreat following the battle on October 11, 1776, proved him to be both brave and daring. By burning the remnants of his fleet on October 13, he denied the British their capture and safely returned the fleet's survivors to Fort Ticonderoga. Arnold's most important achievement in 1776 was the valuable window of opportunity he afforded the Americans—a window that allowed the Americans to strengthen their northern defenses. In 1777 these forces defeated General John Burgoyne's invading armies at Saratoga, an event that persuaded the French to ally with the rebel cause. French assistance was to be a major factor in the eventual overthrow of British colonial rule. Arnold and the crewmen of the small American navy demonstrated the patriotic resolve and rebel determination that would eventually win American independence.

Appendix

CATALOG OF
ARTIFACTS FOUND
ON THE PHILADELPHIA

The following catalog includes all the artifacts reported to have been recovered from the *Philadelphia* in 1935. A total of 719 objects (including the hull) were accessioned into the Museum of History and Technology (now the National Museum of American History) following the Hagglund bequest.[1] Two other objects (an iron round shot for a 12-pounder gun and a shot canister) were later added. A small number of artifacts originally recovered in 1935 are not included in the Smithsonian collection and their whereabouts are unknown. At present, most of the *Philadelphia*'s artifacts are displayed in the Armed Forces History Wing of the National Museum of American History in Washington, D.C., either onboard or adjacent to the gondola. Those not displayed are stored on the fourth floor of the NMAH in the Armed Forces History collections.

Numbers in parentheses next to the artifact descriptions indicate the number of specimens if more than one example was found. Dimensions of objects are indicated if known. Locations of objects found on the *Philadelphia* are also noted where possible.

1. Twelve-Pounder Bow Gun and Slide Carriage, Figs. A.1 and A.2
   Length overall: 102½ inches
   Weight: 3,490 pounds
2. ine-Pounder Broadside Cannons, Figs. A.3 and A.4
   Length overall: 93 inches
   Average weight: 2,192½ pounds
   Found: The starboard gun was jammed against the carriage of the port gun on the midship deck.
3. Wooden 9-Pounder Carriage Trucks (5), Fig. A.5
   Reconstructed diameter: 13 inches
   Reconstructed thickness: 3½ inches
   Found: Presumably, these were lying next to their respective carriages on the midship deck.
4. Iron Carriage Rings (3), Fig. A.6
   A. Carriage Ring with Eyebolt
      Length overall: 9 inches
      Outer diameter of eyebolt: approximately 2 inches
      Inner diameter of eyebolt: approximately 1 inch
      Diameter of shank: ⅞ inch
      Outer diameter of carriage ring: approximately 5⅛ inches
      Inner diameter of carriage ring: approximately 3⅝ inches
   B. Iron Carriage Ring
      Outer diameter of ring: 4¼ inches
      Inner diameter of ring: 3 inches
   C. Iron Carriage Ring (Broken)
      Outer diameter of ring: approximately 4¼ inches
      Inner diameter of ring: approximately 3 inches
5. Iron Keys for Trunnion Plate (7), Fig. A.7
   Length: approximately 3½ inches
   Maximum width: approximately 2 inches
6. Iron Swivel Gun, Figs. A.8, A.9, and A.10
   Length overall: 35¼ inches
   Weight: 160 pounds
   Found: Lying in the bottom of the aft cockpit.
7. Iron Yoke for Swivel Gun, Fig. A.11
   Length overall: 18 inches
   Found: Next to swivel gun in the aft cockpit.

8. Wrought Iron Ring Gauge, Fig. A.12
    Length overall: 13¾ inches
    Outer diameter of ring: 5 ³⁄₁₆ inches
    Inner diameter of ring: 4 ⁷⁄₁₆ inches
    Found: On the midship deck next to port 9-pounder.

9. Wooden Double Shot Gauge for 9- and 12-Pound Shot, Fig. A.13
    Length: 25¼ inches
    Maximum width: 6⅞ inches
    Hole diameters: 4⅛ inches and 4 ¹⁵⁄₁₆ inches
    Found: Resting on the aft deck.
10. Lead Apron
    Found: Lying next to the port 9-pounder.
11. Wooden Tompions (3), Figs. A.14 and A.36
    Length overall: 5 inches
    Diameter: 4¾ inches tapering to 4 inches
12. Gunner's Worm for Swivel Gun, Fig. A.15
    Length overall: 6 inches
    Diameter: 1⅜ inches
13. Rammer Head for 12-Pounder
    Length overall: 4⅜ inches
    Diameter: 4⅜ inches

SHOT

14. Iron Bar Shot, for 12-Pounder Gun, Fig. A.16
    Length overall: 16 ¼ inches
    Diameter of shot hemisphere: 4⅞ inches
    Width of connecting bar: ¹¹⁄₁₆ inch square
    Found: According to Hagglund, this bar shot was found protruding from the muzzle of the bow gun, having slid forward and wedged itself in the tube following the *Philadelphia*'s sinking.
15. Iron Bar Shot, for 9-Pounder Gun, Fig. A.16
    Length overall: 12⅞ inches
    Diameter of shot hemisphere: 3⅞ inches
    Width of connecting bar: ¾ inches square
16. Iron Round Shot, for 24-Pounder Gun, Fig. A.16
    Found: Underneath the forward deck.
17. Iron Round Shot, for 12-Pounder Gun (2), Fig. A.16

Diameter: 4 ⁷⁄₁₆ inches
Found: Resting in one of the bow shot garlands.

18. Iron Round Shot, for 9-Pounder Gun (44), Fig. A.16
Diameter: 4 inches
Found: Piled between the two knees forward of the port 9-pounder.

19. Iron Round Shot, for 6-Pounder Gun, Fig. A.16
Diameter: 3½ inches

20. Iron Round Shot, for 4-Pounder Gun, Fig. A.16

21. Iron Grape- or Swivel-Shot (108)
Diameter: two sizes, 1 ¹⁵⁄₁₆ and 1¾ inches

22. Iron Grapeshot (10)
Diameter: 1 inch

23. Tin Shot Canister with Wooden Sabot, Figs. A.17 and A.18
Length overall: 8⅜ inches
Diameter: 3⅞ inches
Length of sabot: 3 inches
Found: This artifact was recovered from one of the 9-pounder cannons in 1935. The cannon had been loaded with the canister, a 9-pound ball, three wads, and powder.[2]

24. Iron Langrage Fragments (4), Fig. A.19
    A. Length: 1½ inches
       Width: approximately 1 inch
    B. Length: 1⅜ inches
       Width: 1¼ inches
    C. Length: ⅞ inch
       Width: ⅝ inch
    D. Length: approximately ¾ inch
       Width: approximately ¾ inch

SMALL ARMS

25. Wooden Musket Stock (Broken), Fig. A.20
Found: On bottom of the forward cockpit.

26. Musket Barrel Fragment, Fig. A.22
Length: 9½ inches
Width: 1½ inches tapering to 1 inch

27. Brass Trigger Guards (5), Figs. A.21 and A.23
    A. Brass Trigger Guard

Complete guard with tang present on the forward end
B. Brass Trigger Guard
Identical to example A
C. Brass Trigger Guard

Concreted to musket lock assembly
D. Brass Trigger Guard (Broken)
Concreted to musket lock assembly
E. Brass Trigger Guard (Broken)
Width: approximately ½ inch tapering to ¼ inch
28. Wooden Ramrod Fragments (5), Fig. A.24
Length: various, 2¼ inches to 3¾ inches
Diameter: approximately ¹⁵⁄₁₆ inch
29. Brass Ramrod Thimbles (3), Fig. A.25
Length: 1⅜ inches
Diameter: ⅜ inch
30. Brass Rear Ramrod Thimbles (2), Fig. A.26
   A. Length overall: 4⅝ inches
      Length of pipe: 2 inches
      Diameter of pipe: ⅜ inch
   B. Length overall: 2⅝ inches
      Length of pipe: 1⅜ inches
      Diameter of pipe: ⅜ inch
31. Iron Rear Ramrod Thimble (Broken), Fig. A.27
   Length of tang: 4¾ inches
   Width of tang: ¹³⁄₁₆ inch tapering to a round point
32. Bayonet Fragments (9), Fig. A.28
   A. Partial Blade, Shank, and Fragmented Socket
   B. Fragmented Blade and Shank
   C. Complete Blade and Fragment of Shank
   D. Blade Fragment
   E. Blade Fragment with Portion of Shank
   F. Portion of Blade, Shank, and Socket
   G. Blade Fragment with Shank
   H. Blade Fragment with Shank
   I. Blade Fragment with Portion of Shank
   Found: In the forward cockpit.
33. Gunflints (8), Fig. A.29
   A. Length: ¾ inch
      Width: ⅞ inch

B. Length: 1 ³⁄₁₆ inches
   Width: 1¼ inches
C. Length: ⅞ inch
   Width: 1 inch
D. Length: 1 ¹⁄₁₆ inches
   Width: 1 ³⁄₁₆ inches
E. Length: 1 ³⁄₁₆ inches
   Width: 1⅜ inches
F. Length: 1⅜ inches
   Width: 1 ⁷⁄₁₆ inches
G. Length: ⅞ inch
   Width: 1 ⁵⁄₁₆ inches
H. Length: ¹³⁄₁₆ inch
   Width: 1⅛ inches

34. Wooden Cartridge Box Form, Fig. A.30
    Found: In the forward cockpit.

35. Musket Balls and Buckshot, Fig. A.31
    A. Iron Shot (1)
       Diameter: ½ inch
    B. Lead Musket Ball (4)
       Diameter: ¹¹⁄₁₆ inch
    C. Lead Musket Ball (2)
       Diameter: ⅝ inch
    D. Lead Buckshot (349)
       Diameter: ⅜ inch
       Found: In the forward cockpit.

IRON FASTENERS

36. Iron Spikes and Nails, Square (18), Fig. A.32
    A. Length: 7 ¹³⁄₁₆ inches
       Width: ½ inch tapering to ¼ inch
    B. Length: 6½ inches
       Width: ⁹⁄₁₆ inch tapering to ³⁄₁₆ inch
    C. Length: 4¾ inches
       Width: ½ inch tapering to ³⁄₁₆ inch
    D. Length: 4½ inches
       Width: ½ inch tapering to ¼ inch
    E. Length: 4¼ inches

Width: ½ inch tapering to ³⁄₁₆ inch
F. Length: 3 ¹⁄₁₆ inches
   Width: ½ inch tapering to ¼ inch
G. Length: 2¾ inches
   Width: ⁷⁄₁₆ inch tapering to ³⁄₁₆ inch
H. Length: 2 ³⁄₁₆ inches
   Width: ⁵⁄₁₆ inch tapering to ¼ inch
I. Length: 2 ¹⁄₁₆ inches
   Width: ⁵⁄₁₆ inch tapering to ¼ inch
J. Length: 2¾ inches
   Width: ¼ inch tapering to ⅛ inch
K. Length: 3 ⁵⁄₁₆ inches
   Width: ⁵⁄₁₆ inch tapering to ⅛ inch
L. Length: 3 ⁵⁄₁₆ inches
   Width: ⁵⁄₁₆ inch tapering to ⅛ inch
M. Length: 4 inches
   Width: ¼ inch tapering to ⅛ inch
N. Length: 4 inches
   Width: ⅜ inch tapering to ³⁄₁₆ inch
O. Length: 3¾ inches
   Width: ⁷⁄₁₆ inch tapering to ⅛ inch
P. Length: 4 ¹³⁄₁₆ inches
   Width: ⁷⁄₁₆ inch tapering to ⅛ inch
Q. Length: 4¾ inches
   Width: ⁷⁄₁₆ inch tapering to ⅛ inch
R. Length: 4 ⁹⁄₁₆ inches
   Width: ½ inch tapering to ³⁄₁₆ inch

37. Iron Eye Spikes (3), Fig. A.33
   A. Length overall: 9¼ inches
      Outer diameter of eye: 1¾ inches
      Inner diameter of eye: ¾ inch
      Maximum diameter of shank: ¾ inch
   B. Length overall: 7¼ inches
      Outer diameter of eye: 1½ inches
      Inner diameter of eye: ⅝ inch
      Maximum diameter of shank: ⅝ inch
   C. Length overall: 7¼ inches
      Outer diameter of eye: 1½ inches
      Inner diameter of eye: ⅝ inch

Maximum diameter of shank: ⅝ inch

38. Iron Timbering Spike, Round, Fig. A.33
    Length: 13¾ inches
    Diameter of head: 2½ inches
    Diameter of shank: 1¾ inches

TOOLS

39. Iron Ax Heads (4), Figs. A.34 and A.35
    A. Length: 7⅜ inches
       Width of poll: 1½ inches
    B. Length: 8¾ inches
       Width of poll: 1½ inches
    C. Length: 8 inches
       Width of poll: 1⅜ inches
    D. Length: 7 inches (early American ax)
       Width of poll: 1⅜ inches
    Found: In the forward cockpit.

40. Wooden Mallet, Fig. A.36
    Handle length overall: 16¼ inches
    Handle thickness: 1⅜ inches tapering to 1 inch
    Mallet diameter: 4½ inches
    Mallet width: 7½ inches

41. Pitch Brush, Fig. A.38
    Length overall: approximately 11½ inches
    Brush width: approximately 3⅜ inches
    Found: Inside lead pitch dish in the forward cockpit.

42. Lead Pitch Dish, Fig. A.39
    Found: At the bottom of the forward cockpit.

43. Iron Spades, Figs. A.40 and A.41
    A. Length overall: approximately 3½ feet
    B. Length overall: 15 inches
       Length of handle socket: 3½ inches
       Width of blade: 8½ inches tapering to 7¾ inches
       Opening for handle: 1¾ inches
       Found: In the forward cockpit.

44. Iron File, Fig. A.42
    Length overall: 12½ inches
    Length of tang: 2 inches

Width: 1¼ inches
Found: In the forward cockpit.
45. Iron Fascine Knives (2), Figs. A.43 and A.44
    A. Length overall: approximately 14 inches
       Length of blade: approximately 9 inches
       Length of tang: approximately 5 inches
    B. Length overall: approximately 12¼ inches
       Length of blade: approximately 10⅞ inches
       Length of tang: approximately 1¾ inches
       Found: Presumably in the forward cockpit with other
       tools.
46. Iron Chisels (2)
    Length: approximately 15¼ inches
    Blade width: approximately 1¼ inches
    Found: Presumably, these are included among the group of
    small tools recovered from the forward cockpit.
47. Iron Adze Head, Fig. A.45
    Found: In the bottom of the forward cockpit.
48. Grindstone (Broken), Fig. A.46
    Approximately 12 inches in diameter and 4 inches thick.

RIGGING EQUIPMENT

49. Wooden Blocks (4), Fig. A.47
    A. Double Block (12-inch)
    B. Double Block (10-inch)
    C. Single Block (10-inch)
    D. Single Block (8½-inch)
    Found: Inside the forward cockpit.
50. Wooden Sheave
51. Wooden Deadeyes (3), Fig. A.48
    One example is a converted sheave.
52. Iron Hooks and Rope Thimbles (12), Fig. A.49
    A. Hook with Clevis and Rope Thimble
       Length overall: 7¾ inches
       Length of hook: 5 inches
       Thickness of hook shank: ⅞ inch
       Length of clevis: 4¾ inches
       Diameter of clevis at pivot point: approximately 2½ inches

Diameter of thimble: approximately 2⅜ inches

B. Hook and Rope Thimble
   Length overall: 8½ inches
   Thickness of hook shank: 1⅛ inches
   Diameter of thimble: 2¼ inches

C. Hook and Rope Thimble
   Length overall: 6¾ inches
   Thickness of hook shank: ⅞ inch
   Diameter of thimble: 2¼ inches

D. Hook and Rope Thimble
   Length overall: 6¼ inches
   Thickness of hook shank: ⅞ inches
   Diameter of thimble: 2 inches

E. Hook and Rope Thimble
   Length overall: 5½ inches
   Thickness of hook shank: ¾ inch
   Diameter of thimble: 1¾ inch

F. Hook and Rope Thimble
   Length overall: 6½ inches
   Thickness of hook shank: ⅞ inch
   Outer diameter of eye: 3 inches
   Inner diameter of eye: 1¾ inches
   Diameter of thimble: 2 inches
   Width of thimble: 1½ inches

G. Hook
   Length overall: 7¼ inches
   Thickness of shank: approximately ½ inch
   Outer diameter of eye: 2⅝ inches
   Inner diameter of eye: 1¾ inches

H. Hook
   Length overall: 6 inches
   Thickness of shank: ⅞ inch
   Outer diameter of eye: 2⅝ inches
   Inner diameter of eye: 1⅜ inches

I. Rope Thimble (Broken)
   Diameter: 2½ inches

J. Rope Thimble (Broken)
   Diameter: 2⅛ inches

K. Rope Thimble

Diameter: 2½ inches

    L. Rope Thimble

    Diameter: 2¼ inches

53. Iron Hook, Thimble, and Rope Fragment, Fig. A.50   175

ANCHORS

54. Starboard Bow Anchor
    Length overall: 67½ inches
    Distance between arms: 34½ inches
    Length of stock: 62 inches
    Weight: 112 pounds
    Found: Sitting in the mud directly under the starboard cathead.

55. Port Bow Anchor, Fig. A.51
    Length overall: 76½ inches
    Distance between arms: 42½ inches
    Length of stock: 74¼ inches
    Weight: 134 pounds
    Found: Underneath the port cathead.

SWEEPS

56. Sweep Fragments (2)
    Reconstructed length overall: 246 inches
    Blade width: 4 inches
    Length of handle: 11 inches
    Diameter of handle: 2¼ inches decreasing to 1½ inches
    Found: Underneath the forward deck.

NAVIGATIONAL EQUIPMENT

57. Sandglass (Broken), Fig. A.52
    Found: In one of the two stern lockers.

58. Iron Dividers, Fig. A.53
    Surviving length: 6⅛ inches

59. Brick Fireplace (Approximately 64 Bricks), Fig. A.54
    Length of individual brick: 8 inches
    Width of individual brick: 3¾ inches
    Thickness of individual brick: 2¼ inches
    Found: According to Hagglund, the fireplace was located
    on the port side of the hull between the two knees just aft of
    the forward cockpit.[3] Char marks found on the underside of
    he mast partner, however, suggest that the true position
    may have been in the well.[4]

60. Wooden Chopping Block, Fig. A.54
    Diameter: 13 inches
    Thickness: 4 inches

61. Cast-Iron Cooking Kettle, Figs. A.55 and A.56
    Height: 9⅝ inches
    Diameter: 10¾ inches
    Found: In the brick fireplace.

62. Long-Handled, Wrought Iron Frying Pan, Fig. A.57
    Length overall: 25⅜ inches
    Diameter of pan: 13 inches
    Found: In the brick fireplace.

63. Cast-Iron Pot and Bail Fragment, Figs. A.58 and A.59
    Height: 6 ⁷⁄₁₆ inches
    Diameter: 9¾ inches
    Contained traces of ochre and paint brush.

PERSONAL POSSESSIONS

64. Buttons (11), Fig. A.60
    A. Pewter Button (Plain)
       Diameter: ¹¹⁄₁₆ inch
    B. Pewter Button with Star Motif
       Diameter: ¾ inch
    C. Pewter Button with Floral Design
       Diameter: ⅞ inch
    D. Decorated Pewter Button
       Diameter: ¹¹⁄₁₆ inch
    E. Pewter Button (Plain)

Diameter: ⅞ inch

F. Pewter Button of the British Twenty-Sixth Regiment
   Diameter: ⅞ inch
   Found: On the forward deck.

G. Pewter Button (Plain)
   Diameter: ⁹/₁₆ inch

H. Wooden Button Body
   Diameter: ⅝ inch

I. Large brass button
   Diameter: 1⅛ inches

J. Pewter Button Back
   Diameter: ¹¹/₁₆ inch

K. Pewter Button of the British Twenty-Sixth Regiment
   Diameter: ⅞ inch
   Found: On the forward deck.

65. Pewter Spoons (7), Fig. A.61

A. Length overall: 7¾ inches
   Length of bowl: 2⅞ inches
   Width of bowl: 1⅝ inches
   Width of handle: ⅜ inch widening to ⅞ inch

B. Length overall: 7¼ inches
   Length of bowl: 2½ inches
   Width of bowl: 1⅝ inches
   Width of handle: ¼ inch widening to ⅞ inch

C. Length overall: 7¼ inches
   Length of bowl: 3¼ inches
   Width of bowl: 1½ inches
   Width of handle: ⅜ inch widening to ¹³/₁₆ inch

D. Length overall: 7⅝ inches
   Length of bowl: 2¾ inches
   Width of bowl: 1⅝ inches
   Width of handle: ⅜ inch widening to ¹³/₁₆ inch

E. Length overall: 5½ inches
   Length of bowl: 2⅝ inches
   Width of bowl: 1 ¹¹/₁₆ inches
   Width of handle: ⅜ inch

F. Spoon (Broken)
   Length overall: 4 inches
   Length of bowl: 2 ¹⁵/₁₆ inches

Width of bowl: 1⅝ inches
Surviving width of handle: ⅜ inch tapering to ¼ inch

G. Spoon Handle

Length overall: 3⅜ inches
Width of handle: ⁵⁄₁₆ inch widening to ⅞ inch

66. Knee and Shoe Buckles (8), Fig. A.62

A. Intact Brass Shoe Buckle with Chape and Tongue
B. Rectangular Silver Knee Buckle Frame
C. Oval Silver Buckle Frame (Broken)
D. Rectangular Silver Buckle Frame Decorated with Ridges
E. Rectangular Silver Buckle Frame with Circle Motifs
F. Miscellaneous Shoe and Knee Buckles (3)
Found: On the aft deck.

67. Ceramic Cup, Fig. A.63

Height: approximately 3 inches
Diameter: approximately 3½ inches
Found: In one of the two stern lockers.

68. Coarse-Grained Earthenware Fragments (2), Fig. A.64

A. Bowl or Cup Base Fragment
Length: approximately 1½ inches
Width: approximately 1 ⁵⁄₁₆ inches
B. Fragment of Body Sherd
Length: 1 inch
Width: ⅞ inch

69. Leather Shoe Fragments (25), Fig. A.65
Found: Scattered about on the aft deck.

70. Canvas Fragment, Fig. A.66

71. Wooden Canteen
Found: In the forward cockpit.

72. Cuff Links

MISCELLANEOUS FINDS

73. Wrought Iron Strap Hinges (2), Fig. A.67

A. Preserved length: 13⅜ inches
Maximum width: 1½ inches
B. Preserved length: 11⅝ inches
Maximum width: 1⅜ inches

74. Brass Belt Holder, Fig. A.68

Length: 1 $^{13}/_{16}$ inches
Width of arms: ⅛ inch
75. Sulfur Fragments (7), Fig. A.69
76. Medicine Bottle
Found: In one of the two stern lockers.
77. Human Teeth (3), Fig. A.70
Found: On the forward deck.
78. Bone Fragment, Fig. A.71
Length: 1½ inches
Width: ⅝ inch
Found: Inside the cast-iron kettle.
79. Wooden Plugs, Fig. A.37
80. Wooden Cleat,⁵ Fig. A.36
Distance between arms: 13½ inches
Width at base: 4¾ inches
Thickness: 1½ inches
Width of arms: 1½ inches
81. Wooden Powder Horn Plug, Fig. A.72
Length: 1 $^{9}/_{16}$ inches
Maximum width: ⅞ inch
82. Barrel Stave and Barrel End Fragments
83. Firewood
Found: Under the forward deck.
84. Carpenter's Chalk (Fragments)
Found: Underneath the decks during cleaning and recording
operations at the Smithsonian Institution.⁶

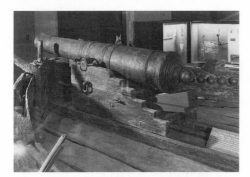

Fig. A.1. Twelve-pounder bow gun and slide carriage. Photograph courtesy of the Smithsonian Institution, NMAH/AFH.

Fig. A.2. Weight stamp of 12-pounder bow gun. Photograph courtesy of the Smithsonian Institution, NMAH/AFH.

Fig. A.3. Howard Hoffman and starboard side 9-pounder. Photograph courtesy of the Smithsonian Institution, NMAH/AFH.

Fig. A.5. Nine-pounder carriage trucks. Photograph courtesy of the Smithsonian Institution, NMAH/AFH.

Fig. A.4. Closeup of markings and touch hole on port side 9-pounder. Photograph courtesy of the Smithsonian Institution, NMAH/AFH.

Fig. A.6. Iron carriage rings. Photograph
courtesy of the Smithsonian Institution, NMAH/
AFH.

Fig. A.7. Iron keys for trunnion plates. Photograph courtesy of the Smithsonian Institution,
NMAH/AFH.

Fig. A.8. Swivel gun, side view. Photograph
courtesy of the Smithsonian Institution, NMAH/
AFH.

Fig. A.9. Swivel gun, top view. Photograph
courtesy of the Smithsonian Institution, NMAH/
AFH.

Fig. A.10. British broad arrow and weight stamp
on swivel gun. Photograph courtesy of the
Smithsonian Institution, NMAH/AFH.

Fig. A.11. (right) Broken swivel gun yoke.
Photograph courtesy of the Smithsonian
Institution, NMAH/AFH.

Fig. A.12. Iron ring gauge. Photograph courtesy of the Smithsonian Institution, NMAH/AFH.

Fig. A.13. Wooden double shot gauge. Photograph courtesy of the Smithsonian Institution, NMAH/AFH.

Fig. A.14. Nine-pounder tompions. Photograph courtesy of the Smithsonian Institution, NMAH/AFH.

Fig. A.15. Swivel gun worm. Photograph courtesy of the Smithsonian Institution, NMAH/AFH.

Fig. A.16. Round and bar shot. Photograph courtesy of the Smithsonian Institution, NMAH/AFH.

Fig. A.17. Grapeshot canister, top view. Photograph courtesy of the Smithsonian Institution, NMAH/AFH.

Fig. A.18. Canister and sabot, bottom view. Photograph courtesy of the Smithsonian Institution, NMAH/AFH.

Fig. A.20. Wooden musket stock. Photograph courtesy of the Smithsonian Institution, NMAH/ AFH.

Fig. A.19. Langrage. Photograph courtesy of the Smithsonian Institution, NMAH/AFH.

Fig. A.22. Musket barrel fragment. Photograph courtesy of the Smithsonian Institution, NMAH/ AFH.

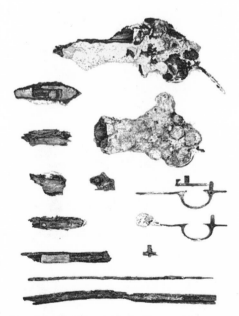

Fig. A.21. Small arms finds. Photograph courtesy of the Smithsonian Institution, NMAH/ AFH.

Fig. A.23. Brass trigger guard. Photograph courtesy of the Smithsonian Institution, NMAH/ AFH.

Fig. A.24. Wooden ramrod fragments. Photograph courtesy of the Smithsonian Institution, NMAH/AFH.

Fig. A.25. Brass ramrod thimbles. Photograph courtesy of the Smithsonian Institution, NMAH/ AFH.

Fig. A.27. Fragment of iron rear ramrod thimble. Photograph courtesy of the Smithsonian Institution, NMAH/AFH.

Fig. A.26. Brass rear ramrod thimble. Photograph courtesy of the Smithsonian Institution, NMAH/AFH.

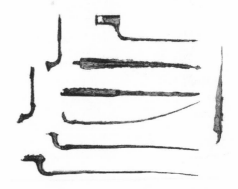

Fig. A.28. Bayonets. Photograph courtesy of the Smithsonian Institution, NMAH/AFH.

Fig. A.29. Gunflints. Photograph courtesy of the Smithsonian Institution, NMAH/AFH.

Fig. A.30. Wooden cartridge box. Photograph courtesy of the Smithsonian Institution, NMAH/ AFH.

Fig. A.31. Buckshot and musket shot. Photograph courtesy of the Smithsonian Institution, NMAH/AFH.

Fig. A.32. (left) Spikes and nails. Photograph courtesy of the Smithsonian Institution, NMAH/ AFH.

Fig. A.33. Eye spikes and timbering spike. Photograph courtesy of the Smithsonian Institution, NMAH/AFH.

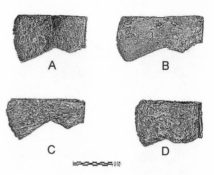

Fig. A.34. Ax heads, side view. Photograph courtesy of the Smithsonian Institution, NMAH/AFH.

Fig. A.35. Ax heads, three-quarters profile view. Photograph courtesy of the Smithsonian Institution, NMAH/AFH.

Fig. A.36. Twelve-pounder and 9-pounder tompions, cleat, and serving mallet. Photograph courtesy of the Smithsonian Institution, NMAH/AFH.

Fig. A.38. Pitch brush. Photograph courtesy of the Smithsonian Institution, NMAH/AFH.

Fig. A.37. Wooden plugs. Photograph courtesy of the Smithsonian Institution, NMAH/AFH.

Fig. A.39. Lead pitch dish. Photograph courtesy of the Smithsonian Institution, NMAH/AFH.

Fig. A.41. Iron spade blade, bottom view. Photograph courtesy of the Smithsonian Institution, NMAH/AFH.

Fig. A.40. Iron spade with wooden handle recovered in 1935. Photograph courtesy of the Smithsonian Institution, NMAH/AFH.

Fig. A.42. Iron file. Photograph courtesy of the Smithsonian Institution, NMAH/AFH.

Fig. A.43. Fascine blades, gunner's worm, tar brush, and iron auger. Photograph courtesy of the Smithsonian Institution, NMAH/AFH.

Fig. A.44. Closeup of fascine blade marking. Photograph courtesy of the Smithsonian Institution, NMAH/AFH.

Fig. A.45. Group of artifacts from 1935 recovery; note adze blade in foreground, right. Photograph courtesy of the Smithsonian Institution, NMAH/AFH.

Fig. A.46. Artifact grouping from 1935 salvage project; note broken grindstone in foreground, center. Photograph courtesy of the Smithsonian Institution, NMAH/AFH.

Fig. A.47. Ten-inch wooden double block. Photograph courtesy of the Smithsonian Institution, NMAH/AFH.

Fig. A.48. Wooden deadeye converted from sheave. Photograph courtesy of the Smithsonian Institution, NMAH/AFH.

Fig. A.49. Iron hooks and rope thimbles. Photograph courtesy of the Smithsonian Institution, NMAH/AFH.

Fig. A.50. Hook, thimble, and rope fragment.
Photograph courtesy of the Smithsonian
Institution, NMAH/AFH.

Fig. A.51. Port anchor. Photograph courtesy of
the Smithsonian Institution, NMAH/AFH.

Fig. A.53. Iron navigational dividers. Photograph courtesy of the Smithsonian Institution,
NMAH/AFH.

Fig. A.52. Sandglass. Photograph courtesy of the
Smithsonian Institution, NMAH/AFH.

Fig. A.54. Wooden chopping block and reconstructed fireplace. Photograph courtesy of the Smithsonian Institution, NMAH/AFH.

Fig. A.55. Cast-iron cooking kettle, front view. Photograph courtesy of the Smithsonian Institution, NMAH/AFH.

Fig. A.56. Cast-iron cooking kettle, side view. Photograph courtesy of the Smithsonian Institution, NMAH/AFH.

Fig. A.57. Long-handled iron skillet. Photograph courtesy of the Smithsonian Institution, NMAH/ AFH.

Fig. A.58. Cast-iron cooking pot, top view. Photograph courtesy of the Smithsonian Institution, NMAH/AFH.

Fig. A.59. Cast-iron cooking pot, side view. Photograph courtesy of the Smithsonian Institution, NMAH/AFH.

Fig. A.61. *Pewter spoons. Photograph courtesy of the Smithsonian Institution, NMAH/AFH.*

Fig. A.60. *Buttons. Photograph courtesy of the Smithsonian Institution, NMAH/AFH.*

Fig. A.62. *Buckles. Photograph courtesy of the Smithsonian Institution, NMAH/AFH.*

Fig. A.63. Ceramic cup. Photograph courtesy of the Smithsonian Institution, NMAH/AFH.

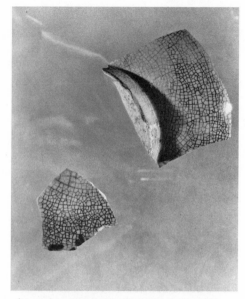

Fig. A.64. Ceramic fragments. Photograph courtesy of the Smithsonian Institution, NMAH/AFH.

Fig. A.65. Shoe fragments. Photograph courtesy of the Smithsonian Institution, NMAH/AFH.

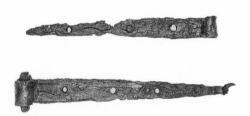

Fig. A.66. Textile fragment. Photograph courtesy of the Smithsonian Institution, NMAH/AFH.

Fig. A.67. Iron half-hinges. Photograph courtesy of the Smithsonian Institution, NMAH/AFH.

Fig. A.68. Brass belt hook. Photograph courtesy of the Smithsonian Institution, NMAH/AFH.

Fig. A.69. Sulfur fragments. Photograph courtesy of the Smithsonian Institution, NMAH/AFH.

Fig. A.70. Human teeth. Photograph courtesy of the Smithsonian Institution, NMAH/AFH.

Fig. A.71. Animal bone found in iron kettle. Photograph courtesy of the Smithsonian Institution, NMAH/AFH.

Fig. A.72. Wooden powder horn plug. Photograph courtesy of the Smithsonian Institution, NMAH/AFH.

NOTES

INTRODUCTION

1. Journal of the Continental Congress, June 17, 1776, in William Bell Clark, William James Morgan, and Michael J. Crawford, *Naval Documents of the American Revolution*, 5:589. The first four volumes of this Navy Department series appeared under the editorship of Clark; the next five, under Morgan; and vol. 10, under Crawford.
2. Schuyler to Washington, May 31, 1776, ibid., 5:317.
3. Schuyler to Gates, July 28, 1776, in Peter Force, *American Archives: A Documentary History of the North American Colonies, Fifth Series*, 1:629.
4. Gates to Schuyler, July 19, 1776, ibid., 1:454.
5. Gates to Arnold, July 17, 1776, in Clark, Morgan, and Crawford, *Naval Documents*, 5:1115.
6. Arnold to Gates, October 12, 1776, ibid., 6:1235.
7. Lorenzo F. Hagglund, "A Page from the Past: The Story of the Continental Gondola *Philadelphia*." *Whitehall Times*, Whitehall, N.Y., October 30, 1936.
8. Howard P. Hoffman, "The Gunboat *Philadelphia*," *Nautical Research Journal* 30 (1984):55.

CHAPTER 1. HISTORY OF THE MILITARY
AND NAVAL EVENTS

1. Russell P. Bellico, *Sails and Steam in the Mountains: A Maritime and Military History of Lake George and Lake Champlain*, 8–9.
2. Frederic F. Van de Water, *Lake Champlain and Lake George*, 35.
3. Earle Newton, *The Vermont Story: A History of the People of the Green Mountain State, 1749–1949*, 19.
4. Van de Water, *Lake Champlain and Lake George*, 75.

5. Arthur B. Cohn, "The Fort Ticonderoga King's Shipyard Excavation," *Bulletin of the Fort Ticonderoga Museum* 14 (1985):339.

6. The site of Fort St. Frédéric was on a low headland, approximately seventy miles south of Lake Champlain's outlet, thrust out toward a bluff on the west shore. According to Frederic Van de Water, the French named the site "Pointe à la Chevelure"—literally "Hair of the Head Point" but by Canadian connotation "Scalp Point." The English, by mistranslation, called it "Crown Point"; see Van de Water, *Lake Champlain and Lake George*, 75.

7. John W. Krueger, "The Fort Ticonderoga King's Shipyard Excavation: An Overview," *Bulletin of the Fort Ticonderoga Museum* 14 (1985):335.

8. Ibid.

9. Charles P. Stacey, *Quebec, 1759, The Siege and the Battle*, 165.

10. Perry Eugene Leroy, "Sir Guy Carleton as a Military Leader during the American Invasion and Repulse in Canada, 1775–1776," 1:6–8. Leroy cites Carleton to Gage, Quebec, February 15, 1767, Transcripts of Colonial Office Records, Correspondence between Governor Carleton and Lord Dartmouth, 1775, Canada, Quebec no. 11, Public Archives of Canada, 295–96.

11. John W. Krueger, "Troop Life at the Champlain Valley Forts during the American Revolution," *Bulletin of the Fort Ticonderoga Museum* 14, no. 3 (summer 1982):161; Krueger cites Haldimand to Gage, May 15, 1774, in K. G. Davies, *Documents of the American Revolution, 1770–1783*, 8:112; Haldimand to Dartmouth, June 1, 1774, in Davies, 7:114.

12. Krueger, "Troop Life," 161.

13. Ibid.; Krueger cites Haldimand to Gage, May 15, 1774, in Davies, *Documents of the American Revolution*, 8:112; Haldimand to Dartmouth, June 1, 1774, ibid., 7:114; Haldimand to Gage, July 6, 1774, in Davies, 7:169; Gage to Dartmouth, August 29, 1774, in Davies, 7:368–69.

14. Krueger, "Troop Life," (summer 1982):161.

15. Krueger, "Troop Life," (summer 1982):161. Krueger cites Dartmouth to Gage, November 2, 1774, in Davies, *Documents of the American Revolution*, 2:177, and Gage to Dartmouth, December 26, 1774, 1:389; Gage to Carleton, March 16, 1775, Gage Papers, Clements Library.

16. Krueger, "Troop Life," (summer 1982):161.

17. Ibid.

18. Ibid.; Krueger cites Gates to Carleton, April 19, 1775, Gage Papers, Clements Library.

19. Krueger, "Troop Life," (summer 1982):161.

20. Ibid.

21. Van de Water, *Lake Champlain and Lake George*, 163.

22. Colonel Henry Knox's List of Cannon at Ticonderoga, December 9, 1775, in Clark, Morgan, and Crawford, *Naval Documents*, 3:21.

23. William M. Fowler, *Rebels under Sail: The American Navy during the Revolution*, 174, 322n; Hugh Hastings, *Public Papers of George Clinton, First Governor of New York, 1777–1795, 1801–1804*, 1:201n.

24. Fowler, *Rebels under Sail*, 322n; Journal Kept by Eleazar Oswald on Lake Champlain, May 11, 1775, in Clark, Morgan, and Crawford, *Naval Documents*, 1:312.

25. Kreuger, "Troop Life," (summer 1982):174.

26. Leroy, "Sir Guy Carleton," 31, citing Carleton to Gage, May 31, 1775, Gage Papers, Clements Library.

27. Fowler, *Rebels under Sail*, 322n; Benedict Arnold to the Massachusetts Committee of Safety, May 19, 1775, in Clark, Morgan, and Crawford, *Naval Documents*, 1:364–66; Oswald's Journal, May 23, 1775, in ibid., 1:513.

28. Fowler, *Rebels under Sail*, 322n; Benedict Arnold to the Massachusetts Committee of Safety, May 23, 1775, in Clark, Morgan, and Crawford, *Naval Documents*, 1:512–13.

29. Fowler, *Rebels under Sail*, 322n.

30. Ibid., 322–23; Ethan Allen to the Continental Congress, May 29, 1775, in Clark, Morgan, and Crawford, *Naval Documents*, 1:563–64; Colonel Benedict Arnold to the Committee of Safety of Massachusetts, May 29, 1775, in ibid., 1:562; Walter Spooner to Governor Jonathan Trumbull, July 3, 1775, in ibid., 1:807–808.

31. Fowler, *Rebels under Sail*, 323n.

32. Bellico, *Sails and Steam*, 120.

33. Schuyler to Franklin, August 23, 1775, in Clark, Morgan, and Crawford, *Naval Documents*, 1:1217; Bellico, *Sails and Steam*, 121.

34. Bellico, *Sails and Steam*, 123, 125–26.

35. The origin of the *Revenge* has been the subject of speculation. Several authors indicate (without reference) that it may have been built at Ticonderoga by an unknown contractor in 1775; see M. Smith, *Navies in the American Revolution*, 1:195–97; Van de Water, *Lake Champlain and Lake George*, 191, 192. Russell Bellico presents a substantiated argument that the row galley captured at St. Jean was taken to Ticonderoga and rigged as a schooner; see Bellico, *Sails and Steam*, 132.

36. Fowler, *Rebels under Sail*, 182–83.

37. Alfred Thayer Mahan, *Major Operations of the Navies in the War of American Independence*, 12.

CHAPTER 2. BUILDING THE AMERICAN FLEET

1. Schuyler to Washington, June 17, 1776, in Clark, Morgan, and Crawford, *Naval Documents*, 5:589.

2. Schuyler to Washington, May 31, 1776, ibid., 5:317.

3. Ibid.

4. Bellico, *Sails and Steam*, 115.

5. Van de Water, *Lake Champlain and Lake George*, 130.

6. Quoted in Edward G, Farmer, "Skenesborough: Continental Navy Shipyard," *United States Naval Institute Proceedings* 90 (1964):161.

7. Schuyler to Wynkoop, May 31, 1776, in Clark, Morgan, and Crawford, *Naval Documents*, 5:317.

8. Philip Schuyler to Hermanus Schuyler, June 7, 1776, ibid., 5:410.

9. Ibid.

10. Schuyler to Washington, June 12, 1776, ibid., 5:494.

11. Ibid., 5:495.

12. Ibid., 5:494.

13. Foster D. Taylor, "The Piscataqua River Gundalow," *American Neptune* 4 (1942):127.

14. Howard I. Chapelle, *History of the American Sailing Navy: The Ships and Their Development*, 101.

15. Hermanus Schuyler to Philip Schuyler, June 13, 1776, Adirondack Museum.

16. Ibid.

17. Schuyler to Washington, June 12, 1776, in Clark, Morgan, and Crawford, *Naval Documents*, 5:494; Journal of the Continental Congress, June 17, 1776, ibid., 5:589–90.

18. John W. Jackson, *The Pennsylvania Navy, 1775–1781: The Defense of the Delaware*, 12.

19. Philip Schuyler to Hermanus Schuyler, June 22, 1776, in Clark, Morgan, and Crawford, *Naval Documents*, 5:680.

20. Ibid.

21. Ibid.

22. Bellico, *Sails and Steam*, 121, 124; Clark, Morgan, and Crawford, *Naval Documents*, 1:1217. See also Benjamin Trumbull, "A Concise Journal or Minutes of the Principal Movements towards St. John's," *Collections of the Connecticut Historical Society* 7 (1899):146.

23. Phillip Schuyler to Benjamin Franklin, August 23, 1775, in Clark, Morgan, and Crawford, *Naval Documents*, 1:1217.

24. Arnold to Washington, May 8, 1776, in George Washington, *The Papers of George Washington*, 4:229.

25. Sullivan to Washington, June 24, 1776, ibid., 5:701–702.

26. Bellico, *Sails and Steam*, 138.

27. Schuyler to Washington, June 24, 1776, in Clark, Morgan, and Crawford, *Naval Documents*, 5:710.

28. Schuyler to Washington, June 25, 1776, ibid., 5:712.

29. Schuyler to Governor Jonathan Trumbull, June 25, 1776, ibid., 5:733.

30. Fowler, *Rebels under Sail*, 189.

31. Ibid., 188–89; John W. Krueger, "Troop Life at the Champlain Valley Forts during the American Revolution," *Bulletin of the Fort Ticonderoga Museum* 14, no. 3 (summer 1982):284.

32. Krueger, "Troop Life," *Bulletin of the Fort Ticonderoga Museum* 14, no. 5 (summer 1984): 284, citing Schuyler to Massachusetts Assembly, June 25, 1776, in Peter Force, *American Archives: A Documentary History of the North American Colonies, Fourth Series*, 4:1074–75; Resolve of Massachusetts Assembly, July 1, 1776, in Force, *American Archives, Fifth Series*, 1:303–304; Resolve of Massachusetts General Court, July 1, 1776, in Clark, Morgan, and Crawford, *Naval Documents*, 5:848–49.

33. Varick to McKesson, May 1, 1776, in Clark, Morgan, and Crawford, *Naval Documents*, 4:1362; Minutes of the New York Committee of Safety, May 8, 1776, ibid., 4:1460.

34. Sullivan to Schuyler, June 19, 1776, in Clark, Morgan, and Crawford, *Naval Documents*, 5:613.

35. Hermanus Schuyler to Philip Schuyler, June 30, 1776, Adirondack Museum.

36. Ibid.

37. Schuyler to Officer Bringing Carpenters from Massachusetts and Connecticut to Skenesborough, July 4, 1776, in Clark, Morgan, and Crawford, *Naval Documents*, 5:915.

38. Resolves of a Council of War Held at Crown Point, July 7, 1776, ibid., 5:961.

39. Colonel John Trumbull to Governor Jonathan Trumbull, July 12, 1776, ibid., 5:1035–36; Gates to Hancock, July 16, 1776, ibid., 5:1099.

40. Arnold to Gates, July 10, 1776, ibid., 5:1008–1009.

41. Ibid.; Anthony Wayne, "The Wayne Orderly Book," *Bulletin of the Fort Ticonderoga Museum* 11 (1963):94.

42. Arnold to Gates, July 10, 1776, in Clark, Morgan, and Crawford, *Naval Documents*, 5:1009.

43. Hartley to Arnold, July 10, 1776, ibid., 5:1009.

44. Ibid.

45. Force, *American Archives, Fifth Series*, 1:629; Schuyler to Washington, June 24, 1776, in Clark, Morgan, and Crawford, *Naval Documents*, 5:710.

46. Gates to Schuyler, July 19, 1776, in Force, *American Archives, Fifth Series*, 1:454.

47. Gates to Arnold, July 13, 1776, in Clark, Morgan, and Crawford, *Naval Documents*, 5:1057.

48. Cooke to Hancock, July 15, 1776, ibid., 5:1097.

49. Gates to Hancock, July 16, 1776, ibid., 5:1099–1101.

50. Ibid.

51. Jeduthan Baldwin, *The Revolutionary Journal of Col. Jeduthan Baldwin, 1775–1778*, 62–63.

52. Hermanus Schuyler to Schuyler, July 24, 1776, Adirondack Museum; Arnold to Schuyler, July 24, 1776, in Clark, Morgan, and Crawford, *Naval Documents*, 5:1197.

53. H. Schuyler to P. Schuyler, July 24, 1776, Adirondack Museum.

54. Jackson, *Pennsylvania Navy*, 18.

55. H. Schuyler to P. Schuyler, July 24, 1776, Adirondack Museum.

56. Arnold to P. Schuyler, July 24, 1776, in Clark, Morgan, and Crawford, *Naval Documents*, 5:1198.

57. Varick to Hughes, August 3, 1776, ibid., 6:35.

58. P. Schuyler to Varick, July 25, 1776, ibid., 5:1211.

59. Jacobus Van Zandt to Varick, July 31, 1776, ibid., 5:1307.

60. Varick to Washington, August 3, 1776, ibid., 6:33.

61. Ibid., 6:33–34.

62. Varick to P. Schuyler, August 3, 1776, ibid., 6:34.

63. Force, *American Archives, Fifth Series*, 1:582.

64. H. Schuyler to P. Schuyler, June 30, 1776, Adirondack Museum.

65. Ibid., July 26, 1776, Adirondack Museum; Force, *American Archives, Fifth Series*, 1:679.

66. Cornelius Wynkoop to Gates, July 30, 1776, in Clark, Morgan, and Crawford, *Naval Documents*, 5:1284.

67. Baldwin, *Revolutionary Journal*, 64–65.

68. Ibid.

69. Arnold to Schuyler, July 30, 1776, in Clark, Morgan, and Crawford, *Naval Documents*, 5:1282.

70. Ibid.

71. Wayne to Franklin, July 31, 1776, ibid., 5:1306.

72. Arnold to Gates, August 7, 1776, ibid., 6:98.

73. Ibid.

74. Gates to P. Schuyler, October 11, 1776, Force, *American Archives, Fifth Series*, 2:1000.

75. Arnold to P. Schuyler, July 24, 1776, in Clark, Morgan, and Crawford, *Naval Documents*, 5:1197.

76. Arnold to Gates, August 7, 1776, ibid., 6:98.

77. Arnold to P. Schuyler, August 8, 1776, ibid., 6:120.

78. H. Schuyler to P. Schuyler, August 10, 1776, Adirondack Museum.

79. Gates to Trumbull, August 11, 1776, in Clark, Morgan, and Crawford, *Naval Documents*, 6:145.

80. Ibid.

81. Norman K. Risjord, *Jefferson's America, 1760–1815*, 42.

82. H. Schuyler to P. Schuyler, August 25, 1776, Adirondack Museum.

83. P. Schuyler to Hancock, August 29, 1776, in Clark, Morgan, and Crawford, *Naval Documents*, 6:348.

84. H. Schuyler to P. Schuyler, September 2, 1776, Adirondack Museum.

85. Ibid.; Henry Sewall, "The Diary of Henry Sewall," *Bulletin of the Fort Ticonderoga Museum* 9 (1963):78.

86. Gates to P. Schuyler, September 30, 1776, in John P. Butler, *Papers of the Continental Congress, 1774–1789*, 2:419–26.

87. P. Schuyler to Gates, October 11, 1776, in Force, *American Archives, Fifth Series* 2:1000; Gates to Arnold, October 12, 1776, Gates Papers, Box 19, New York City Public Library.

88. Arnold to Gates, October 10, 1776, in *Bulletin of the Fort Ticonderoga Museum* 4, no. 7 (1938):41–42.

CHAPTER 3. BUILDING THE BRITISH FLEET

1. Vice Admiral Samuel Graves to Philip Stephens, September 26, 1775, in Clark, Morgan, and Crawford, *Naval Documents*, 2:210; Fowler, *Rebels under Sail*,196, 325n.

2. George Jackson to John Pownall, January 9, 1776, in Clark, Morgan, and Crawford, *Naval Documents*, 3:490.

3. Ibid.; Fowler, *Rebels under Sail*, 325n; Lords Commissioners, Admiralty, to Lord George Germain, February 6, 1776, in Clark, Morgan, and Crawford, *Naval Documents*, 4:890–91.

4. Elizabeth Cometti, *The American Journals of Lt. John Enys*, 16.

5. Sullivan to Schuyler, June 19, 1776, in Clark, Morgan, and Crawford, *Naval Documents*, 5:613; Leroy, "Sir Guy Carleton," 2:443.

6. Fowler, *Rebels under Sail*, 199.

7. Douglas to Stephens, July 21, 1776, in Clark, Morgan, and Crawford, *Naval Documents*, 5:1168.

8. Howard I. Chapelle, *The History of American Sailing Ships*, 75–76.

9. Douglas to Starke, July 7, 1776, in Clark, Morgan, and Crawford, *Naval Documents*, 5:957.

10. Douglas to Stephens, July 23, 1776, ibid., 5:1184.

11. "A Draught of the Carleton Rebuilt at St. Johns on Lake Champlain 1776," in Clark, Morgan, and Crawford, *Naval Documents*, 5:1256; Chapelle, *History of American Sailing Ships*, 76.

12. J. F. Wasmus, *An Eyewitness Account of the American Revolution and New England Life: The Journal of J. F. Wasmus, German Company Surgeon, 1776–1783*, 30.

13. Journal of Robert Barwick, in Clark, Morgan, and Crawford, *Naval Documents*, 2:1104.

14. Arnold to Gates, September 16, 1776, ibid., 6:857.

15. Bellico, *Sails and Steam*, 145.

16. Chapelle, *History of American Sailing Ships*, 76.

17. Bellico, *Sails and Steam*, 145.

18. Douglas to Pownoll, September 23, 1776, in Clark, Morgan, and Crawford, *Naval Documents*, 6:951.

19. Leroy, "Sir Guy Carleton," 2:449.

20. James Murray Hadden, *Hadden's Journal and Orderly Books: A Journal Kept in Canada and upon Burgoyne's Campaign in 1776 and 1777*, 539.

21. Douglas to Stephens, July 23, 1776, in Clark, Morgan, and Crawford, *Naval Documents*, 5:1184.

22. Hadden, *Hadden's Journal*, 539–40.

23. Douglas to Stephens, July 23, 1776, in Clark, Morgan, and Crawford, *Naval Documents*, 5:1185; Fowler, *Rebels under Sail*, 199.

24. Fowler, *Rebels under Sail*, 199, 326n; Captain Charles Douglas to Philip Stephens, July 23, 1776, in Clark, Morgan, and Crawford, *Naval Documents*, 5:1184.

25. Hadden, *Hadden's Journal*, 169–71.

26. Clark, Morgan, and Crawford, *Naval Documents*, 6:883–84.

27. Fowler, *Rebels under Sail*, 201.

28. Wasmus, *Eyewitness Account*, 31.

29. Douglas to Pownoll, October 10, 1776, in Morgan and Clark, *Naval Documents*, 6:1193–94.

30. Douglas to Stephens, October 21, 1776, ibid., 4:1344.

31. "A Draught of the Thunderer Built at St. Johns on Lake Champlain 1776," in Clark, Morgan, and Crawford, *Naval Documents*, 6:1437; Chapelle, *History of American Sailing Ships*, 76.

32. Chapelle, *History of American Sailing Ships*, 76.

33. Douglas to Stephens, October 21, 1776, in Clark, Morgan, and Crawford, *Naval Documents*, 4:1344; Fowler, *Rebels under Sail*, 326.

34. Cometti, *American Journals*, 16; Wasmus, *Eyewitness Account*, 25.

35. Wasmus, *Eyewitness Account*, 28.

36. Leroy, "Sir Guy Carleton," 2:457; Hadden, *Hadden's Journal*, 15–16; George Pausch, *Journal of Captain George Pausch, Chief of the Hanau Artillery during the Burgoyne Campaign*, 80–81.

CHAPTER 4. THE AMERICAN FLEET PREPARES FOR CONFRONTATION

1. Gates's Orders to Brigadier General Benedict Arnold, August 7, 1776, in Clark, Morgan, and Crawford, *Naval Documents*, 6:95.

2. Wynkoop had been recommended by Schuyler and the New York Committee of Safety for the command in March. Minutes of the New York Committee of Safety, March 23, 1776, in Clark, Morgan, and Crawford, *Naval Documents*, 4:476; Schuyler to Wynkoop, May 7, 1776, ibid., 4:1440.

3. Arnold to Gates, August 17, 1776, ibid., 6:216.

4. Arnold to Captains Seamon and Primere, August 17, 1776; Wynkoop to Arnold, August 17, 1776; Arnold to Wynkoop, August 17, 1776, ibid., 6:215.

5. Arnold to Gates, August 17, 1776, ibid., 6:216.

6. Wynkoop to Gates, August 17, 1776, ibid., 6:216–17; Gates to Arnold, August 18, 1776, ibid., 6:223.

7. Bayze Wells, "Journal of Bayze Wells," 268.

8. Gates to Schuyler, August 18, 1776, in Clark, Morgan, and Crawford, *Naval Documents*, 6:223.

9. Schuyler to Hancock, August 29, 1776, ibid., 6:348.

10. Gates to Schuyler, August 18, 1776, ibid., 6:223.

11. Gates to Arnold, September 5, 1776, ibid., 6:708.

12. Arnold to Gates, August 31, 1776, ibid., 6:371; Gates to Arnold, September 19, 1776, ibid., 6:902; Arnold to Gates, September 21, 1776, ibid., 6:925–26.

13. Arnold to Gates, August 16, 1776, ibid., 6:205; Arnold to Potts, August 18, 1776, ibid., 6:222.

14. Gates to Arnold, August 23, 1776, ibid., 6:283.

15. Ibid.

16. Ibid.

17. Wells, "Journal," 267–68.

18. Ibid.; Baldwin, *Revolutionary Journal*, 65.

19. Wells, "Journal," 270.

20. Ibid., 269–70.

21. Ibid., 270.

22. Arnold to Gates, August 31, 1776, in Clark, Morgan, and Crawford, *Naval Documents*, 6:371.

23. Wells, "Journal," 271.

24. Arnold to Gates, August 31, 1776, in Clark, Morgan, and Crawford, *Naval Documents*, 6:371.

25. Wells, "Journal," 271–72.

26. Ibid., 272–73.

27. Arnold to Gates, September 2, 1776, in Clark, Morgan, and Crawford, *Naval Documents*, 6:654.

28. Gates to Arnold, September 5, 1776, ibid., 6:708.

29. Wells, "Journal," 273–74.

30. Ibid.

31. Ibid.

32. Arnold to Gates, September 7, 1776, in Clark, Morgan, and Crawford, *Naval Documents*, 6:734.

33. Ibid.

34. Wells, "Journal," 275.

35. Arnold to Gates, September 7, 1776, in Clark, Morgan, and Crawford, *Naval Documents*, 6:734.

36. "Last night we had no molestation from the enemy. Our batterys are almost compleat, & the brig has sent on shore to git fasshines to hang over her sides, so as to atteck the fort at the time the batterys are opened." See Samuel Jenks, "Samuel Jenks: His Journal of the

Campaign in 1760," *Proceedings of the Massachusetts Historical Society,* 2d ser., 5 (1889–90).

37. Arnold to Gates, September 7, 1776, in Clark, Morgan, and Crawford, *Naval Documents,* 6:734; Baldwin, *Revolutionary Journal,* 74–75.
38. Wells, "Journal," 275.
39. Baldwin, *Revolutionary Journal,* 73.
40. Arnold to Gates, September 7, 1776, in Clark, Morgan, and Crawford, *Naval Documents,* 6:734–35.
41. Gates to Arnold, September 12, 1776, ibid., 6:791–92.
42. Ibid.
43. Wells, "Journal," 276.
44. Ibid., 277.
45. Ibid., 278.
46. Arnold to Gates, September 18, 1776, in Clark, Morgan, and Crawford, *Naval Documents,* 6:884.
47. Gates to Arnold, September 12, 1776, ibid., 6:791–92.
48. Arnold to Gates, September 18, 1776, ibid., 6:884.
49. Wells, "Journal," 278.
50. Arnold to Gates, September 7, 1776, in Clark, Morgan, and Crawford, *Naval Documents,* 6:735.
51. Wells, "Journal," 279; Baldwin, *Revolutionary Journal,* 77.
52. Arnold to Gates, September 21, 1776, in Clark, Morgan, and Crawford, *Naval Documents,* 6:925.
53. Wells, "Journal," 279.
54. Arnold to Gates, September 21, 1776, in Clark, Morgan, and Crawford, *Naval Documents,* 6:926.
55. Arnold to Gates, September 7, 1776, ibid., 6:735.
56. Wells, "Journal," 279.
57. Ibid.
58. Krueger, "Troop Life," (summer 1982):180.
59. Wells, "Journal," 280.

CHAPTER 5. THE BATTLE OF VALCOUR ISLAND

1. Christopher Ward, *The War of the Revolution,* 1:392.
2. Force, *American Archives, Fifth Series,* 2:440.
3. Ibid., 2:835.
4. Ibid.
5. Wells, "Journal," 280.
6. Force, *American Archives, Fifth Series,* 2:835.
7. James Arnold, captain of the *Congress,* has sometimes been confused with Benedict Arnold. James Arnold had served as a company commander in Colonel Joshua Wingate's New Hampshire regiment. At least thirteen men from Arnold's company were drafted to man the

Philadelphia. The company's first lieutenant, Joshua Grant, was given command of the *Connecticut.*

8. Force, *American Archives, Fifth Series,* 2:835.

9. "Examination of Sergeant Stiles," in Clark, Morgan, and Crawford, *Naval Documents,* 5: 96.

10. Force, *American Archives, Fifth Series,* 2:835.

11. Arnold to Gates, October 7, 1776, in *Bulletin of the Fort Ticonderoga Museum* 4, no. 7 (1938):36.

12. Clark, Morgan, and Crawford, *Naval Documents,* 6:1081.

13. Persifer Frazer to Polly Frazer, September 21, 1776, in "Letters from Ticonderoga, 1776," *Bulletin of the Fort Ticonderoga Museum* 10 (1962) 6:450–51.

14. Gates to Arnold, October 3, 1776, *Bulletin of the Fort Ticonderoga Museum* 4, no. 7 (1938):32.

15. William Digby, *The British Invasion from the North: Digby's Journal of the Campaigns of Generals Carleton and Burgoyne from Canada, 1776–1777,* 154.

16. Arnold to Gates, October 10, 1776, *Bulletin of the Fort Ticonderoga Museum* 4, no. 7 (1938):41–42.

17. Jahiel Stewart notes that the time was seven o'clock. Pascal de Angelis states eight o'clock. See Donald H. Wickman, "A Most Unsettled Time on Lake Champlain: The October 1776 Journal of Jahiel Stewart," *Vermont History* 64, no. 2 (1996):92; Charles M. Snyder, "With Benedict Arnold at Valcour Island: The Diary of Pascal De Angelis," *Vermont History* 42, no. 3 (1974)198.

18. Waterbury to Gates, October 24, 1776, in Force, *American Archives, Fifth Series,* 2:1224.

19. E. Vale Smith, "Diary of Colonel Edward Wigglesworth," 357.

20. Arnold to Gates, October 12, 1776, in Clark, Morgan, and Crawford, *Naval Documents,* 6:1235. General Arthur St. Clair states in a letter to James Wilson on October 15, 1776, that the British had "2 Gondolas rigged as Sloops carrying 3, 12 prs each," Historical Society of Pennsylvania; "The Battle of Valcour Island 1776"; painting by Henry Gilder (Windsor Castle, Royal Library, Her Majesty Queen Elizabeth II); Snyder, "With Benedict Arnold at Valcour Island," 198.

21. Arnold to Gates, October 12, 1776, in Clark, Morgan, and Crawford, *Naval Documents,* 6:1235.

22. Bellico, *Sails and Steam,* 152.

23. Digby, *British Invasion,* 152–53.

24. J. Robert Maguire, "Dr. Robert Knox's Account of the Battle of Valcour, October 11–13, 1776," *Vermont History* 46, no. 3 (1978):147. Knox's account of the engagement is contained in a portion of a letter written to an unknown person on October 29, 1776, and is reproduced in Maguire's study.

25. Ibid., 148.

26. John Schank, John Starke, and Edward Longcroft, "An Open Letter to Captain Pringle," *Bulletin of the Fort Ticonderoga Museum* 1 (1928):14–20.

27. Ibid.; Snyder, "With Benedict Arnold at Valcour Island," 143.

28. Snyder, "With Benedict Arnold at Valcour Island," 198.

29. Force, *American Archives, Fifth Series*, 2:1038; Butler, *Papers of the Continental Congress*, 3:163; Samuel Adams to Sally (Preston) Adams, October 14, 1776, Sol Feinstone Collection of the American Revolution, reel no. 1, no. 23; Schank, Starke, and Longcroft, "An Open Letter to Captain Pringle," 18.

30. Hadden, *Hadden's Journal*.

31. Schank, Starke, and Longcroft, "An Open Letter to Captain Pringle," 18.

32. Ibid.

33. Pausch, *Journal*, 82–85.

34. Hadden, *Hadden's Journal*, 23.

35. John A. Barton, "The Battle of Valcour Island, from *The Life of Admiral Viscount Exmouth*, by Edward Osler, Esq., London, 1835," *Bulletin of the Fort Ticonderoga Museum* 2, no. 5 (1930–32):164.

36. According to Edgar S. Maclay, Lieutenant Dacres of the *Carleton* was the father of James R. Dacres, who was the commander of the *Guerrière* when it was captured by the *Constitution* in 1812; see Maclay, *A History of the United States Navy from 1775 to 1894*, 1:53.

37. Wickman, "A Most Unsettled Time," 92.

38. Hadden, *Hadden's Journal*, 23.

39. Barton, "The Battle of Valcour Island," 163–64.

40. Ibid., 165–66.

41. Maguire, "Dr. Robert Knox's Account," 144.

42. Ibid., 142–43.

43. Schank, Starke, and Longcroft, "An Open Letter to Captain Pringle," 18.

44. Cometti, *American Journals*, 19.

45. Hadden, *Hadden's Journal*, 23.

46. Pausch, *Journal*, 82–85.

47. Ibid.

48. Arnold to Gates, October 12, 1776, in Clark, Morgan, and Crawford, *Naval Documents*, 6:1235; Bellico, *Sails and Steam*, 153.

49. Philip K. Lundeberg, *The Gunboat* Philadelphia *and the Defense of Lake Champlain in 1776*, 29.

50. Arnold to Gates, October 12, 1776, in Clark, Morgan, and Crawford, *Naval Documents*, 6:1235. Jeduthan Baldwin notes in his journal that "a Gundalow Stript & Sunk by our men in the Bay of Bellcour"; see Baldwin, *Revolutionary Journal*, 80–81. "[W]e lost 3 vessels, one we sank after taking out all on board, a schooner run aground & was burnt, another went off to the Eastward & has not been seen since";

see Jeduthan Baldwin, "The Baldwin Letters," *American Monthly Magazine* 6 (1895):193.

51. Arnold to Gates, October 12, 1776, in Clark, Morgan, and Crawford, *Naval Documents*, 6:1235.

52. Wickman, "A Most Unsettled Time," 92.

53. Cometti, *American Journals*, 20.

54. Digby, *British Invasion*, 166.

55. Wasmus, *Eyewitness Account*, 32.

56. Hadden, *Hadden's Journal*, 23, 24.

57. Arnold to Gates, October 12, 1776, in Clark, Morgan, and Crawford, *Naval Documents*, 6:1235.

58. Pausch, *Journal*, 82–85.

59. Hadden, *Hadden's Journal*, 24.

60. Winslow C. Watson presents an argument suggesting that Arnold led his fleet around the north end of Valcour; see "Arnold's Retreat after the Battle of Valcour," *Magazine of American History* 6 (1881):414–17.

61. Force, *American Archives, Fifth Series*, 2:1224.

62. Wickman, "A Most Unsettled Time," 92.

63. Lundeberg, *The Gunboat* Philadelphia, 31.

64. Cometti, *American Journals*, 20.

65. Gardner W. Allen, *A Naval History of the American Revolution*, 172–73, citing *London Chronicle*, November 23, 1776.

66. Schank, Starke, and Longcroft, "An Open Letter to Captain Pringle," 14.

67. Hadden, *Hadden's Journal*, 24–26.

68. Arnold to Gates, October 12, 1776, in Clark, Morgan, and Crawford, *Naval Documents*, 6:1235.

69. Smith, "Diary of Colonel Edward Wigglesworth," 358.

70. "Att light we clost to the Four Brothers and the schooner, sloop and 2 gallies in sight, the wind southerly; and we beat up and came to, and anchor[ed] under the western shore and stoped our leaks and refreshed ourselves, and lay there till half after one at night, when 2 of the gundeloes came along and we hailed them; and they told us that one of our gundeloes was taking water *[New Jersey]* and the other sunk *[Providence]*. Whereupon we gott underway, and beat down the rest of the night"; see Snyder, "With Benedict Arnold at Valcour Island," 198.

71. Cometti, *American Journals*, 21–22.

72. "The first [October 11, 1776] we lost 3 vessels, one we sank after taking out all on board, a schooner run aground & was burnt, another went off to the Eastward & has not been seen since"; see Baldwin, "The Baldwin Letters," 193; Persifer Frazer notes correctly that the British took two vessels (the *New Jersey* and the *Lee*); see Frazer, "Letters from Ticonderoga," (1962):453.

73. Sewall, "Diary of Henry Sewall," *Bulletin of the Fort Ticonderoga Museum* 80.

74. Frazer, "Letters from Ticonderoga," (1962):453.

75. Allen, *A Naval History*, 176. Allen cites the *London Chronicle*, November 26, 1776.

76. Wickman, "A Most Unsettled Time," 94.

77. Smith, "Diary of Colonel Edward Wigglesworth," 358.

78. Snyder, "With Benedict Arnold at Valcour Island," 199.

79. Waterbury to Gates, February 26, 1777, in Clark, Morgan, and Crawford, *Naval Documents*, 2:1224–95.

80. Waterbury to Gates, October 24, 1776, in Force, *American Archives, Fifth Series*, 2:1224.

81. Force, *American Archives, Fifth Series*, 2:1069.

82. Allen, *A Naval History*, 176; Allen cites the *London Chronicle*, November 26, 1776.

83. Waterbury to Gates, February 26, 1776, in Clark, Morgan, and Crawford, *Naval Documents*, 7:1295.

84. Haldimand Papers, Correspondence with General Gage, 1758–1777, Special Collections, John C. Pace Library, University of West Florida, Pensacola, microfilm.

85. Baldwin, *Revolutionary Journal*, 81.

86. Bellico, *Sails and Steam*, 158.

87. Arthur B. Cohn, "An Incident Not Known to History: Squire Ferris and Benedict Arnold at Ferris Bay, October 13, 1776," *Vermont History* 55 (1987):3.

88. "Dear General I intended sending the foregoing from Button Mould Bay, but waited for a Boat that I had Sent to this place. . . . [Y]esterday at Noon we left Button Mould Bay, & arived here last night" (Button Mould Bay was the name formerly applied to Ferris Bay); see Arnold to Gates, September 2, 1776, in Clark, Morgan, and Crawford, *Naval Documents*, 6:654.

89. James Wilkinson, *Memoirs of My Own Times*, 1:91–92.

90. Knox's report of this incident is found in a fragment of a letter presumed to be an English correspondent of Knox's. The letter was written on October 29, 1776, from Crown Point, New York, and is in the possession of J. Robert Maguire; see Maguire, "Dr. Robert Knox's Account."

91. Jahiel Stewart, Diary, Revolutionary War Pension Records, National Archives and Records Administration, Washington, D.C.; see entry for October 11, 1776.

92. Digby, *British Invasion*, 176.

93. Ward, *War of the Revolution*, 1:396.

94. Hadden, *Hadden's Journal*, 34.

95. William Briggs, an American seamen belonging to the captured *Washington* reported the information October 17, 1776 after his release; see John Almon, ed., *The Remembrancer, or Impartial Repository of Public Events, 1775–1784* (London: J. Almon, 1775–84 [University of Central Florida, Microfiche]), 135.

96. Ward, *War of the Revolution*, 1:397.

97. Force, *American Archives, Fifth Series*, 2:1040–41.

98. Digby, *British Invasion*, 169–72.

99. Baldwin, *Revolutionary Journal*, 82.

100. John Trumbull, *Autobiography, Reminiscences, and Letters of John Trumbull from 1756 to 1841*, 36.

101. Paul R. Reynolds, *Guy Carleton: A Biography*, 106.

102. Bellico, *Sails and Steam*, 162; Gates to Trumbull, October 21, 1776, in Force, *American Archives, Fifth Series*, 2:1192.

103. Bellico, *Sails and Steam*, 162–63.

104. Mahan, *Major Operations of the Navies*, 19; Allen, *A Naval History*, 170.

105. Bellico, *Sails and Steam*, 163.

106. Arthur St. Clair to James Wilson, October 15, 1776, Historical Society of Pennsylvania.

CHAPTER 6. SALVAGING THE PHILADELPHIA

1. *Burlington Daily News*, "Special Historical Tabloid," August 3, August 10, 1935.

2. *Burlington Free Press*, January 3, 1966.

3. Peter S. Palmer, *History of Lake Champlain*, 109.

4. Robert G. Skerrett, "Wreck of the *Royal Savage* Recovered," *United States Naval Institute Proceedings* 61 (1935):1646.

5. *Burlington Free Press*, January 3, 1966.

6. Skerrett, "Wreck of the *Royal Savage*," 1659.

7. Ibid., 1651.

8. Ibid.

9. Ibid., 1652.

10. Art Cohn, personal communication, 1995.

11. Memorandum, March 26, 1963, record no. 229338.237, *Philadelphia* File, Accession no. 229338, Department of Armed Forces History, Division of Naval History, National Museum of American History, Smithsonian Institution. This file contains numerous items and is several hundred pages in length. All items are under the general accession number 229338; most, but not all, letters and memos contained in the file are distinguished by a decimal number after the accession number. Hereinafter, items from this file are cited by name, number, or both, followed by *Philadelphia* file, NMAH.

12. Hagglund, "A Page from the Past," 17.

13. Ibid.

14. Record no. 229338.237, *Philadelphia* file, NMAH.

15. Jenifer Bergen, et al., "Raising the Philadelphia," *Lake Champlain Horizons* 1 (1988):5.

16. Hagglund, "A Page from the Past," 17.

17. Ibid.

18. Ibid., 24.

19. Ibid., 19.

20. Baldwin, *Revolutionary Journal*, 74–75; Frazer, "Letters from Ticonderoga, (1962):451.

21. Hagglund, "A Page from the Past," 19.

22. Ibid., 20.

23. Ibid.

24. Baldwin, *Revolutionary Journal*, October 13, 1776:80, "this morning a Messinger came from the fleet about ten o'clock with a letter from Genl. Arnold informing that he had with his fleet been ingaged with the Enemies fleet 2 Day that we have lost a large schooner *[Royal Savage]* run aground & burnt by the enemy a Gundalow stript & sunk by our men in the Bay of Bellcour."

25. In November, 1779, the British salvaged most of the guns from the *Royal Savage*, but no mention is made in the historical record of any salvage attempt on the *Philadelphia*. See Bellico, *Sails and Steam*, 192.

26. Hagglund, "A Page from the Past," 21.

27. According to Harold Langley, curator of Armed Forces History at the Smithsonian Institution, all the faunal material recovered from the *Philadelphia*, with the exception of the human teeth, was later identified as nonhuman.

28. Bergen, et al., "Raising the *Philadelphia*," 5; *Burlington Daily News*, "Special Historical Tabloid," August 10, 1935.

29. *Burlington Daily News*, "Special Historical Tabloid," August 10, 1935.

30. Ibid.

31. Record no. 229338.237, *Philadelphia* file, NMAH.

32. Erick Tichonuk, personal communication, 1995.

33. Record no. 229338.237, *Philadelphia* file, NMAH.

34. Hagglund, "A Page from the Past," 23.

35. Bergen, et al., "Raising the *Philadelphia*," 6.

36. Hagglund, "A Page from the Past," 23.

37. Frank Taylor to Mr. Graf, October 16, 1939, *Philadelphia* file, NMAH.

38. *Burlington Free Press*, January 3, 1966.

39. Bergen, et al., "Raising the *Philadelphia*," 6.

40. Bellico, *Sails and Steam*, 196–97.

41. John Hayward, *Gazetteer of Vermont*, 97.

42. Bellico, *Sails and Steam*, 200.

43. Ibid.

44. Ibid.

45. Ibid., 201.

46. Record nos. 229338.026 and 229338.007, *Philadelphia* file, NMAH.

47. Record no. 229338.019, *Philadelphia* file, NMAH.

48. Ibid.

49. Ibid.

50. Record no. 229338.018, *Philadelphia* file, NMAH.

51. Record no. 229338.031, *Philadelphia* file, NMAH.
52. Ibid.
53. Record nos. 229338.030 and 229338.026, *Philadelphia* file, NMAH.
54. Record no. 229338.091, *Philadelphia* file, NMAH.
55. Peter Schaufler to Frank Kiendl, record no. 229338.103, *Philadelphia* file, NMAH.
56. Ibid.
57. *Whitehall (N.Y.) Times,* June 1, 1961.
58. Ibid.
59. Record nos. 229338.184 and 229338.194, *Philadelphia* file, NMAH.
60. Record no. 229338.194, *Philadelphia* file, NMAH.
61. *Troy (N.Y.) Record,* July 22, 1961.
62. *Whitehall (N.Y.) Times,* June 1, 1961.
63. Ibid., May 25, 1961.
64. *Whitehall (N.Y.) Banner,* July 14, 1961.
65. D. W. Grattan and R. W. Clarke, "Conservation of Waterlogged Wood," 167–68.
66. A. Rosenqvist, "The Oseburg Find, Its Conservation and Present State," 77–88; A. Rosenqvist, "The Stabilization of Wood Found in the Viking Ship of Oseberg: Parts 1 and 2," *Studies in Conservation* 4 (1959):13–22, 62–77.
67. Donny L. Hamilton, *Basic Methods of Conserving Underwater Archaeological Material Culture,* 27.
68. Grattan and Clarke, "Conservation of Waterlogged Wood," 170; Alfred J. Stamm, "Dimensional Stabilization of Wood with Carbowaxes," *Forest Products Journal* 6, no. 5 (1956):201–204.
69. Mendel L. Peterson to Mr. F. A. Taylor, "Subject: Use of Carbowax," May 25, 1961, record no. 229338.174, *Philadelphia* file, NMAH.
70. Record no. 229338.186, *Philadelphia* file, NMAH.
71. Record no. 229338.189, *Philadelphia* file, NMAH.
72. Record no. 229338.323, *Philadelphia* file, NMAH.
73. "Press Release for Final Movement of Gundelo *Philadelphia,*" December 5, 1961, record no. 229338.227, *Philadelphia* file, NMAH.
74. Lundeberg, *The Gunboat* Philadelphia, 43.
75. Charles H. Olin to Philip Lundeberg, September 26, 1963, *Philadelphia* file, NMAH.
76. Beth Richwine, personal communication, 1996.

CHAPTER 7. CONSTRUCTING THE PHILADELPHIA

1. Hoffman, "The Gunboat *Philadelphia,*" 59.
2. Ibid.
3. Ibid., 61.
4. Howard P. Hoffman, *A Graphic Presentation of the Continental Gondola*

Philadelphia: *American Gunboat of 1776*, "Profile and Sail Plan—Historical Information," sheet 1.

5. Schuyler to Washington, June 12, 1776, in Clark, Morgan, and Crawford, *Naval Documents*, 5:494; Hermanus Schuyler to Philip Schuyler, June 30, 1776, Adirondack Museum.

6. Hoffman, *A Graphic Presentation*, "Bibliography, Discussion of Design, Cordage Table and Photographs," sheet 2.

7. Ibid.

8. Bayreuther, William A., "Hull Construction of the Continental Gondola *Philadelphia*: Description and Comments," 5.

9. Hoffman, *A Graphic Presentation*, "Bottom Planking and Framing Structure," sheet 4.

10. Hoffman, "The Gunboat *Philadelphia*," 61.

11. Hoffman, *A Graphic Presentation*, "Bottom Planking and Framing Structure," sheet 4.

12. Ibid., "Additional Structural Details," sheet 5.

13. Ibid., "Bottom Planking and Framing Structure," sheet 4.

14. Ibid., "Frame Details and Lines Drawing," sheet 3.

15. Ibid., "The Gunboat *Philadelphia*," 61.

16. Hoffman, *A Graphic Presentation*, "Additional Structural Details," sheet 5.

17. Hoffman, "The Gunboat *Philadelphia*," 64.

18. Hoffman, *A Graphic Presentation*, "Frame Details and Lines Drawing," sheet 3.

19. Ibid., "Sails, Sailmaking, Deadeyes, Collars, and Hull Cross Section Views," sheet 12.

20. Ibid., "Additional Structural Details," sheet 5.

21. Ibid., "Sails, Sailmaking, Deadeyes, Collars and Hull Cross Section Views," sheet 12.

22. Ibid., "Additional Structural Details," sheet 5.

23. Hermanus Schuyler to Philip Schuyler, July 26, 1776, Adirondack Museum.

24. Hoffman, *A Graphic Presentation*, "Complete Structural Assembly and Details," sheet 6.

25. Ibid.

26. Wells, "Journal," 275; Arnold to Gates, September 7, 1776, in Clark, Morgan, and Crawford, *Naval Documents*, 6:734.

27. Hoffman, *A Graphic Presentation*, "Spars, Sailmaking, Deadeyes, Collars, and Hull Cross Section Views," sheet 10.

28. Ibid., "Complete Structural Assembly and Details," sheet 6.

29. Ibid., "Additional Structural Details," sheet 5.

30. Ibid., "Bibliography, Discussion of Design, Cordage Table, and Photographs," sheet 2.

31. William A. Bayreuther III, "Revolutionary War Gunboat Construction: The Lake Champlain Continental Gondolas of 1776," 11.

32. Benedict Arnold, "Dimensions for Two Gondolas to Be Built at Chamblé," *History of American Sailing Ships*, 683.

CHAPTER 8. THE PHILADELPHIA ARTIFACT COLLECTION

1. Hoffman, *A Graphic Presentation*, "Guns and Ammunition," sheet 14.
2. Harold L. Peterson, *Round Shot and Rammers*, 41.
3. Hoffman, *A Graphic Presentation*, "Guns and Ammunition," sheet 14.
4. Spencer C. Tucker, *Arming the Fleet: U.S. Navy Ordnance in the Muzzle-Loading Era*, 265.
5. Lundeberg, *The Gunboat* Philadelphia, 57.
6. *Guide to the Royal Danish Arsenal Museum: The Cannon Hall*, 20.
7. Hagglund, "A Page from the Past," 22.
8. Tucker, *Arming the Fleet*, 114.
9. Hoffman, *A Graphic Presentation*, "Bibliography, Discussion of Design, Cordage Table, and Photographs," sheet 2.
10. Spencer C. Tucker. "U.S. Navy Gun Carriages from the Revolution through the Civil War," *American Neptune* 47 (1987):109.
11. Ibid.; Marion V. Brewington, "American Naval Guns, 1775–1785," *American Neptune* 3 (1943):157.
12. Tucker, *Arming the Fleet*, 91.
13. Colonel Henry Knox's List of Cannon at Ticonderoga, December 9, 1775, in Clark, Morgan, and Crawford, *Naval Documents*, 3:21.
14. Arnold to Washington, May 8, 1776, ibid., 4:1455; Baldwin, *Revolutionary Journal*, 65.
15. Hartley to Gates, October 11, 1776, *Bulletin of the Fort Ticonderoga Museum* 4, no. 7 (1938):41.
16. Wasmus, *Eyewitness Account*, 37, 43n.
17. Arnold to Schuyler, July 30, 1776, in Clark, Morgan, and Crawford, *Naval Documents*, 5:1282.
18. Spencer C. Tucker, "American Naval Ordnance of the Revolution," *Nautical Research Journal* 22, no. 1 (1976):20–21.
19. Hoffman, *A Graphic Presentation*, "Guns and Ammunition," sheet 14.
20. Tucker, *Arming the Fleet*, 98.
21. Tucker, "American Naval Ordnance," 27.
22. Varick to Washington, August 3, 1776, in Clark, Morgan, and Crawford, *Naval Documents*, 6:33.
23. Gates to Arnold, September 12, 1776, in Clark, Morgan, and Crawford, *Naval Documents*, 6:792.
24. Kevin J. Crisman, personal communication, 1997.
25. Hoffman, *A Graphic Presentation*, "Ammunition, Aprons, Barrels, Chests, Gauges, and Side Arms," sheet 16.
26. Ibid.
27. Tucker, *Arming the Fleet*, 265.

28. Hoffman, *A Graphic Presentation*, "Ammunition, Aprons Barrels, Chests, Gauges and Side Arms," sheet 16.

29. Ibid., "Guns and Ammunition," sheet 14.

30. Hagglund, "A Page from the Past," 25; "Inventory of Objects and Relics Recovered in Raising the Gundelo 'Philadelphia,'" record no. 229338.177, *Philadelphia* file, NMAH.

31. Hoffman, *A Graphic Presentation*, "Guns and Ammunition," sheet 14.

32. Lorenzo F. Hagglund, "The Continental Gondola *Philadelphia*," *United States Naval Institute Proceedings* 62 (1936):666–67.

33. Ibid., 21.

34. Gladys Hagglund to Philip Lundeberg, July 23, 1961, record no. 229338.209, *Philadelphia* file, NMAH.

35. Tucker, *Arming the Fleet*, 95.

36. Ivor Noël Hume, *A Guide to Artifacts of Colonial America*, 217.

37. Harold L. Peterson. "Lock, Stock and Barrel: Being a Survey of the Shoulder Weapons and Guns of the Continental Army," *American History Illustrated* 11 (1968):31–33.

38. Robert H. McNulty. "A Study of Bayonets in the Department of Archaeology, Colonial Williamsburg, with Notes on Bayonet Identification" In Audrey Noël Hume, et. al., *Five Artifact Studies* (Williamsburg, Va.: Colonial Williamsburg Foundation, 1973), 58.

39. Ibid.; see fig. 2, no. 2, 59.

40. Ibid., 56–57, and fig. 4, no. 6, 63.

41. Hagglund, "The Continental Gondola *Philadelphia*," 668.

42. Peterson, "Lock, Stock and Barrel," 27, 36.

43. Hoffman, *A Graphic Presentation*, "Fittings for Hull and Mast Cap," sheet 9.

44. Carl P. Russell, *Firearms, Traps, and Tools of the Mountain Men*, 260.

45. Ibid.

46. Similar knives were recovered from the British sloop *Boscawen*; see Kevin J. Crisman, "The Fort Ticonderoga King's Shipyard Excavation: The Artifacts," *Bulletin of the Fort Ticonderoga Museum* 14, no. 6 (1985):391.

47. Hoffman, "The Gunboat *Philadelphia*," 65.

48. Hoffman, *A Graphic Presentation*, "Sails, Sailmaking, Deadeyes, Collars, and Hull Cross Section Views," sheet 12.

49. Ibid., "Fittings for Hull and Mast Cap," sheet 9.

50. Ibid., "Anchors, Fireplace and Cooking Utensils," sheet 13.

51. Ibid.

52. Ibid., "Awning Structure, Bow Rails, Fascines, and Sweeps," sheet 7.

53. Hagglund, "A Page from the Past," 20.

54. Philip Lundeberg, personal communication, 1996.

55. Gates to Arnold, September 5, 1776, in Clark, Morgan, and Crawford, *Naval Documents*, 6:708.

56. Hagglund, "A Page from the Past," 25; Philip Lundeberg, personal communication, 1996.

57. Hoffman, *A Graphic Presentation*, "Anchors, Fireplace and Cooking Utensils," sheet 13.
58. Philip Lundeberg, personal communication, 1996.
59. Hagglund, "A Page from the Past," 22; Montgomery to Schuyler, December 5, 1775, in Clark, Morgan, and Crawford, *Naval Documents*, 2:1277.
60. Dan Jenkins, *Military Buttons of the Gulf Coast, 1711–1830*, 44.
61. *Burlington Free Press*, "Special Historical Tabloid," August 10, 1935.
62. Merry W. Abbitt, "The Eighteenth-Century Shoe Buckle," 34.
63. Hagglund, "A Page from the Past," 25.
64. Philip Lundeberg, personal communication, 1996.
65. C. Keith Wilbur, *Revolutionary Medicine, 1700–1800*, 18.
66. Wells, "Journal," 278.
67. Hagglund, "A Page from the Past," 23.
68. Mark Hartmann, personal communication, 1996.
69. Hagglund, "A Page from the Past," 27.
70. Hoffman, *A Graphic Presentation*, "Ammunition, Aprons, Barrels, Chests, Gauges, and Side Arms," sheet 16.
71. Kevin Crisman, personal communication, 1997.
72. Philip Lundeberg, personal communication, 1996.

CHAPTER 9. THE CREW OF THE PHILADELPHIA

1. Arnold to Schuyler, July 24, 1776, in Clark, Morgan, and Crawford, *Naval Documents*, 5:1197.
2. Fowler, *Rebels under Sail*, 195, 325n; Benedict Arnold to Philip Schuyler, July 24, 1776, in Clark, Morgan, and Crawford, *Naval Documents*, 5:1197–98; General Order of Major General Philip Schuyler, July 23, 1776, in Clark, Morgan, and Crawford, *Naval Documents*, 5:1186–87.
3. Arnold to Schuyler, July 24, 1776, in Clark, Morgan, and Crawford, *Naval Documents*, 5:1197.
4. Wayne, "The Wayne Orderly Book," 101.
5. Arnold to Gates, August 7, 1776, in Clark, Morgan, and Crawford, *Naval Documents*, 6:98.
6. Krueger, "Troop Life," (summer 1984):285.
7. Arnold to Schuyler, July 24, 1776, in Clark, Morgan, and Crawford, *Naval Documents*, 5:1197; Arnold to Gates, July 25, 1776, ibid., 5:1210; Trumbull to Schuyler, August 13, 1776, ibid., 6:165; Trumbull to Washington, August 16, 1776, ibid., 6:203; Trumbull to Hancock, August 22, 1776, ibid., 6:265.
8. Schuyler to Trumbull, July 31, 1776, in Force, *American Archives, Fifth Series*, 1:696–97; Trumbull to Schuyler, August 13 and August 22, 1776, ibid., 1:937, 1:1115–16; Trumbull to Washington, August 16, 1776, in Clark, Morgan, and Crawford, *Naval Documents*, 6:203–204;

Varick to Schuyler, August 3, 1776, ibid., 34; Varick to Eddy, August 3, 1776, ibid., 34–35; Payrolls, ibid., 984–86.

9. Krueger, "Troop Life," (summer 1984):287.

10. Gates to Arnold, September 5, 1776, in Clark, Morgan, and Crawford, *Naval Documents*, 6:708.

11. Krueger, "Troop Life," (summer 1984):287.

12. Brigadier General Benedict Arnold's Supply Requisition, in Clark, Morgan, and Crawford, *Naval Documents*, 3:96.

13. Arnold to Gates, October 10, 1776, *Bulletin of the Fort Ticonderoga Museum* 4, no. 7 (1938):41–42.

14. Lundeberg, *The Gunboat* Philadelphia, 19.

15. Ibid., 46.

16. Ibid.

17. Thomas Lynch Montgomery, *Pennsylvania Archives, Fifth Series*, 5:327; John B. Linn and William H. Egle, *Pennsylvania Archives, Second Series*, 1:45–50.

18. Captain Benjamin Rue, Pension Records, Revolutionary War Orderly Books, M853, roll 20, book 147, 156, National Archives, Washington, D.C.

19. Wayne, "The Wayne Orderly Book,"108.

20. Presumably, the James McIntires were father and son. Historical records indicate they were both from Portsmouth, N.H.; Philip Lundeberg, personal communication, 1996.

21. "Pay Roll of Captain Benjamin Rue's Crew Belonging to the Gondola *Philadelphia*," October 16, 1776, typescript at the Lake Champlain Maritime Museum, Basin Harbor, Vt. The original is on display next to the *Philadelphia* at the National Museum of American History, Smithsonian Institution, Washington, D.C.

22. Captain Benjamin Rue, pension records, roll 20, book 147, 156.

23. Wayne, "The Wayne Orderly Book,"110.

24. Persifer Frazer to Polly Frazer, August 6, 1776, in "Letters from Ticonderoga," *Bulletin of the Fort Ticonderoga Museum* 10, no. 5 (1961):393–94.

25. Arnold to Gates, in Clark, Morgan, and Crawford, *Naval Documents*, 6:884.

26. Captain Benjamin Rue, pension records, roll 20, book 147, 156.

27. Ibid.; Lundeberg, *The Gunboat* Philadelphia, 49.

28. Jackson, *Pennsylvania Navy*, 342.

29. Lundeberg, *The Gunboat* Philadelphia, 50.

30. Hazel Spencer Phillips, *The Golden Lamb*, 47.

31. Lundeberg, *The Gunboat* Philadelphia, 47.

32. James C. Neagles, *Summer Soldiers: A Survey and Index of Revolutionary War Courts-Martial*, 84.

33. Lundeberg, *The Gunboat* Philadelphia, 47.

34. Wynkoop to Gates, July 30, 1776, in Clark, Morgan, and Crawford, *Naval Documents*, 5:1284.
35. The King's Rangers, http://www.cam.org/%7Edmonk/index.html.
36. Lorenzo Sabine, *Biographical Sketches of Loyalists of the American Revolution, with an Historical Essay*, 1:227; Lundeberg, *The Gunboat Philadelphia*, 47.
37. Haldimand Papers, Correspondence with General Gage, 1758–77.

CHAPTER 10. THE PHILADELPHIA II

1. Arthur B. Cohn, "Afterword: Building and Sailing the Replica," 61.
2. One of the first projects undertaken by the museum was the replication of an eighteenth-century bateau, an important type of military vessel on Lake George and Lake Champlain during the French and Indian Wars and the American Revolution. Based on archaeological examples excavated from Lake George, New York, in 1960, the replica bateau *Perseverance* launched in 1987 provided an excellent model to evaluate eighteenth-century construction techniques. While being tested for handling and sailing abilities, the *Perseverance* became the subject of a Vermont Public Television documentary; see Lake Champlain (Basin Harbor, Vt.) Maritime Museum Newsletter, fall–winter 1993–94 (hereinafter cited as LCMM Newsletter). To fulfill the documentary film crew's need for an authentic vessel that would dramatize the northeastern Vermont logging industry, museum boatbuilders also assembled a traditional log-driving bateau for the movie *Where the Rivers Run North*. These replica vessels have been incorporated into the growing collection of watercraft on display at the museum.
3. LCMM Newsletter, fall–winter 1993–94.
4. Cohn, "Afterword," 68.
5. Ibid., 69.
6. LCMM Newsletter, fall–winter 1993–94.
7. Cohn, "Afterword," 70.
8. *The Philadelphia Project*, Crossroads Video, Vermont Public Television, 1991.
9. Cohn, "Afterword," 72.
10. Ibid.
11. Donald Dewees, personal communication, 1995.
12. Cohn, "Afterword," 77.
13. LCMM Newsletter, fall 1991.
14. Cohn, "Afterword," 77–80.
15. LCMM Newsletter, fall–winter 1992.
16. Roger Taylor, personal communication, 1995.
17. Cohn, "Afterword," 84.

18. Roger Taylor, personal communication, 1995.
19. Cohn, "Afterword," 82–84, 78.
20. Roger Taylor, personal communication, 1995.

CHAPTER 11. CONCLUSION

1. "Last Missing Gunboat of 1776 Squadron Discovered," http://www.lcmm.org/pages/NauticalGunBoat9707.html.
   In 1999 the lakewide survey of Lake Champlain was in its fourth year under the direction of Art Cohn. As of that date, the project had surveyed more than 160 square miles of the lake's bottom; LCMM Newsletter, fall–winter 1999–2000, p. 1. Veteran researchers include Fred Fayette, Peter Barranco, geologists Patricia and Tom Manley, Kathy Baumann, Matt Hommeyer, Anna Cotton, Ric Gifford, and volunteers Bibs Francis, Chuck St. John, Joe LaMountain, and Bob Phoenix. Additional team members include LCMM staff: Nautical Archaeologist/Conservator David Robinson, Education Specialist Erick Tichonuk, Pierre LaRocque, and Don Dewees.
2. LCMM Newsletter, fall–winter 1999–2000, p. 5.
3. "LCMM to Develop Gunboat Management Plan," http://www.lcmm.org/pages/NauticalNavy Plan9809.html; "Planning Underway for Future of Newly Discovered Revolutionary War Gunboat," http://www.lcmm.org/pages/NauticalSurvey9907a.html.
4. "Benedict Arnold's Last Gunboat: Management Plan Progresses," http://www.lcmm.org/pages/NauticalNavyPlan9906.html.
5. LCMM Newsletter, fall–winter 1999–2000, p. 4.
6. Ibid.; Art Cohn, personal communication, 1995.
7. U.S. Senator Patrick Leahy statement at the "Key to Liberty" opening in Washington, D.C., cited in LCMM Newsletter, fall–winter 1999–2000, p. 4.
8. James Kirby Martin, *Benedict Arnold, Revolutionary Hero: An American Warrior Reconsidered.*

APPENDIX: CATALOG OF ARTIFACTS FOUND
ON THE PHILADELPHIA

1. Memorandum, January 30, 1962, *Philadelphia* file, NMAH.
2. Hagglund, "A Page from the Past," 21.
3. Ibid., 25.
4. Philip Lundeberg, personal communication, 1996.
5. Dimensions are reconstructed from Clarence Hope, "Pencil Sketches of *Philadelphia*," notebook on file at the Lake Champlain Maritime Museum, Basin Harbor, Vt.
6. Philip Lundeberg, personal communication, 1996.

GLOSSARY

AMIDSHIPS Position on a vessel halfway between stem and stern or from side to side.

BALLAST Rock or other heavy material placed low in a vessel's hold to provide greater stability.

BATEAU A rowing boat similar to a flat-bottomed double-ended skiff.

BEAM Maximum width of a vessel.

BILGES The portions of a hull below the waterline where water tends to collect.

BITTS Strong wooden uprights firmly attached in pairs onto the deck or in the cap rail of a vessel for securing cables and other heavy lines.

BUTT BLOCK A small wooden block fastened directly over the juncture of two planks.

BUTT JOIN To place end to end or side to side without over-lapping.

CANT FRAMES The frames in the ends of a vessel that are placed obliquely to the centerline.

CAPRAIL A timber placed at the upper edge of a vessel's side to cover the top of the frames.

CATHEADS Projecting timbers near the bow of a vessel to which the anchor is hoisted and secured.

CEILING The internal planking of a vessel.

COAMING The raised boundary or curb of a hatchway, cockpit, etc.

COCKPIT The space inside the coaming, lower than the deck.

DECK BEAM One of the horizontal transverse timbers of a vessel that support the deck and hold the vessel together.

EYEBOLT A bolt with a looped head.

FASCINES Long bundles of sticks or wood bound together and fixed to the sides of a vessel; used for protection against boarding and sniper fire.

FLOOR TIMBER A frame timber placed transversely in the bottom of a vessel.

FRAME A transverse timber to which the side planking and ceiling are fastened.

GONDOLA A flat-bottomed and double-ended vessel, 40 to 60 feet in length, usually fitted with a single mast set with a square course and topsail.

GUDGEON A socket for a rudder pintle.

HAWSE PIPE The tube through which an anchor cable passes.

KEEL The lowest lengthwise member of a vessel's framework to which the stem, sternpost, and floors are attached.

KEEL PLANK A center line hull plank substantially thicker than the rest of the bottom planking and used in place of a keel.

KEELSON A line of timber placed inside a vessel along the floor timbers and parallel to the keel, to which it is bolted, so as to fasten the floors and the keel together.

LIMBER HOLE One of a series of square holes cut on the underside of floor timbers allowing bilge water to pass to a bailing well.

LODGING KNEE A horizontal, angled timber used to reinforce a deck beam and the side of a hull.

MIDSHIPS Same as *amidships.*

MOLDED DIMENSION The dimensions of timbers as seen from the sheer and body views of a vessel.

OAKUM Hemp fiber obtained by untwisting old rope; used in caulking a vessel's seams.

PINTLE A pin forming part of the hinge of a rudder, usually attached to the rudder and fitting into a ring or gudgeon on the sternpost.

PORT SIDE The left-hand side of a vessel when facing the bow.

RABBET Deep groove or channel cut into a piece of timber to receive the edge of a plank.

RADEAU A large sailing scow with rounded sides and square-shaped bow and stern.

SCANTLINGS The dimensions of all the structural parts of a vessel regarded collectively.

SCARF To join the ends of two timbers forming one longer piece, the ends being chamfered, halved, notched, or cut away to fit together neatly.

SCHOONER Sailing vessel with at least two masts, with all lower sails rigged fore and aft.

SHEER The fore-and-aft curvature from bow to stern of a vessel's deck as shown in side elevation.

SHOT GARLAND A wooden rack with hollows cut into it for supporting round shot for cannons.

SHROUDS A set of ropes forming part of the standing rigging of a vessel.

SIDED DIMENSION The dimension measured across an outer frame surface or the measurement of nonmolded timber surfaces.

SLOOP A single-masted fore-and-aft rigged vessel.

STANCHION An upright support post for deck beams.

STARBOARD SIDE The right-hand side of a vessel when facing the bow.

STEM The curved upright bow timber of a vessel, into which the planks of the bow are joined.

STERNPOST The straight timber at the aft end of a vessel used to support the rudder.

STRAKE Continuous row of planking running fore and aft along a vessel's side.

SWEEP A long, heavy oar used to propel small sailing vessels.

THOLE PIN Wooden peg inserted in pairs in a vessel's cap rail to hold and guide a sweep or oar.

TREENAILS A wooden peg usually fashioned from seasoned hardwood; used in fastening a ship's side and bottom planks to the frames.

WALE One of a number of strakes of extra thick and strong planks used to stiffen the outer hull.

BIBLIOGRAPHY

Abbitt, Merry W. "The Eighteenth-Century Shoe Buckle." In Audrey Noël
    Hume, Merry W. Abbitt, Robert H. McNulty, Isabel Davies, and Edward
    Chappell, *Five Artifact Studies*, 25–53. Williamsburg, Va.: Colonial
    Williamsburg Foundation, 1973.

Adams, Samuel. Papers. Sol Feinstone Collection of the American Revolu-
    tion, Philadelphia, American Philosophical Society. Microfilm.

Allen, Gardner Weld. *A Naval History of the American Revolution*. 2 vols.
    Boston: Houghton Mifflin, 1913.

Almon, John, ed. *The Remembrancer, or Impartial Repository of Public Events,*
    1775–1784. London: J. Almon, 1775–84. University of Central Florida,
    Orlando. Microfiche.

Arnold, Benedict. "Dimensions for Two Gondolas to Be Built at Chamblé."
    In Howard I. Chapelle, *The History of American Sailing Ships*, 683. 1935.
    Reprint, New York: Bonanza Books, 1985.

Baldwin, Jeduthan. "The Baldwin Letters." *American Monthly Magazine* 6
    (1895):193–97.

———. *The Revolutionary Journal of Col. Jeduthan Baldwin, 1775–1778*.
    Edited with memoir and notes by Thomas Williams Baldwin. 1906.
    Reprint, New York: New York Times and Arno Press, 1971.

Barton, John A. "The Battle of Valcour Island, from the *Life of Admiral*
    Viscount Exmouth, by Edward Osler, Esq., London, 1835." *Bulletin of the*
    Fort Ticonderoga Museum 2, no. 5 (1930–32):163–68.

Bayreuther, William A. "Hull Construction of the Continental Gondola
    Philadelphia: Description and Comments." Typescript on file in the
    Nautical Archaeology Library, Texas A&M University, College Station,
    Tex., 1981.

———. "Revolutionary War Gunboat Construction: The Lake Champlain
    Continental Gondolas of 1776." In Paul F. Johnston, ed., *Proceedings of*
    the Sixteenth Conference on Underwater Archaeology, 10–12. Society for
    Historical Archaeology, Special Publications Series, no. 4, 1985.

Bellico, Russell P. *Sails and Steam in the Mountains: A Maritime and Military History of Lake George and Lake Champlain*. Fleischmanns, N.Y.: Purple Mountain Press, 1992.

Bergen, Jenifer, Trudy Caswell, Christine Mazzaferro, and Anthony Scuderi. "Raising the *Philadelphia*." *Lake Champlain Horizons* 1 (1988).

Brewington, Marion V. "American Naval Guns, 1775–1785." *American Neptune* 3, no. 1 (January 1943):11–18.

———. "American Naval Guns, 1775–1785: Part II." *American Neptune* 3, no. 2 (April 1943):148–58.

Bulletin of the Fort Ticonderoga Museum, 4, no. 7 (1938).

Burlington Daily News, "Special Historical Tabloid," August 3, 1935; August 10, 1935.

Burlington Free Press, January 3, 1966.

Butler, John P., ed. *Papers of the Continental Congress, 1774–1789.* 5 vols. Washington, D.C.: U.S. Government Printing Office, 1978.

Chapelle, Howard I. *The History of American Sailing Ships.* 1935. Reprint, New York: Bonanza Books, 1985.

———. *The History of the American Sailing Navy: The Ships and Their Development.* New York: Bonanza Books, 1949.

Clark, William Bell, William James Morgan, and Michael J. Crawford, eds. *Naval Documents of the American Revolution.* 10 vols., to date. Washington: Naval Historical Center, 1964–.

Cohn, Arthur B. "Afterword: Building and Sailing the Replica." In Philip K. Lundeberg, *The Gunboat* Philadelphia *and the Defense of Lake Champlain in 1776*, 61–84. Basin Harbor, Vt.: Lake Champlain Maritime Museum, 1995.

———. "The Fort Ticonderoga King's Shipyard Excavation: 1984 Field Season Report." *Bulletin of the Fort Ticonderoga Museum* 14 (1985):337–56.

———. "An Incident Not Known to History: Squire Ferris and Benedict Arnold at Ferris Bay, October 13, 1776." *Vermont History* 55 (1987):2–17.

Cometti, Elizabeth, ed. *The American Journals of Lt. John Enys.* Syracuse, N.Y.: Syracuse University Press, 1976.

Crisman, Kevin J. "The Fort Ticonderoga King's Shipyard Excavation: The Artifacts." *Bulletin of the Fort Ticonderoga Museum* 14, no. 6 (1985):375–436.

Davies, K. G., ed. *Documents of the American Revolution, 1770–1783.* 21 vols. Shannon: Irish University Press, 1972–81.

Digby, William. *The British Invasion from the North: Digby's Journal of the Campaigns of Generals Carleton and Burgoyne from Canada, 1776–1777.* 1887. Reprint, with introduction and notes by James Phinney Baxter, New York: Da Capo Press, 1970.

Farmer, Edward G. "Skenesborough: Continental Navy Shipyard." *United States Naval Institute Proceedings* 90 (1964):160–62.

Force, Peter, comp. *American Archives: A Documentary History of the North American Colonies, Fifth Series.* 3 vols. Washington, D.C.: M. St. Clair Clark and Peter Force, 1848–53.

———. *American Archives: A Documentary History of the North American Colonies, Fourth Series.* 6 vols. Washington, D.C.: M. St. Clair Clark and Peter Force, 1837–46.

Fowler, William M., Jr. *Rebels under Sail: The American Navy during the Revolution.* New York: Charles Scribner's Sons, 1976.

Frazer, Persifer. "Letters from Ticonderoga, 1776." *Bulletin of the Fort Ticonderoga Museum* 10, no. 5 (1961):386–94.

———. "Letters from Ticonderoga, 1776." *Bulletin of the Fort Ticonderoga Museum* 10, no. 6 (1962):450–59.

Gage Papers. William L. Clements Library. Ann Arbor, Michigan.

Gates, Horatio. Papers. New York Public Library, Box 19.

Grattan, D. W., and R. W. Clarke. "Conservation of Waterlogged Wood." In Colin Pearson, ed., *Conservation of Marine Archaeological Objects.* London: Butterworth, 1987:164–206.

Guide to the Royal Danish Arsenal Museum: The Cannon Hall. Copenhagen: Tøjhusmuseet, 1948.

Hadden, James Murray. *Hadden's Journal and Orderly Books: A Journal Kept in Canada and upon Burgoyne's Campaign in 1776 and 1777.* 1884. Reprint, Freeport, N.Y.: Books for Libraries Press, 1970.

Hagglund, Lorenzo F. "The Continental Gondola *Philadelphia.*" *United States Naval Institute Proceedings* 62 (1936):655–69.

———. "A Page from the Past: The Story of the Continental Gondola *Philadelphia.*" *Whitehall (N.Y.) Times,* October 30, 1936.

Haldimand, Frederick. Papers. Correspondence with General Gage, 1758–1777. Special Collections, John C. Pace Library, University of West Florida, Pensacola. Microfilm.

Hamilton, Donny L. *Basic Methods of Conserving Underwater Archaeological Material Culture.* Washington, D.C.: U.S. Department of Defense Legacy Resource Management Program, 1996.

Hammond, Isaac Weare, comp. *The State of New Hampshire: Rolls of the Soldiers in the Revolutionary War.* Vol.1 of the war rolls; vol. 14 of the series. Concord, N.H.: Parsons B. Cogswell, State Printer, 1885.

Hastings, Hugh, ed. *The Public Papers of George Clinton, First Governor of New York, 1777–1795, 1801–1804.* 10 vols. Albany, N.Y.: State of New York, 1899–1914.

Hayward, John. *Gazetteer of Vermont.* Boston: Tappan, Whittemore, and Mason, 1849.

History of Oneida County, New York. Philadelphia, Pa.: Everts and Fariss, 1878.

Hoffman, Howard P. *A Graphic Presentation of the Continental Gondola Philadelphia, American Gunboat of 1776.* Washington, D.C.: Smithsonian Institution, 1982.

———. "The Gunboat *Philadelphia:* A Continental Gondola of 1776 and Her Model." *Nautical Research Journal* 30 (1984):55–67.

Hope, Clarence. "Pencil Sketches of *Philadelphia.*" Notebook on file at the Lake Champlain Maritime Museum, Basin Harbor, Vt., n.d.

Jackson, John W. *The Pennsylvania Navy, 1775–1781: The Defense of the Delaware.* New Brunswick, N.J.: Rutgers University Press, 1974.

Jenkins, Dan. *Military Buttons of the Gulf Coast, 1711–1830.* Mobile, Ala.: Museum of the City of Mobile, 1973.

Jenks, Samuel. "Samuel Jenks: His Journal of the Campaign in 1760." *Proceedings of the Massachusetts Historical Society,* 2d ser., 5 (1889–90):353–91.

Krueger, John W. "The Fort Ticonderoga King's Shipyard Excavation: An Overview." *Bulletin of the Fort Ticonderoga Museum* 14, no. 6 (fall 1985): 335–36.

———. "Troop Life at the Champlain Valley Forts during the American Revolution." *Bulletin of the Fort Ticonderoga Museum* 14, no. 3 (summer 1982):158–83.

———. "Troop Life at the Champlain Valley Forts during the American Revolution." *Bulletin of the Fort Ticonderoga Museum* 14, no. 5 (summer 1984):277–310.

Lake Champlain (Basin Harbor, Vt.) Maritime Museum Newsletter. Fall 1991; fall–winter 1992; fall–winter 1993–94; and fall–winter 1999–2000.

Leroy, Perry Eugene. "Sir Guy Carleton as a Military Leader during the American Invasion and Repulse in Canada, 1775–1776." 2 vols. Ph.D. diss., Ohio State University, 1960. Ann Arbor, Mich.: University Microfilms.

London Chronicle, November 23, 1776.

Linn, John B., and William H. Egle, eds. *Pennsylvania Archives, Second Series.* 2 vols. Harrisburg, 1880.

Lundeberg, Philip K. *The Gunboat* Philadelphia *and the Defense of Lake Champlain in 1776.* Basin Harbor, Vt.: Lake Champlain Maritime Museum, 1995.

———. Interview with the author, Washington, D.C., August, 1996.

Maclay, Edgar Stanton. *A History of the United States Navy from 1775 to 1894.* 2 vols. New York: D. Appleton, 1895.

Maguire, J. Robert. "Dr. Robert Knox's Account of the Battle of Valcour, October 11–13, 1776." *Vermont History* 46, no. 3 (1978)141–50.

Mahan, Alfred Thayer. *Major Operations of the Navies in the War of American Independence.* 1913. Reprint, New York: Greenwood Press, 1969.

Martin, James Kirby. *Benedict Arnold, Revolutionary Hero: An American Warrior Reconsidered.* New York: New York University Press, 1997.

McNulty, Robert H. "A Study of Bayonets in the Department of Archaeology, Colonial Williamsburg, with Notes on Bayonet Identification." In Audrey Noël Hume, Merry W. Abbitt, Robert H. McNulty, Isabel Davies, and Edward Chappell, *Five Artifact Studies*, 54–77. Williamsburg, Va.: Colonial Williamsburg Foundation, 1973.

Montgomery, Thomas Lynch, ed. *Pennsylvania Archives, Fifth Series.* 8 vols. Harrisburg, 1906.

Newton, Earle. *The Vermont Story: A History of the People of the Green Mountain State, 1749–1949.* Montpelier, Vt.: Vermont Historical Society, 1949.

Neagles, James C. *Summer Soldiers: A Survey and Index of Revolutionary War Courts-Martial.* Salt Lake City, Utah: Ancestry Inc., 1986.

Noël Hume, Ivor. *A Guide to Artifacts of Colonial America.* New York: First Vintage Books, 1991.

Palmer, Peter S. *History of Lake Champlain.* 1886. Reprint, Harrison, N.Y.: Harbor Hill Books, 1983.

Pausch, George. *Journal of Captain George Pausch, Chief of the Hanau Artillery during the Burgoyne Campaign.* Translated by William L. Stone. 1886. Reprint, Albany, N.Y.: Arno Press, 1970.

"Pay Roll of Captain Benjamin Rue's Crew Belonging to the Gondola *Philadelphia*," October 16, 1776. Typescript, Lake Champlain Maritime

Museum, Basin Harbor, Vt. Original on display next to the *Philadelphia*,
National Museum of American History, Smithsonian Institution,
Washington, D.C.

Peterson, Harold L. "Lock, Stock, and Barrel: Being a Survey of the
Shoulder Weapons and Guns of the Continental Army." *American History
Illustrated* 11 (1968):31–33.

———. *Round Shot and Rammers.* South Bend, Ind.: South Bend Replicas,
1969.

Philadelphia File. Accession no. 229338. Department of Armed Forces
History, Division of Naval History, National Museum of American
History, Smithsonian Institution.

The Philadelphia *Project.* Crossroads Video, Vermont Public Television,
1991.

Phillips, Hazel Spencer. *The Golden Lamb.* Oxford, Ohio: Oxford Press, 1958.

Reynolds, Paul R. *Guy Carleton: A Biography.* New York: William Morrow,
1980.

Risjord, Norman K. *Jefferson's America, 1760–1815.* Madison, Wisc.:
Madison House, 1991.

Rosenqvist, A. "The Oseburg Find, Its Conservation and Present State."
ICOMOS Symposium on the Weathering of Wood. Ludwigsburg, ICOMOS.
Paris (in English) 1969, 77–88.

———. "The Stabilization of Wood Found in the Viking Ship of Oseberg:
Parts 1 and 2." *Studies in Conservation* 4 (1959).

Rue, Captain Benjamin. Pension Records. Revolutionary War Orderly
Books. National Archives, Washington, D.C.

Russell, Carl P. *Firearms, Traps, and Tools of the Mountain Men.* Albuquerque:
University of New Mexico Press, 1996.

Sabine, Lorenzo. *Biographical Sketches of Loyalists of the American Revolution,
with an Historical Essay.* 2 vols. Boston: Little Brown, 1864.

Schank, John, John Starke, and Edward Longcraft. "An Open Letter to
Captain Pringle." *Bulletin of the Fort Ticonderoga Museum* 1 (1928):14–20.

Schuyler, Hermanus. Extracts of forty-three letters from Hermanus
Schuyler to Philip Schuyler. Adirondack Museum, Blue Mountain Lake,
N.Y. Microfilm.

Secretary of the Commonwealth of Massachusetts. *Massachusetts Sailors and
Soldiers of the Revolutionary War.* 17 vols. Boston: Wright and Potter
Printing, 1896–1908.

Sewall, Henry. "The Diary of Henry Sewall." *Bulletin of the Fort Ticonderoga
Museum* 9 (1963):75–92.

Skerrett, Robert G. "Wreck of the *Royal Savage* Recovered." *United States
Naval Institute Proceedings* 61 (1935):1646–52.

Smith, E. Vale. "Diary of Colonel Edward Wigglesworth." In *History of
Newburyport.* Newburyport, Mass.: E. Vale Smith, 1854.

Smith, Myron J. Jr. *Navies in the American Revolution: A Bibliography.* 2 vols.
Metuchen, N.J.: Scarecrow Press, 1973.

Snyder, Charles M. "With Benedict Arnold at Valcour Island: The Diary of
Pascal De Angelis." *Vermont History* 42, no. 3 (1974):195–200.

Stacey, Charles P. *Quebec, 1759: The Siege and the Battle.* 1959. Reprint,
Toronto: Macmillan, 1984.

Stamm, Alfred J. "Dimensional Stabilization of Wood with Carbowaxes." *Forest Products Journal* 6, no. 5 (1956):201–204.

St. Clair, Arthur. Letter to James Wilson, October 15, 1776. Historical Society of Pennsylvania, Philadelphia.

Stewart, Jahiel. Diary. Revolutionary War Pension Records. National Archives and Records Administration, Washington, D.C. Transcribed by Don Wickman, Rutland, Vt.

"Supplies for the Galley *Washington*." *Bulletin of the Fort Ticonderoga Museum* 4 (1936):21–22.

Taylor, Foster D. "The Piscataqua River Gundalow." *American Neptune* 4 (1942):127–39.

Trumbull, Benjamin. "A Concise Journal or Minutes of the Principal Movements towards St. John's." *Collections of the Connecticut Historical Society* 7 (1899):137–73.

Trumbull, John. *Autobiography, Reminiscences, and Letters of John Trumbull from 1756 to 1841*. New Haven, Conn.: B. L. Hamlen, 1841.

Troy (N.Y.) Record, July 22, 1961.

Tucker, Spencer C. "American Naval Ordnance of the Revolution." *Nautical Research Journal* 22, no. 1 (1976)21–30.

———. *Arming the Fleet: U.S. Navy Ordnance in the Muzzle-Loading Era*. Annapolis, Md.: Naval Institute Press, 1989.

———. "U.S. Navy Gun Carriages from the Revolution through the Civil War." *American Neptune* 47 (1987):108–18.

Van de Water, Frederic F. *Lake Champlain and Lake George*. New York: Bobbs-Merrill, 1946.

Ward, Christopher. *The War of the Revolution*. Edited by John Richard Alden. 2 vols. New York: Macmillan, 1952.

Washington, George. *The Papers of George Washington*. Edited by W. W. Abbot and Dorothy Twohig. Revolutionary War Series. 6 vols. Charlottesville: University Press of Virginia, 1992.

Wasmus, J. F. *An Eyewitness Account of the American Revolution and New England Life: The Journal of J. F. Wasmus, German Company Surgeon, 1776–1783*. Translated by Helga Doblin; edited and introduction by Mary C. Lynn. Contributions in Military Studies, no. 106. New York: Greenwood Press, 1990.

Watson, Winslow C. "Arnold's Retreat after the Battle of Valcour." *Magazine of American History* 6 (1881):414–17.

Wayne, Anthony. "The Wayne Orderly Books." *Bulletin of the Fort Ticonderoga Museum* 11 (1963):94–204.

Wells, Bayze. "Journal of Bayze Wells." *In Orderly Books and Journals Kept by Connecticut Men While Taking Part in the American Revolution, 1775–1778*. Vol. 7. Hartford: Connecticut Historical Society, 1899.

Whitehall (N.Y.) Banner, July 14, 1961.

Whitehall (N.Y.) Times, October 30, 1936; May 25, 1961; June 1, 1961.

Wickman, Donald H. "A Most Unsettled Time on Lake Champlain: The October 1776 Journal of Jahiel Stewart." *Vermont History* 64, no. 2 (1996)89–98.

Wilbur, C. Keith. *Revolutionary Medicine, 1700–1800*. Chester, Conn.: Globe Pequot Press, 1980.

Wilkinson, James. *Memoirs of My Own Time*. 3 vols. 1816. Reprint, New York: AMS Press, 1973.

INDEX

STUDIES IN
NAUTICAL ARCHAEOLOGY

Mark, Samuel. *From Egypt to Mesopotamia: A Study of Predynastic Trade Routes.* 1997.

Martin, Lillian Ray. *The Art and Archaeology of Venetian Ships and Boats.* 2001.

Mott, Lawrence V. *The Development of the Rudder: A Technological Tale.* 1997.

Oertling, Thomas J. *Ships' Bilge Pumps: A History of Their Development, 1500–1900.* 1996.

Simmons, Joe J. III. *Those Vulgar Tubes: External Sanitary Accommodations aboard European Ships of the Fifteenth through Seventeenth Centuries.* 1997.

JOHN R. BRATTEN works as a nautical archaeologist and conservator at the Archaeology Institute of the University of West Florida. He holds a Ph.D. in anthropology from Texas A&M University. He has done extensive field work at archaeological sites in the United States, the Middle East, and the Caribbean. Bratten has published numerous articles in this field.

ISBN 1-58544-147-3

90000